$24.95

D0927866

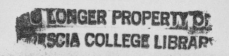

THE CAUSES OF THE PRESENT INFLATION

THE CAUSES OF THE PRESENT INFLATION

An Interdisciplinary Explanation of Inflation in Britain, Germany and the United States

Andrew Tylecote

A Halsted Press Book

John Wiley & Sons
New York

First published 1981 by
THE MACMILLAN PRESS LTD
London and Basingstoke
Companies and representatives
throughout the world

First published in the USA by
Halsted Press, a Division of
John Wiley & Sons, Inc.

Printed in Hong Kong

Library of Congress Cataloging in Publication Data

Tylecote, Andrew.
    The causes of the present inflation.

"A Halsted Press book."
Bibliography: p.
Includes index.
    1.   Inflation (Finance) – Great Britain.
    2.   Inflation (Finance) – Germany, West.
    3.   Inflation (Finance) – United States.
    I.   Title.
HG229.T94   1980   332.4′1′09048   80-15798

ISBN 0–470–26953–7

Contents

67230

List of Figures

Preface

This book puts forward a new theory of inflation. That involves it in the fiercest and perhaps most complex debate in modern economics; yet it has been written in a way which should be easily understood by the layman. To those of my colleagues who judge a work by the sophistication of its mathematics, and the intellectual Groucho Marxes who think no club worth joining unless it does its best to keep them out, that must seem ridiculous and perverse. Not at all. It was the only way the job could be done, and if it had had to be done any other way it would hardly have been worth doing. Modern economics is enmeshed in technical jargon and intellectual gadgetry. To begin with, our jargon cut us off from the layman; then it cut us off from the rest of the social sciences; now that each little section of the subject has spawned its own, it cuts us off from each other. Even within the intellectual ghettos of our subdivisions – labour economics, monetary economics, and so forth – the methods we are expected to use have become so sophisticated that most can only find time to master them by neglecting the background of the problems they are meant to solve.

Yet the most urgent economic problems are not problems in labour economics, or monetary economics; they are not even problems in economics – they concern the social sciences as a whole. With inflation our petty divisions between subjects become ridiculous. The prices a firm charges are a matter for the industrial economist; its wages are the preserve of the labour economist. What if the wages it pays depend on the prices it charges? Worse, what if they also depend on the social relationships of its workers – on the rivalries among them, on their jealousies of other groups, on their attitudes towards their work and their employer? Economists, as economists, have little to say about such things; but how, in the present segregation of their subject, can they make use of the insights of sociologists, psychologists, and political scientists?

There are two ways of putting the other social sciences to work. One is to study these subjects; I had studied history, philosophy, politics and sociology before I turned in earnest to economics. The other is to set out one's ideas in plain English, so that experts in such fields can see what sociological, psychological, political, historical assumptions are being made, and how they affect the conclusion reached; the way is then open for their contribution. That is what I have tried to do. If I have succeeded, then I shall not be very much disappointed to be told that many of these assumptions are questionable, even wrong. That is probably inevitable; what is not inevitable, but disastrous, is that economists should go on feeding arbitrary assumptions into their theories without anyone to tell them their mistakes. Garbage in, garbage out.

But this book straddles countries as well as disciplines. Any explanation of inflation is bound to suggest international comparisons – why is country A's experience so different from country B's? – and I felt from the beginning I must make them. At first I planned to base the book on a comparison of Britain and West Germany – the two countries I knew best, and with a very different experience of inflation – leaving other Western countries in the background. As I wrote, however, I found a third country, the United States, gradually forcing its way into the limelight. In the end I realised why: first, because of its sheer importance, and second, more strangely, because the Anglo-German contrast I had set out to draw was not as clear cut as I had thought; in some important respects it looked now more like a convergence. The deepest contrast was in fact between the two European countries, Britain and Germany, on the one hand, and the United States on the other. So I decided to recast the book to base it on a triangular comparison between the three countries; but I also write in some detail about other important West European countries (France, Italy, the Netherlands and Sweden) and the perspective of the book is very much European.

If it is hard to explain changes in inflation in one country, it is harder to explain them in several; and to try also to explain variations between countries, all in one book, may seem insanely ambitious, once one recognises (as I do) that most of the complex differences between countries, economic, social and political, are relevant. But I do not claim to give an exhaustive explanation for any of these things, still less to offer predictions which are accurate, or remedies which are certain to work. My main aim is more modest, on the face of it – in a sense as ambitious: to change the shape and language of the argument. We have failed so far to understand inflation because we have put the wrong questions, in the wrong words, to the wrong people. If we look at the real world, where organisations, their internal politics and external rivalries, are as important as markets, where behaviour has motives which are as much social as economic; if we ask our questions about it in plain English – or rarer still, plain German – and insist on answers in the same; if we put the questions to those best equipped to answer them, whether they are psychologists, historians, sociologists, political scientists, or even (who knows) economists; if – above all – we *connect* the answers; then, in the end, we shall succeed. This book is a beginning.

ANDREW TYLECOTE

Acknowledgements

This book has benefited from the influence of some who taught me, at Oxford and Sussex, before it was thought of: A. H. Halsey, Derek Robinson, Chris Freeman, and above all, George Richardson and Eprime Eshag, who have protected many young economists from an old paradigm. Econometric work to test my theories was generously financed by the Houblon-Norman Fund of the Bank of England, and the Social Science Research Council, and efficiently carried out by my two research assistants, Ann Anson and David Newlands. Manchester University, by making me Hallsworth Fellow in 1976–7, gave me invaluable time, and stimulating discussion. Prof. C. C. von Weizsäcker, with his assistant Paul Gerhard Schröder, gave me generous academic hospitality and advice in Bonn during 1978, as did Prof. Karl-Georg Zinn at Aachen; this period in Germany was partly financed by the Social Science Research Council and Deutsche Forschungsgesellschaft. At various points on my travels I received valuable help from Åke Källquist of Swedish Radio, Prof. Manfred Hein of the Free University of Berlin, Dr Manfred Piecka and others at the Deutsche Gewerkschaftsbund, and my friend Dr Jürgen Helm. Nearer home, I have had vital support from the SSRC Industrial Relations Research Unit at Warwick University: from seminars given and attended there, and from members of the Unit, in particular William Brown and Keith Sisson. At Sheffield, Brian McCormick, successive heads of department, and many other colleagues have been considerate and helpful. Dr George Wagner gave me valuable advice.

Most of all, I am grateful to friends and colleagues of various disciplines and several countries, who read and criticised successive drafts: Elspeth McVeigh, Simon French, Paul Gerhard Schröder, John Westergaard, Marian Mackie, and Joan Robinson; also to John Winckler and Anne-Lucie Norton, of Macmillan. Since I did not take all their advice, it can scarcely make them in any way responsible for what emerged. I must also thank Mr Keuner, of Brecht's *Verträger des Wissens*, for some advice which I did take. I thank Edith Gillett, Patricia Wynter, and above all Sheila Watts for their patience and efficiency in typing the various drafts. They read what they were typing, enjoyed it, and were its first critics.

Perhaps I should also thank Geoffrey Howe, Keith Joseph, and Margaret Thatcher for economic policies well designed to test my theory; but they will get their thanks from the British electorate.

January 1980   ANDREW TYLECOTE
West Berlin

List of Abbreviations

Abbreviations used in the Endnotes, Figures and Bibliography

PERIODICALS

AER	*American Economic Review*
BJIR	*British Journal of Industrial Relations*
BOUIES	*Bulletin of the Oxford University Institute of Economics and Statistics*
BPEA	*Brookings Papers on Economic Activity*
CJE	*Cambridge Journal of Economics*
DEG	*Department of Employment Gazette*
Eca.	*Economica*
EHR	*Economic History Review*
EJ	*Economic Journal*
EPR	*Economic Policy Review*
ERP	*Economic Report of the President*
ESE	*United Nations Economic Survey of Europe*
FT	*Financial Times*
JEL	*Journal of Economic Literature*
LBR	*Lloyds Bank Review*
NIER	*National Institute Economic Review*
OEP	*Oxford Economic Papers*
QJE	*Quarterly Journal of Economics*
RES	*Review of Economic Studies*
REStats.	*Review of Economics and Statistics*
St. J.	*Statistisches Jahrbuch der Bundesrepublik Deutschland*

ORGANISATIONS

AEA	American Economic Association
AFL/CIO	American Federation of Labor/Congress of Industrial Organisations
BLS	Bureau of Labor Statistics (US)
CBI	Confederation of British Industry
CIR	Commission on Industrial Relations (UK)

CUP	Cambridge University Press
DAE	Department of Applied Economics (Cambridge)
DE	Department of Employment (UK)
DGB	Deutsche Gewerkschaftsbund
HMSO	Her Majesty's Stationery Office
IEA	Institute of Economic Affairs (UK)
ILO	International Labor Organisation
NBER	National Bureau for Economic Research (US)
NEDO	National Economic Development Office (UK)
NIESR	National Institute of Economic and Social Research (UK)
OECD	Organisation for Economic Cooperation and Development
OUP	Oxford University Press
PEP	Political and Economic Planning (UK)
St. B.	Statistisches Bundesamt
TUC	Trades Union Congress (UK)

OTHER

DP, Occ. Pap.	Discussion Paper, Occasional Paper
Res. Pap., WP	Research Paper, Working Paper
EA	Employers' Association
NY	New York
RC	Royal Commission
TU	Trade Union
UP	University Press

1 Old Doctrines and a New Theory

1.1 INTRODUCTION

The language of economics is littered with the husks of dead theories. Words have their modern meanings, but their outer forms embody the ideas of the economists who first used them. Often that does no harm, but there are some words which act as carriers for old theories, slipping them unseen into our thoughts, where they stay unnaturally alive. I shall have to use three of these vampire words again and again: inflation, deflation, reflation. The best protection, the economist's garlic and crucifix, is a cold clear definition of the word, and a warning of what theory lurks within.

Inflation, deflation, reflation; they sound alike, as they were meant to, but the first now means something quite different from the others. Inflation is a general and continuing rise in prices – nothing more (here at least). Deflation here is action to bring about a general fall in the level of economic activity; reflation is the opposite of deflation. But inflation and deflation *sound* like opposites, and reflation like renewed inflation, and the result is to imply that a rise (or fall) in economic activity and a rise (or fall) in prices go together – something which was taken for granted by the economists who first used these words, but (to put it mildly) is not obvious now. With that said, we can use them, and add another term, wage inflation. For us this means a general and continuing rise in wages, not 'inflation *caused* by wage rises' (this whole book is about causes; they can wait).

Yet most of this book – an explanation of inflation, rising *prices* – is spent explaining wage inflation – rising *wages*. Does that not imply that the second causes the first? It does, certainly, imply that there is a causal connection. As I shall argue later, wages have a great effect on prices, as do prices on wages. Thus the term 'the wage-price spiral'. It would be futile to try to analyse only wage inflation or only (price) inflation. Any explanation of one must in some way, at some

1

stage, involve or imply an explanation of the other. I lay the stress on wages because that is the more difficult part. It is also, fortunately, the more interesting.

The particular difficulty, and the special interest, of wages arise from the same problem. Wages are a price, but the price of a most unusual commodity, the labour of human beings; and since the abolition of slavery the seller of each human being's labour has been that same human being. I shall argue that these peculiarities make the forces at work in the setting of wages quite different from those which affect other prices. This proposition underlies all the arguments in this book, and it is an unorthodox one – few economists treat prices and wages as so sharply distinct. Some of my other 'initial propositions', or assumptions, will be at least as unorthodox. This is dangerous, for ideas starting from unorthodox assumptions risk being rejected through sheer misunderstanding, the reader being so used to the old ones that he goes on making them unconsciously, so that the new ideas, not fitting the old assumptions, seem nonsensical. In this case the danger is acute, for the orthodox assumptions have for a century provided the framework of ideas within which economists – and anyone with even a smattering of economics – are trained to see the world. They live within the very language; the 'vampire' words which I warned against just now, are their servants. My best chance of avoiding misunderstanding, I think, is to bring the orthodox set of assumptions out into the open at the beginning, and point the contrast with mine. I shall describe the orthodox set as *neoclassical* (although not all those who use them may like that label) for they can be traced back to the school of economists which we now know by that name.[1]

The neoclassical school had its heyday in the Golden Age of the Western market economy, before the First World War. They claimed to stand in the tradition of the 'classical' economist Adam Smith: rejecting many later developments of classical economics (notably by David Ricardo and Karl Marx) they stressed that part of Smith's work which praised the operation of competition and market forces, left to themselves. The neoclassical economy was a marvellous self-balancing system in which many different commodities were exchanged for one another, via money, in interconnected markets. The price of each was settled by the supply and demand for it; if the supply increased, or demand diminished, the price would fall, until enough buyers had been attracted or sellers driven away to bring the market back into balance. That was as true for labour as it was for cauliflowers: both commodities were traded by competing buyers and sellers whose over-riding motive, called 'economic rationality', was the pursuit of maximum profit. Strictly speaking, workers sold labour for maximum 'utility', but it made little difference.[2]

Of course, if some firm (or union) could corner the market for a particular type of good (or labour), it could drive up the price by restricting the supply. Such monopolisation was known, and deplored, but it was not the rule, and even where it existed it was always under threat from the entry of new competitors into the market, attracted by the higher price. Nor could monopolists ignore wider market forces: in a boom they would, being 'rational', generally charge more than in a slump. So far as prices and wages in general were concerned, the matter was quite simple: they were fixed by the forces of supply and demand operating in the markets for goods, and for labour.[3]

It is easy to see why the neoclassical theory of prices and wages was popular before 1914. It was an optimistic theory which supported the *status quo*, in an optimistic period when the *status quo* seemed worth supporting.[4] And wages and prices were generally stable, in most countries, while unemployment was never high for long; so it seemed to fit the facts.

After 1914 the world was never so optimistic again. The change was naturally smallest in the United States, which actually gained from the war; business there was much as usual until 1929. Reflecting this prosperity, economics did not change much either. On the continent of Europe, on the other hand, the old order was shattered; but precisely because of the scale of disruption – social, political and economic – economists were not much inclined to question neoclassical theory.[5] It had, after all, been designed for *normal* times, which they hoped would soon return. It was in Britain that the neoclassical school faced its most serious challenge. For in Britain, social and political 'normality' returned, more or less, soon after the war, but there was something wrong with the economy. Well before 1929 there was mass unemployment, depressed profits, and near-stagnant production.[6]

It turned out that the theory which had originally served to reassure, could now be adapted to apportion blame. The great Cambridge economist Pigou pointed the finger at the unions. They were much stronger than before the war; and real wages were a good deal higher. The unions must be artificially holding wages up above their equilibrium (or 'economic') level, thus causing a surplus of labour.

Now Pigou started from the assumption that there was an

economic wage . . . a wage rate . . . such that . . . all able-bodied
workers desiring work are able to find it.

It followed that

> If . . . we put the actual level of wages above the economic
> level, employment is necessarily restricted and output is cut down
> correspondingly. . . . If the percentage of unemployment stands,
> over a considerable period, substantially above 3 or 4 per cent, there is
> a strong presumption that the general level of wages has been put
> above the economic level. That presumption is, in my judgement,
> warranted at the present time [1926].[7]

If the unions could be persuaded – or forced – to stop interfering with
the market mechanism, all would be well, and mass unemployment
would disappear. Keynes, almost alone, disagreed – first rather prag-
matically, for he was a neoclassical economist by training; but slowly he
moved towards direct conflict with his mentors.[8] In the *General Theory*
(published in 1936) he showed how even assuming competitive markets,
there was no reason to expect full employment always, or indeed ever.[9]
The great hole this knocked in neoclassical macroeconomics was later
enlarged by Piero Sraffa, Joan Robinson and others, who began work
on a new structure to replace it.[10] But Keynes was a practical man,
concerned to solve the problems of the Slump which by now had
brought mass unemployment to the whole Western world, not seeking
to overthrow an intellectual dynasty. After 1936 he was mainly a policy-
maker, and content to leave the neoclassical school to adapt an old
theory to new policies.

They did the job ingeniously. Samuelson, for example, soon explained
that it was wage rigidity, due to union power, which prevented the
economy settling automatically at full employment, and he gave the
credit for this discovery, not to Pigou, but to Keynes.[11] Such
Keynesians, as they led Keynes' ideas back into the neoclassical fold,
came to no definite conclusions about why wages behaved in this way.
Now that government reflation seemed enough to solve the problem of
unemployment, wage flexibility was no longer needed, and there wasn't
much point in discussing why we didn't have it. But wages could only be
ignored so long as they were, if not flexible, at least more or less stable.
So they were, in the 1930s. In the 1940s they began to rise quickly, but
under the special circumstances of wartime excess demand that was
hardly surprising. Moreover prices were rising faster than wages.

Practical policy-makers were happy to use price controls and union-backed wage restraint as short-term expedients, while theoretical purists looked the other way, and pondered the problems of peace.

In most of the Continental countries the special circumstances lasted well into the 1950s, and by the time they faded, so had inflation. Like unemployment after the First World War, inflation after the Second was most discussed where it was least easily explained. In the US 'normality' was quickly restored, yet inflation was disturbingly high in 1946–7. If inflation had greatly increased since the last period of full employment (in the 1920s) so had union power; thus the role of unions in inflation attracted attention – and hostility.[12] There was a wave of anti-union legislation; then both union strength and inflation fell sharply,[13] and in the 1950s the focus of concern with both moved to Britain. For Britain emerged from post-war shortages without much of a fall in wage inflation, which remained irritating if not alarming.[14] Some British economists took this as showing that demand and supply were now unimportant; others decided to re-examine their effects.[15]

The relation between unemployment and wages was seen against a background which differed in two important ways from that of the 1920s. In economic theory, the level of unemployment was accepted as something the authorities could and should control. That the Keynesian revolution had achieved. In economic policy, it was accepted, particularly in the new social democracies of Europe, that 'full' employment must be maintained. That did not mean no unemployment at all, but it did limit the amount which was permissible. Economists, then, were inclined to look for a theory which, though not too far from the old one, did not imply a solution which went beyond these new limits.

In 1958 Phillips met these requirements.[16] He said little, in fact, about the causes of inflation – the Phillips Curve has been called a curve without a theory – he merely claimed, from British experience, to have found a rather stable relationship between the level of unemployment and the rate of wage inflation. Higher unemployment, lower wage inflation. The Curve traced out the choices open to the policy-maker. If x per cent unemployment was the most his electorate would tolerate, then he would have to accept y per cent inflation. If he (or they) insisted on lower inflation, then he (and they) would have to put up with higher unemployment.

The policy implications of the Curve were acceptable. If you took it neat, then it expressed the disadvantages of post-war social democracy, but did not imply that the arrangement had to be scrapped. The present combination of low unemployment and modest inflation seemed tolerable, and as it was vague about causes, the Curve left 'practical men' a lot of latitude to try to reduce inflation without raising unemployment. They might, for example, try to reduce labour shortages by an 'active manpower policy' on the Swedish model – giving workers new skills and encouraging them to move where the skills were required. They might even use more direct measures like voluntary or compulsory incomes policy – the expedients of the 1940s.

By the late 1960s, however, inflation was rising again in the United States, and seriously worrying American economists. There were neoclassical economists there who had been less affected by the 'Keynesian Revolution' than anyone in Britain, and had no social-democratic inhibitions. Led by Milton Friedman and his 'Chicago School' they worked out a theory of wage inflation which was clearly consistent with neoclassical tradition. That tradition laid down that the forces of supply and demand determined the *real* wage decreed by the employer or agreed with the union.[17] What money wage that amounted to, depended on prices; to be more precise, on *expected* prices, for wages were not adjusted day by day, but fixed for a year or more ahead, and so one had to allow for expected price increases during that period.[18] (This was most relevant in the US, where wage contracts are generally for two or three years.) So a rise in money wages could be explained by a rise in the pressure of demand for labour, *or* by the expectation of price rises; or both. Thus, if wage inflation slackened, but did not stop, during the brief and mild recessions of the 1950s and 1960s, that was because employers and workers went on expecting price rises.

Price expectations worked like inertia in physics – they would keep inflation going just as a satellite's inertia keeps up its speed in space, but they were not the original cause; that was excess demand. Like the satellite's rockets, demand had got the inflationary circle moving. If the cause was reversed, and there was an excess supply of labour, that would act like a braking rocket on the satellite, gradually slowing it down. If supply just balanced demand (at the 'natural rate of unemployment') then the process would move at a constant speed.[19] But if excess demand were kept up – if the main rockets went on firing – there would be continuous acceleration into hyperinflation and disaster.[20]

This 'expectations-augmented Phillips Curve' was extremely persuasive to economists. It explained why inflation could go on rising even when demand had been falling: as long as unemployment was still below the 'natural rate' the main rockets were still firing. Even when unemployment was so high as to be clearly above the natural rate, inflation would not decelerate sharply, if a long history of rising prices had made 'inflationary expectations' *ingrained*; but if one went on braking, inflation would stop in the end. So the remedy was to raise unemployment until inflation slackened, and keep it high until inflation stopped. (Friedman and other monetarists recommended that this should be done by restricting the money supply; I explain why in Chapter 4, Section 3. A similar deflationary effect could be had by cutting government spending or, more arguably, by raising taxation.) Governments found the 'monetarist' diagnosis unattractive because the deflation prescribed was nasty, but as the alternative remedies seemed to fail, the monetarists increasingly got their way; and by the mid-1970s their theory of inflation was dominant too.

Whom the gods will destroy they give all he asks for. The criticisms of Keynes, Kalecki, Sraffa, Joan Robinson, in the realm of High Theory,[21] have not seriously hurt neoclassicism, for few economists, let alone laymen, understand the argument, or much care. Inflation is different. Politicians and public demand explanations – Low Theory – and solutions. Economists, who pride themselves on being useful, have had to offer them. Governments, growing desperate, have tried them: as inflation rose in the 1970s they gradually conceded more and more to the harshest neoclassical doctrine. The result has been merely to turn a single crisis, of high inflation, into a double crisis, of high inflation and high unemployment. Finance ministers of the West assembled together have admitted to each other and the world that they did not know how they got into this mess, nor how they could get out of it. Neoclassical policies have failed, and have been shown to have failed, and that makes the theory behind them vulnerable. What is needed now is a coherent alternative: an explanation which can convincingly account for our present predicament using a different pattern of key assumptions and basic propositions. This book is meant to offer just such an alternative.

Let me now set out my assumptions. (Having called the old set Neoclassical, I shall call mine Post-Keynesian, with apologies to anyone else who uses the term differently.) These assumptions are about *motives*, and *circumstances*.

Motives

Human beings do not normally try to maximise anything; they set themselves targets, and try to achieve them by the easiest and most obvious means. For as Simon and March have pointed out

Finding the optimal alternative is a radically different problem from finding a satisfactory alternative. . . . An example is the difference between searching a haystack to find the sharpest needle in it, and searching the haystack to find a needle sharp enough to sew with. To optimise requires processes several orders of magnitude more complex than those required to satisfice. . . . Most human decision-making, whether individual or organisational, is concerned with the discovery and selection of satisfactory alternatives; only in exceptional cases is it concerned with the discovery and selection of optimal alternatives . . . optimising is replaced by satisficing – the requirement that satisfactory levels of the criterion variables be attained.[22]

This applies to profits as much as to any other 'criterion variable': even if their 'optimum' is to maximise profits, the managers of a large firm cannot and will not constantly search through the haystack of possible decisions to find that one 'optimum' needle, which maximises profits. But they can and will keep an eye on the implications of their decisions for profits, and try to achieve a certain 'satisfactory' level, or target, of profitability. In that sense all managers of large firms are satisficers; but I shall use the word satisficer more narrowly, to describe managers who set themselves and their subordinates profit targets which are not usually difficult to reach. I shall use (profit) 'maximiser' for those who set profit targets high, and when they are reached, raise them. For the post-Keynesian, it is an open – and important – question, how far are the managers (and others) he is concerned with, (profit) maximisers? And in so far as they are satisficers, what do they try to achieve once they have reached their profit targets? I start to grapple with this question in Chapter 2.

Where wages are concerned, motives will be particularly complex, for the commodity being bought and sold is tied up with the deepest emotions, with self-respect and self-expression. And on the workers' side, the organisations involved are more complex than on the managers'. For owners, who are supposed to control firms, and have the property right to do so, are, as seems natural, at the top of the pyramid of power; but ordinary workers, who are supposed to control unions, and have the democratic right to do so, are at the *bottom* of the union pyramid. This makes for complex and unstable relationships of power within unions, and makes it more difficult to explain and predict their objectives and methods.

Circumstances

The neoclassical assumption is that the profit-maximising firms and 'utility-maximising' workers are operating within markets which are normally perfectly competitive or, failing that, monopolistic. The 'pattern' case for post-Keynesians is quite different. With *prices*, firms are assumed to be selling their goods in oligopolistic markets, that is, with a limited number of competitors. This change is surprisingly important, because with oligopoly everything depends on the *relationship with competitors*. This relationship in turn depends on a variety of factors, and the balance of demand and supply is not usually the most important of them. If the relationship among competing firms is *cooperative*, prices will be set just below the level which might attract other firms into the market. (This will be the rule for monopolists, too.) The result, as I shall argue in Chapter 2, is that prices (and indirectly wages) will behave in a thoroughly un-neoclassical way.

Wages are settled by collective bargaining – negotiation – between employers and unions. This creates a situation where there is neither a competitive market for labour, nor monopoly (nor, for that matter, oligopoly). If the employer fails to agree with the union he cannot go and buy his labour from some other union; nor can the union 'sell' to some other employer. In a word, each is stuck with the other; if they cannot agree, there will be a strike (or lock out) until they do. Such a situation is called 'bilateral monopoly', and it has been recognised for a long time that it has quite different rules from the standard competitive or monopoly case.[23] Here it is the relationship between the bargainers which is all-important. There is, however, a second case the post-Keynesian must recognise: the non-union employer. He is normally an oligopoly or monopoly buyer in his particular labour market, and may set his wages much as he sets his prices, but he will probably have to bear in mind the possibility of unionisation if his workers feel ill-treated. This in fact may make him very like the post-Keynesian monopolist who dare not price too high for fear of a 'new entrant'; *he* dare not pay too *low* for fear of unionisation. So here too a lot depends on the employer's relationship with his workers, even if they are not unionised.

Most neoclassical economists would probably concede that the post-Keynesian assumptions are a good deal more realistic than their own – many are not above borrowing some of them on occasion. However, they would argue that for building *general* theories of how the economy works, the cold simplicity of their own assumptions is much more useful.

It is hard enough making general theories as it is, without starting from difficult assumptions like oligopoly or bilateral monopoly which beg questions rather than answer them. In any case, does it matter that one's assumptions are unrealistic? The important thing, surely, is to be *scientific*, and for the scientist the all-important thing is to have a logical theory, starting from clear assumptions, that leads to clear predictions which turn out, when tested, to be correct.[24] You only change the assumptions if the predictions turn out not to fit the facts. The proof of the pudding is in the eating, or to put it another way, never mind the quality, feel the fit.

I believe this is a misunderstanding of scientific method. Natural scientists take great pains, by careful observation, to make their assumptions as realistic as possible. Having done so, they build their theory, and test its predictions. Happily for them, they can usually do so by repeated, controlled experiment. Economists, who hardly ever can, have instead to compare their predictions with whatever scraps of (usually unreliable) information they can cobble together. The statistical methods for doing this are all unreliable, and the most notoriously unreliable of them is the one most used to test theories of inflation, time-series regression analysis.[25] Clearly, where it is difficult to judge what comes out of one's theory, it makes sense to take special care over what goes in. Adam Smith and Alfred Marshall, from whom the neoclassical economists claim descent, certainly took care to make their assumptions realistic.[26] We should copy them.

Still, a problem does arise in building general theories. Assumptions simple enough to work with cannot be entirely realistic for the whole field one is covering (mine are no exception). But this is a problem which the natural scientists have been grappling with for centuries, and we can learn from their experience. The most general scientific theories of all are the patterns, the frameworks of key assumptions and basic propositions, which are shared by all the members of each scientific school and used by them in all their work.[27] Such patterns (or 'paradigms') are most difficult to judge by the accuracy of their predictions, for these are very numerous and diverse. When schools compete, a whole generation of scientists may have to give a life's work before the implications of a new pattern can be worked out in detail, and tested. They will scarcely want to make this commitment without some way of judging beforehand whether they have picked the winner.

The way the natural scientists resolve these conflicts of competing schools is to use a much broader conception of 'fit' than conventional statisticians recognise.[28] They know, or can quickly find out, many things, across a wide range of human experience. Any theory they may think up makes assumptions, yields predictions, has implications or corollaries across much of this field (the more general the theory, the wider the field). To judge it, they can compare these assumptions, etc., with the facts at their disposal. Social scientists can do much the same, if they are prepared to change their modern habits. They are trained to specialise, to keep each to his own patch, and there to dig deep, and build high. But for this purpose they must range widely. 'The economist whose search for causes brings him up against convention, mood, passion or culture [must no longer say] "At this point I stop: you must send for another trade". When the actual way in which decisions are reached in the board room or across the bargaining table has been discussed, it has been said that economics as such has nothing to contribute. Down with "economics as such". . . . Where an economic problem arises, let us observe whatever seems significant, and follow clues to causes wherever they may lead.' (That, I am glad to say, was part of a Presidential Address, by E. H. Phelps Brown, to the Royal Economic Society.)[29]

One advantage of the natural scientist is the wealth of established 'facts' at his disposal. For the social scientist the best way of amassing 'facts' with which to build or judge a theory, is history. Phelps Brown draws a parallel here with medicine: 'Clinical intuition (which doctors value) has been defined as reasoning from experience not consciously recalled; and history is vicarious experience . . . we ought to value . . . the insight of the historian more than the rigour of the mathematician.'[30]

In a phrase, in judging a theory we should reason in three directions rather than one. First, we should reason upwards, that is to say compare the theory's predictions with the facts – the usual statistical procedure, but applied along a broad front. We can see, for example, how far our theory of inflation can explain trends, fluctuations and variations in inflation within and between many different countries at various times. Second, we should reason downwards, comparing the assumptions with reality. Does collective bargaining seem to be normal in most industries? Where it is not, do employers seem to take account of settlements negotiated elsewhere? . . . Third, we should reason sideways; that is, first uncover the basic propositions on which the theory is based – theories of collective bargaining, of pricing under oligopoly, etc. – then see how well these explain other questions – strike patterns, say, or the size of profit margins. To sum up the process, it is like exploring a tree, starting from a bough. You work upwards and outwards, towards the twigs and the leaves; you work downwards towards the roots; and having found the main trunk, you go up it to explore other boughs.[31]

This method of judgement, with its triple set of criteria, can be made as systematic as the conventional one, with its single set, but in essence it is the test which any intelligent person uses when he is offered a new idea to explain something. He tries to work out its implications for the areas with which he is familiar, to see how far they are consistent with what he already knows, or believes, reasoning upwards, downwards and sideways. If the consistency is not obvious at some point he may come back, 'But in that case, how would you account for x; how could your explanation be squared with y?' If there are answers, and they are convincing, then he may conclude, 'yes, that seems to fit'.

'It seems to fit' – that is the accolade. It is the end of a process of reasoning which is truly scientific: it seeks to connect what was previously separate, to transform disorder into ordered patterns, and thus, to make sense of the world. (Explanations built on false assumptions are not scientific – they are nonsensical, like trees with fine leaves and no roots.) My aim in this book is to make such patterns and connections, and to make it possible for the reader to join in the procedure I have described – asking of every assumption whether from his experience or knowledge it seems reasonable, and of every idea whether it can help to explain the world he knows, and answer the questions he has already been asking himself.

Such an aim makes the style and structure of the book all-important. What matters is the pattern I am putting forward, and the best way to see its shape clearly is to read fast; lingering over each tree, one may miss the wood. (But each will stand scrutiny, later.) So wherever possible anything which would impede the flow of the argument has been cut out of the main text. Many substantiations, reservations, qualifications have been banished to the notes and appendix at the end of the book. There is not one mathematical equation in the main text. (For modern economists, it is only a fault to be illiterate, but it is criminal to be innumerate, so I should stress that in the appendix, mathematical explanations are used wherever they make for rigour or speed, and there is some econometrics.) I do, however, use one standard theoretical gambit: I begin with a set of assumptions which are too simple, so as to show the shape of the argument or introduce a concept, and then make them more complicated and realistic later. I have also to make a number of controversial assumptions in the early stages which are only justified later in the book. Both ploys require some patience, but not much, for I will not keep you long.

1.2   A BARGAINING THEORY OF WAGES[32]

> When a Trade Union demands an advance in wages, or resists
> a reduction, it sets before the employer an alternative: either
> he must pay higher wages than he would have paid on his own
> initiative (and this generally means a prolonged reduction in
> profits) or on the other hand he must endure the direct loss
> which will probably follow from a stoppage of work . . . one
> alternative will generally bring him less loss than the other. If
> resistance appears less costly than concession, he will resist; if
> concession seems cheaper, he will meet the Union's claim.
> J. R. Hicks (1933), *Theory of Wages*, p. 131.

To resist or to concede, that is the question. But that puts the choice a
little too simply, as black or white, when the world is made of shades of
grey. How grimly to resist, how much to concede – that is what the
employer must decide. I shall describe his decision in terms of his
negotiating policy, or *bargaining stance*; in terms of the *toughness* or
softness of his stance. A tough stance has the aim of conceding little – the
emphasis is on resistance, in spite of the costs of resistance; a soft stance
is designed to avoid those management resistance *costs*, at the price of
conceding more. It is clear that a tough stance makes for a low wage
increase, a soft stance for a higher one; but the outcome depends not
only on the employer, but also on the union's behaviour – which can
also be described in terms of bargaining stance. If the union takes a
tough stance, that means it aims for a high wage increase, in spite of the
costs of this policy (including the cost of carrying on a strike). For
symmetry I will call these costs *union resistance costs* – the costs of
resisting the employer. To avoid these costs, the union may take a soft
stance – be ready to accept a small wage increase; that involves some
sacrifice of wages, which is the *union's* cost of concession.

If we know the stances of both sides, employer and union, we know
the outcome, more or less: if the employer's stance is tough, the union's
soft, the wage increase will be low; if the union's is tough, the employer's
soft, the increase will be high. If both stances are soft, or both tough, the
increase will be somewhere between; in the tough : tough case we can
expect a strike, on the way to the agreement.

How, in turn, can we explain or predict the stance each side takes?
First, from their resistance and concession costs. 'If resistance appears
less costly than concession, he will resist. . . .' What are these costs
composed of?

The Employer

Let us look first at a firm operating in a competitive market in which the price at which it can sell its goods is fixed, more or less, by forces beyond its control. Its concession cost is simply the increase in its wage bill, for its profit will be reduced by that amount. On the other hand, a firm in a less competitive market may choose to pass part or all of the increase on to the customer, and even if that leads to some loss of sales, the cost of the concession, taken as a whole, will presumably be rather less than in the first case. And if competing firms agree to copy the increase, or their workers force them to do so, then *they* will have higher costs too and our firm may be able to pass the rise on in higher prices with little or no loss of sales.

The employer's resistance cost can be divided into two parts, *direct* and *indirect*. A tough policy may lead to a strike, or some other form of action meant to force his hand – an overtime ban, say, or a go-slow. That inflicts *direct* resistance costs; since these costs result from concerted action, they imply unionisation, but there are other unpleasant consequences of keeping wages down which do not: a low wage is known to lower morale and productivity, increase absenteeism and the 'quit rate' and make good workers harder to recruit. All these are *indirect* resistance costs, and can equally affect non-union firms. Non-union firms have an extra indirect resistance cost: the risk of their workers unionising in response to a low wage increase.

If we want to explain the wages of a *non-union* firm, there is no need to look any further – it will simply pick the increase which it expects to cost least, taking concession and (indirect) resistance costs together. If, for example, it faces a labour shortage or its workers seem discontented and on the point of joining a union, it will probably give a big increase; if it faces a highly competitive market or its labour costs are a particularly high proportion of its total costs, it will be inclined to be mean.

The complication with a unionised firm is that it has to take account of direct resistance cost, and that depends on *what the union will do*. It is not enough to know, say, how many customers would be lost through an *x* weeks strike (*strike cost*) but also whether a particular stance would result in an *x* weeks strike. The firm can hardly expect to know that definitely, so the best it can hope to do is to make an educated guess about the likelihood as well as the cost of such a strike, and be ready to revise the guess, and its stance, as the bargaining (or the strike) proceeds. The likelihood of a strike depends on the union's stance, so we, and the firm, have to ask what determines that.

The Union[33]

The easiest way to approach the union's costs is to treat the union for the moment purely as the representative of its members, so that its costs are their costs. In that case, union concession costs are what the workers lose in wages by not getting a higher increase. Thus there will always be union concession costs, whatever the situation, but they will vary according to the value the workers set on higher wages. If, for example, they can expect to be in the job for many years to come, they will lose a lot by accepting a low increase; therefore they have high concession costs. That, of course, will tend to make the union's stance tough. But then there are the costs of resistance. *Indirect* resistance cost is the loss the workers may suffer as a result of an increase in the wage – in practice, the loss of a job. If the wage increase seems likely to lead to many redundancies, and workers cannot expect to get equally good jobs elsewhere, then indirect resistance costs will be high, and that will soften the union stance. *Direct* resistance cost, finally, is the loss workers must suffer through the strike (or other 'industrial action') they have to endure in order to win a better settlement. This will depend on their *strike costs*, which would, for example, be high if the union had no strike fund and the workers no savings, or prospects of other support; but it will depend equally on how long the strike would have to be – whether the employer would cave in without it, at one extreme, or stick out for months, at the other. That brings us back full circle, to the employer's stance. (For a graphic summary of the argument see Fig.1.1.)

Expectations, objectives and organisations

Till now, I have ignored or skirted several difficulties. The first is the problem of uncertainty, information and expectations. Neither the union nor the employer know exactly or certainly what their concession, indirect resistance or direct resistance costs will be. It is what they *think* they will be that counts – their *expectations*; but their expectations will rarely be very far from the truth. Management's concession cost depends on its relationship with its competitors and its customers – which it should know well; and on its own cost structure – which it should know even better. Its resistance cost depends on the degree of discontent among the workforce, the need for new labour, the damage a strike would do. . . . Managers should be able to assess these things. Likewise, the union should know roughly what resources the workers

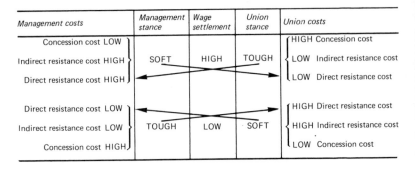

Note: Read towards the centre from each side. Costs (as perceived) determine stances which in turn determine the settlement; thus e.g. HIGH union concession cost makes for a TOUGH union stance which makes for a HIGH wage settlement. Stances affect the other side's direct resistance cost; thus e.g. a TOUGH union stance makes for HIGH management direct resistance cost - the arrow shows cause-and-effect.

FIGURE 1.1 The basics of a bargaining theory of wages[34]

have for a strike, and certainly the state of its own finances. It makes matters a little more difficult, that resistance cost for each side depends partly on what the other side will do; but even if he lacks direct information about the other side, as to the costs I have just been discussing, an experienced negotiator can usually tell how anxious his opponent is for a settlement. Where there is clear evidence that negotiators are misinformed or uncertain, one must of course take that into account; but otherwise I shall work on the general assumption that each side knows roughly what its costs are, and that if we too can find out, we shall have a good explanation of wage settlements.

The second problem concerns objectives. In the last paragraph I may seem to have slipped into the neoclassical assumption about them. To choose the stance you expect to *cost least* is in effect to choose that which will give most profit, surely? It depends what one means by *cost*. I shall take it as something much broader than *financial* cost; as anything one dislikes. For example, a peaceable manager with a horror of conflict will have relatively high direct resistance costs, and will therefore take a relatively soft stance. This view of cost can take account of *targets* too. Suppose workers have decided that *x* per cent is the minimum increase they are entitled to get, and that anything less is an insult (perhaps because others have got *x* or more). Then this is their target increase, and up to it they will have high concession costs, and a tough stance. In much the same way, managers who have a target level of profitability will have low concession costs so long as they are clearly above target; so their stance will be soft. (But as I have said in the Introduction, once a manager is above a target, he may choose to raise it, or be forced to do so.)

I shall soon show that differences in objectives play an indispensable part in explaining differences in inflation. What makes for the widest variations in objectives is that unions and employers are not single individuals, but groups, and very complex groups at that. Unions are representative institutions which have members with diverse interests, and a hierarchy of different levels, any or all of which may deal with management; firms are organisations which belong in principle to a number of shareholders and are run by a hierarchy of management levels, any or all of which may deal with the union. Between the union president and the newest member, between a majority shareholder, or chairman of the employers' association, and a foreman, lie wide differences of interests, attitudes and perceptions. This creates a problem which sociologists have pointed out to me more than once: if there is one thing that they all agree on, it is that groups, such groups above all, do not behave like individuals. Yet this theory of wages does treat the two sides to the negotiation, by implication, very much as if they were individuals.

It would have been easier to respond to this criticism if sociology had offered any clear theory of how groups do behave. For lack of such a theory, I have had to find my own answer to the problem. The procedure is to analyse each side from two points of view: first, to look at the *power structure* and try to make some useful generalisations about the distribution of power within firms, employers' associations, unions in different countries and industries, and at different times; second, to ask how resistance and concession costs tend to vary between the different sections and levels on both sides. Thus we may be able to say, for example, that in a certain situation a level of management with relatively high resistance costs and low concession costs played a particularly important role in setting wages, and that this made for high wage increases. It is a crude procedure, and more complex than it sounds, but it seems the best available. I begin to use it in Chapter 2, Section 1.

Conclusion

My theory of wages is quite different from neoclassical theories, that is clear. But one should not exaggerate the differences. Although they are not normally used by neoclassical economists, concepts like bargaining stance, resistance and concession cost, do not as such contradict their theories, and indeed supply-and-demand theories of wages have occasionally been dressed up in bargaining sheep's clothing. It all depends on what you assume determines resistance and concession cost; and I shall not deny that market forces have an important role. Yet the form of the theory is all-important. It frees us to look far beyond market forces, at a wide range of political, social, psychological and economic factors, then provides a main focus for what we find. That focus is the negotiating relationship – a *power* relationship – between workers and unions on the one hand, and employers on the other. This book is built around it.

1.3   THE WAGE-PRICE, WAGE-WAGE SPIRAL

In Chapters 2 and 3 I shall look at the features of firms and unions which affect their bargaining stances, and thus their wages. On the management side, for example, these include technology, market structure, and the organisation and objectives of management. But no industry, still less firm, least of all plant, stands alone. Inflation is a spiral process, in which wages affect prices, prices affect wages, and the wages of one group affect those of another. Before looking with a narrow focus at any part of it, we must have at least a broad picture of the links within the whole.

The Wage-Wage Spiral

To see the links between the wages of different groups, let us take as an example an imaginary firm in the car industry, which I shall call British Fordsler. BF is of course in the habit of negotiating wage increases at regular intervals. Now consider what would happen to those negotiations if from this moment on no-one else's workers, anywhere in the economy, won an increase in wages – this year, next year, ever.

The first point for both sides at BF to note is that because its wage increases are not going to be copied in future – not even at Vauxland or Chrysall, its main rivals – they are very unlikely to affect anyone else's prices, so that in turn the prices it can charge will not change.[35] To begin with, this may not matter; a wage increase may improve morale and recruitment, and cut labour turnover, so that costs do not rise. But at some stage labour productivity is going to rise just about as high as good wages can bring it; any further wage rise beyond that point means an

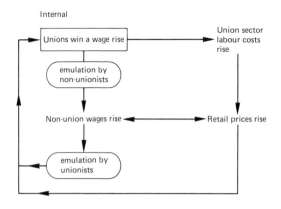

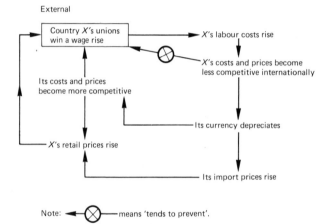

FIGURE 1.2 The internal and external spirals of inflation

equal reduction in profits. Thus we expect management's bargaining stance to grow progressively tougher.[36]

On the union side, the opposite is happening. Every increase they get makes British Fordsler workers better off, both in absolute terms and relative to other workers. While they may have begun with some discontent about past price rises or unfair 'relativities' as against other workers, they will now be more and more content with their position; and they will have to take into account rising indirect resistance costs – the fear of losing their jobs if BF's cars, and thus their labour, are 'priced out of the market'. At some point their indirect resistance cost will exceed their concession cost – i.e. they wouldn't want an increase even if the firm was ready to concede it without a strike. So the workers' bargaining stance progressively softens.

It is clear that before long the process of wage inflation at British Fordsler will grind to a halt. The forces which combine to stop it are, in the last analysis, just two.

First is the fact that wages are increasing faster than elsewhere. Sooner or later, in any firm, that is bound to make management's stance tougher, and the union's softer, until the rate of increase comes down to the average; the opposite will happen where wage increases are unusually low.[37]

The other force toughens management's stance from the beginning or rather from the moment it is perceived: BF's *isolation*. No concession BF makes is going to budge any other firm an inch, and thus give BF more room to raise prices; so the whole increase in labour costs counts as concession cost, as it would not have done if there had been any imitation of the settlement. This isolation would have depressed BF's wages even if the wage increases others were giving had been the same as BF's, or greater.

In a fully unionised economy neither of these forces will have a strong depressing effect on wages. Individual firms, individual industries, will not be *isolated*, but closely *linked*; as I shall show in Chapter 3, Section 3, the wage increases given by A increase the pressure on B, C and D to give an increase too; this *emulation* cuts A's concession cost. And for every firm which pays above the average and is held back by that fact, there is another firm which is pushed forward because it is paying less than the average. But if only a small proportion of the labour force is unionised, the unionised firms are likely to feel much more isolated, and also to be paying well above average (the 'union differential'); that will tend to hold their wage increases down.

The relative size of the *union* and *non-union sectors* is important, but there is more to it. The non-union sector, or a large part of it, may in fact emulate the union sector: non-union employers may keep carefully in line with union wages (or at least wage increases) for fear that otherwise their workers may unionise, or work less well out of discontent, or simply quit. The more they feel obliged to behave like this, the less isolated is the union sector. And because of such emulation, or through shortage of labour, the 'union differential' may be small even though the non-union sector is large. Lastly, supposing non-union firms do pay lower wages, and do not 'emulate', they will depress union firms' wage increases much more if they are direct competitors than if they are in some quite unrelated industry.

Union and non-union sectors, then, are rather like hostile confederations of states. Any state unlucky enough to be in an area dominated by the 'other side' must adopt many of its customs, for fear of worse – the worst being, in the union sector, going out of business, and in the non-union sector, unionisation. Where the union 'confederation has generally the upper hand, then most of the 'non-union' side must behave more or less as if they were unionised; where the non-union confederation is dominant, the union sector will tend to copy it. This relationship is the more important because it has changed a great deal over time, and varies quite as much between countries today. In the USA in the 1920s the union sector was very small; in Sweden now, the non-union sector is. In my triangular comparison between Britain, West Germany and the USA, we shall see a great difference between the union sector's minority situation in the USA, and its majority situation in the other two countries.[38]

The Wage-Price Effect

How does inflation affect prices; how much do prices increase – other things being equal – for every 1 per cent increase in the average level of money wages in the economy? The neatest way to an answer is by seeing how the increase affects each of the four components of prices: wage costs, indirect taxes, import costs, and the profit margin. The first is easy: wages up, wage costs up: one for one, straight away. Indirect taxes are almost as quickly dealt with. All, or almost all, a government's revenue from taxation goes to pay the wages and prices which are rising. If the other components of prices go up 1 per cent – as I shall show they all will – then it will want 1 per cent more revenue. Even if the system of indirect taxation is not designed to provide this automatically, there will be little difficulty in raising tax rates. 'Nothing is certain but death and taxes'; they will not lag behind for long.

Import costs, on the other hand, seem not at all affected by the wage increase: but they are, in due course. We can see how, in the process of explaining what happens to profit margins.

Firms will probably have a *target* for their profit margin (see Chapter 1, Section 1 and Chapter 2), and it will probably be expressed in real terms – so if costs go up by 1 per cent, they will want to raise margins by 1 per cent as well. We shall see in Chapter 2, Section 3 that this will present no problem so long as their competitors have had much the same increase in cost; they will then raise prices together. But their foreign competitors may not have had the same cost increases, and on markets where foreign firms are important, and buyers are price-conscious, it may be necessary to hold back until these competitors are ready to raise prices too.

Fortunately, the wage increase will solve even this problem in time. An example will show how. Suppose Britain trades only with Germany, and British wages rise faster than German. Then British costs get out of line with those in Germany. British goods become less competitive, exports fall and imports rise, and the British balance of payments moves into deficit. That must lead, sooner or later, to a fall in the value of the pound – devaluation – against the mark, which brings British costs back into line. With dearer marks, importers have to raise sterling prices, which allows British producers to do so too; and British exporters now get more sterling for the marks they earn.

So profit margins rise, back to their old real value. And we now see what causes the increase in import costs: the devaluation, itself due to the wage increase. In recent years, with floating exchange rates, such a devaluation has become almost automatic. Governments will usually choose to nudge the rate down to avoid too great a loss of competitiveness, and if they do not, private operators on the foreign exchange market will drive it down as soon as they see the effect on the balance of payments; in fact they are learning to anticipate this by watching movements of costs. So a wage rise now feeds back into import costs, and profit margins, more quickly than before.[39]

And so, in time, and other things being equal, a 1 per cent rise in wages means a 1 per cent rise in prices; that is (to phrase it more clearly) if wages rise by 1 per cent more than they would otherwise have done, prices too will rise by 1 per cent more than they would otherwise have done.[40]

The Price-Wage Effect

If we could now find the same effect of prices on wages as of wages on prices, we would have a perfect wage-price spiral – and a perfectly alarming one – for a 1 per cent rise in price inflation would produce a 1 per cent rise in wage inflation which would feed back into a *further* 1 per cent rise in price inflation, and so on up. As I showed in the Introduction, this is precisely the monetarists' view, because they assume that wage bargaining is about *real* wages; if price inflation quickens, that presumably gives a lower real wage increase than had been agreed, so when the bargainers next meet they will increase money wages even more so as to get that real increase *this* time. Indeed the acceleration might itself accelerate as soon as the bargainers got used to it; perhaps at first you bargain assuming constant prices; then you find prices rise but at least assume price *inflation* constant; then you find inflation rises but assume the acceleration of inflation constant; then. . . .

It is a plausible nightmare and gives a basic understanding of the spectacular cases of *hyperinflation*. But I believe that at lower rates of inflation it is not quite accurate, because bargainers do not automatically raise wage settlements by 1 per cent for every 1 per cent rise in price inflation, even when they have had time to find out about it. This is not because they suffer from 'money illusion' – the illusion that the money increase is a real increase; even once they have come to assume the inflation will go on, they may not *fully* allow for it. The reason is that they are only partly concerned with real wages – the firm with the real cost of labour, the union with the purchasing power of earnings; within certain limits they may be more concerned with *relative* wages – the firm worrying in case they are higher than its competitors', or lower than other employers', the union determined that they should at least match those of 'comparable groups' (see Chapter 3, Section 3). In that case the effect of wages on wages is as important as that of prices, and instead of a perfect wage-price-wage spiral we have an imperfect one, with a wage-wage effect helping to drive it.[41]

There may be little difference in the outcome – we can go to hell along either road, and just about as fast – but there is a difference in the mechanics. It is a difference which helps to explain the emphasis of this book: if the step from wage inflation to price inflation is in a sense automatic, once one has allowed for increases in productivity, while the step from prices to wages is not, then one may need to take a little longer to see what does determine wages. But – please – it does not imply that wages, or unions, 'cause' inflation; that prices, or management, do not. The role of prices is central, and manifold. What price a firm is charging determines its profit margin and thus affects its concession costs (particularly if it is a satisficer, happy with a limited margin). How far and how easily it could raise its price to pass on a wage increase, will affect its concession costs even more. I shall deal first, then, with prices, later with wages. If that means looking at management before unions, so much the better, for management, again, has the central role. The unions only deal with wages, and naturally always try to raise them; management's position is more delicately balanced: should it hold down prices and please its customers, at the expense of its workers, or raise wages and please its workers at the expense of its customers? In any case, as I shall show in Chapter 3, one can understand very little about a country's unions without understanding its managers first.

2 The Management Side

2.1 BRITISH SATISFICERS AND GERMAN MAXIMISERS: THE OBJECTIVES AND ORGANISATION OF MODERN FIRMS

> 'The directors of such [joint-stock] companies . . . being the managers rather of other people's money than of their own, it cannot be well expected, that they should watch over it with the same anxious vigilance with which the partners in a private copartnery frequently watch over their own. Negligence and profusion, therefore, must always prevail, more or less, in the management of such a company.
>
> Adam Smith, *Wealth of Nations*, vol. 2, pp. 264–5.

How far is Adam Smith's pessimistic view of 'professional' management – as satisficers, in my language – true today? The answer is important, for it affects management's bargaining stance. The answer also turns out to be quite different, between Britain on the one hand, and Germany and the United States on the other. That makes it fascinating.

The controversy about the objectives of management hinges on the relationship between the owners of a firm's capital – that is, its shareholders and bankers – and its managers. If the latter are left to run the firm as they choose it is easy to see that they may do so in a way which does not suit the interests of the owners. But the owners are not helpless: if they take enough trouble over supervision they can use their property right to make the managers act in their interests; and if owners in general take enough trouble they can arrange institutions which will make the task of supervision easier. Before we can fully explain – and even quite believe – the differences between modern managers, we must understand the differences between owners, in their organisation, their attitudes, their traditions. For that we need history. I begin, as seems right, with Britain's.

Britain

The most important peculiarity of British social and political history is the character of the landowners. The early success of the British Industrial Revolution was due more than anything to the old landowning upper class. Unlike his Continental counterparts, the British landowner was well disposed towards industry. He provided it with much of its finances; through his control of the state, he protected it from threats to its markets and removed obstacles which blocked its expansion; his younger sons, denied a share of his lands, would often invest their own energies in it, as well as their 'portion'. Not least, by accepting the *nouveau riche* into Society, he gave industrialists an incentive to accumulate.

There was the rub. No sooner had a manufacturer made his money than he was absorbed. At first, Dissenters were excluded from this welcome on religious grounds, and provided a large proportion of the manufacturers, but by the mid-19th century the religious barrier too was crumbling, and landowners and industrialists were rapidly merging into a new upper class. In that new upper class, fatally, it was the landowners who set the tone for the rest. Why? The obvious reason is that holding the high ground of Society they could dictate terms – they accepted the newer rich on condition they obeyed the old rules. But a class without a *raison d'être* makes a poor model for imitation. The British landowners found their new *raison d'être* just in time – imperialism.

The Empire made the aristocratic model irresistible, for it provided a glamorous and even useful outlet for all the old aristocratic qualities, in war, diplomacy, administration, even farming. Rich manufacturers bought country estates for themselves, and a classical education for their sons; they disdained technical education, improved methods, or new investment, for they had set their hearts on the great game of Empire. The worst of it was, they continued to prosper – the Empire and the British sphere of influence in Latin America provided markets for the products they should have updated and outlets for the profits they should have ploughed back into their factories. Not until the late 1920s did British industry in general face a serious crisis through failure to meet international competition; that crisis was short-lived, since after 1931 it enjoyed twenty years of protection and Imperial Preference before gradually returning to the harsh test of free trade. By that time the manufacturing families had almost all given up the running of their firms to professional managers, and were rapidly selling their shareholdings to the financial institutions of the City, to which we must now turn.

Parallel to manufacturing, but separate from it, grew up the great financial institutions of the City of London. They left most of the business of providing industry with funds to the provincial capital markets which flourished in the 18th and 19th centuries – lenders on these had a better knowledge of the firms involved and were well able to raise the modest sums required. The City lent on a grander scale, to governments; for railways and canals; for commerce; and for the dazzling variety of lucrative ventures which blossomed in the Empire and the Americas up to the First World War.

Then the world changed, and foreign lending became less attractive and more difficult. At the same time, new institutions moved their headquarters to the City from the provinces: the great clearing banks, which traditionally provided industry with most of what short-term finance it needed, and the insurance companies. After the Second World War, the banks steadily expanded their lending to industry; and the insurance companies, together with the pension funds, rapidly bought up the majority of the shares of large industrial firms. But it was typical of these institutions, of the City's traditions, and of the attitudes of British society, that this enormous capital stake was built up in ways calculated to minimise both risk and the opportunity for control. The banks preferred to lend short-term, the insurance companies to buy small stakes in a wide range of big firms. There was no tradition of exercising control; they did not set out to gain it; when they realised that (as a group) they had it for the taking they preferred not to take it; and when they found a firm they had invested in, in a state that cried out for intervention, they did not know how to go about it. Large private shareholders could have given the institutions a lead, as we shall see they often do in the USA; but in Britain the 'activist' private shareholder had died as the manufacturing families acquired their Oxford accents. And so the control of industry was left to the professional managers.

There are two broad types of top manager in British industry, which I will call the Officer and the NCO. The NCO has come up from lower management (or below) through native ability or determination or luck; he has not been trained or educated for top positions, and what he has learnt has been practical and specialised, either in a technical subject or in a technique like accountancy. Such men tended to be the first to rise to fill the vacuum left by the founding families, simply because they were there, but when large firms in the 1940s and 1950s set out deliberately to recruit and promote 'leadership material', they looked elsewhere. They looked to the Officer type, who already dominated the professions, politics and the Civil Service. His education was the old, glamorous, imperial kind, in dead languages or abstract disciplines, typified by the Oxford or Cambridge 'arts' degree. Though this background tended to instil a disdain for industry, industry admired it. The Officer type, who already ran everything else in Britain, was now brought in to run industry, in uneasy partnership with the NCO.

Between them these two types had all the faults imaginable in a top manager. The Officer had something of the same indifference to industry, and ignorance of it, that the old industrial families had shown before they gave up control. (It was men with a similar education and attitudes who dominated the City, which helps to explain their reluctance to intervene.) The NCO knew and probably cared about industry, or rather the compartment of it in which he had worked, but was unprepared for leadership, and for dealing with financiers and the other gods in the lofty world to which he had risen. He was thus likely to be rather timid – as was the Officer if he had the wit to see how little he knew. These qualities will seem the more striking after we have looked at top management in Germany. I shall try to show that they made British top managers peculiarly unsuited to the autonomy which the owners of industry allowed them.

The Ownership and Control of West German Industry

The contrast with West Germany could scarcely be more complete. The divorce of ownership from control has simply not happened. There are professional managers at the top of many large firms, but a multitude of pressures combine to make them act in the interests of the owners. First, a large proportion of top managers even now have a major share stake in the business, or belong to families which do. There is still a very high concentration of share ownership; even in many of the large firms a family or individual holds a controlling interest. These *Unternehmer* or 'entrepreneurial' families take a good deal of trouble to *exercise* control, as their participation in management suggests.

However, the most important constraint on management is probably the all-pervading influence of the banks, above all the Big Three, the *Grossbanken* (Deutsche, Dresdner, Commerz). The banks, led by the Big Three, combine a staggering range of functions. They control the Stock Exchanges, act as shareholders, underwrite capital issues, lend short, medium and long term funds, allocate state investment subsidies – but their main power stems from two other features of German industry, the *Aufsichtsrat* and *Depotstimmrecht*. The Aufsichtsrat is a supervisory board of non-executive directors with formidable powers – and duties – to oversee the Vorstand (executive board). The key post is held by the Chairman, who is bound to maintain continuous supervision over the firm and has a full-time secretariat to help him do it. The banks are strongly represented on the Aufsichtsräte, and the Big Three hold most of the Chairmanships of the larger firms.

The Aufsichtsrat gives the banks access to information, without which power cannot be exercised, but the power itself is based above all on Depotstimmrecht, the use of proxy votes 'deposited' by shareholders (mainly with the Big Three). Bank holdings of industrial shares are modest, and although the Big Three have a higher proportion of their assets in equities than the rest do, there are few major firms where this gives them a controlling interest; but by using proxy votes and where necessary forming coalitions, with family owners and one another, they wield great power, which they have not hesitated to use to turn out unsatisfactory managements.

It is the combination of roles which is all-important. From their men on the Aufsichtsrat the banks find out if anything needs to be done. Bank officials on other Aufsichtsräte, and the banks' well-staffed Technical Departments, can help to decide what changes need to be made, even find the men to make them. Once the banks are sure of their ground (they are wary nowadays of accusations of abuse of power) it is almost futile for the Vorstand to resist. The firm could be refused loans, effectively barred from the capital market, and if necessary voted out of office by the banks' proxies, or by a coalition of banks and major private shareholders.

The close relation between owners and managers in Germany, like the loose relation in Britain, can be best understood by way of history.

The Historical Background of West German Management

The German industrial revolution was made by a coalition of the state with the urban middle class (from which most industrialists came) without the support of the old landowning class (in Prussia called Junkers). For the rapid expansion which was planned, and achieved, German industry needed a great deal of trained manpower and capital. To provide the first, a superb system of technical education was developed, including the *Technische Hochschulen*. To provide the second, the joint-stock banks (the ancestors of today's Big Three) were set up, largely by the industrialists themselves (as Siemens founded the

Deutsche Bank) and for their purposes: 'The joint-stock bank was not merely a credit organisation but a politico-economic agency for converting Germany into an industrial state.'[1] The interventionist policy of the banks is not new – they were doing almost exactly the same in the late 19th century.

The early surge of expansion and investment is perhaps less impressive than the fact that it was maintained. For that, ironically, we have to thank the Junkers and the semi-feudal nature of the Hohenzollern state. The highest positions in politics, diplomacy and war were closed to the Unternehmer and the rest of the middle class; as a result, as the historian Sombart put it in 1905,

> With us there is no diversion of talent into the field of politics, as in other countries. Neither the rich, nor what is more important, the gifted members of the middle class are withdrawn from economic life to devote themselves to politics.[2]

When the Empire collapsed in 1918, the Unternehmer began tentatively to explore the power vacuum it had left, but a succession of economic crises kept their hands full (note that the neglect of industry by the British manufacturers dates from a period of mild prosperity). In 1933 came the Nazis, who for all that they received support from industrialists, did not (in general) belong to that class. Their system rather resembled the imperial one: the Unternehmer was to be lord in his own firm, and to have a voice in his industry, but let him not stray outside it.

Only when the Nazi regime too had collapsed, and what remained of the old structure of German society with it, did the Unternehmer see the chance, and the urgent need, to assert themselves in politics. For 'due to the destruction of old elites, the importance of the Unternehmer for the formation of a new *élite* group has increased'.[3] 'At stake is a new balance of society and State, that is, the establishment of a new industrial society which is shaped by the Unternehmer.'[4] That was their new ambition, and they realised it. Their social isolation in the old order had helped to make them cohesive, devoted to industrial progress, and well-educated to achieve it. They now used their power to remake West German society very much in their own image. We shall see later what this meant for the unions; in the present context the important aspect is their concern for education. They set out to make it not only teach useful subjects, but spread useful attitudes – attitudes which recognised the importance of business leadership and the need for profit.

Objectives Compared

Objectives cannot be seen, or measured; the most one can do is to find out whether the predictions which can be made about them, from history and present circumstances, fit the way managers are observed to behave.

A strong commitment to owners' interests is to be expected from German managers, since they are trained and promoted in a system dominated by owners. Any who turn out to lack this commitment can be efficiently replaced: candidates for the Vorstand of a large firm are largely recruited from the Vorstände of smaller firms, where Aufsichtsrat bankers will have been able to observe their qualities as top managers. And what *are* the owners' interests? The determined pursuit of profit, long-term, so that dividends and share values may grow, and grow. The British manager, on the other hand, is reared in a society which gives scant glory to the aggressive pursuit of industrial profit, and if he shows little interest in this there does not seem much that the owners, i.e., bankers and shareholders, are able or willing to do to change his attitude or replace him.

I am not suggesting that the average British top manager is lazy or negligent. On the contrary; he is probably a decent and overworked man, and for all the modern talk of social responsibility is likely to put his shareholders' interests first. The danger is that he will favour policies which suit himself and his colleagues and involve the minimum disturbance to established routine. The men he chooses for promotion, likewise, will be cautious types who seem to 'fit in', rather than arrogant young men with disruptive ideas. His instinct will be to stay out of trouble and to make sure that profits are kept above a certain minimum level, in the short term at any rate – else there might be trouble from shareholders or take-over bidders, and a shortage of funds for investment; and there must be *enough* invested for a gentle rate of growth which will keep management as a whole happy. The more distant future – even five years ahead – matters less; he may have retired by then.

Let us look at this man in action. Hannah and Kay have found that the sharp increase in overall concentration in British industry since 1950 was entirely due to mergers, and that very few of these could be justified on the grounds of technical economies of scale. Why such a taste for merger? The ambitious British manager finds fast growth through investment too risky, when he can use mergers to build a corporate empire based on established products and entrenched market shares.

Mergers reduce the danger of competition, dilute the holdings of inconveniently large shareholders, and make the firm too large for many potential take-over bidders. The result has been that British industry has evolved into a hotchpotch of ramshackle conglomerates, which though large by international standards have small plants, and out-of-date products and equipment.

German firms, on the other hand, are if anything smaller than British, but with larger plants and a much higher rate of investment per man. Why? The German owner wants growth, in order to increase profit – but *internal* growth. The Unternehmer dislikes growth by merger, since by diluting his shareholding that would weaken his control. Traditionally, mergers have been resisted by owners and forced through by the banks when they seemed the only way to technical economies of scale. (The banks could then look forward to financing the large new plants needed to make the most of these economies.) Many reasons given for mergers in Britain cut very little ice in Germany. Financial economies of scale? Even small German firms have excellent access to long term bank finance. Is an injection of new management needed? No need for a merger – the banks will find the men and force the change. Product rationalisation? In the mid-1950s the product structure of the steel industry was rather confused. Discreet intervention led by the Deutsche Bank persuaded each firm to concentrate on its strengths, and leave the rest to its rivals.

Employers' Associations

We can now explain the very important differences between British and West German employers' associations (EAs). German EAs have been strong ever since the beginning of the century, when trade unions first became a threat. They include more than 90 per cent of all West German firms, tightly organised in regional and industrial associations which themselves belong to a national body, the BDA. The BDA is no loose central lobbying association, but has a 'so rigidly hierarchical, altogether bureaucratic, mechanism for the wielding of power that it would be plainly impossible to visualise anything more centralised, tightened, irresistible'.[5] The employers' associations carry out almost all wage bargaining, and keep individual firms under strict discipline.[6] Compare the British EAs, which were also strong at the turn of the century. They are now loose associations which negotiate with unions at industry level, while the most important wage bargaining in most of industry goes on at plant or firm level, which few EAs even try to control.[7]

Why is there such a difference? We have to ask who gains, and who loses, from a firm's decision to participate in a strong employer organisation. The greatest gainers are the *other* firms – will the firm have their interests at heart? In Germany, yes, because of the Unternehmer tradition of solidarity, and the power of banks with a stake in the whole industry; in Britain, there is no such cement to bind firms together. The greatest losers are the managers of large firms, who will have more difficulty in keeping the peace within their walls if they have to yoke their bargaining policy to decisions taken by others with different interests. In Britain, these managers are now more or less autonomous – they can act to suit their own convenience; in Germany, managers are firmly controlled by owners, and *they* will probably decide that on a long view, the industry must hang together if it is not to hang separately.[8]

The Role of Lower Management

The division of power between lower management and top management is as important as that between the firm and the EA, and for the same reason – it affects the balance of resistance and concession cost.

Compare the lower manager with his superior. Normally the managers at plant or shop-floor level who can influence wages are line management (i.e. production managers and foremen) and personnel managers. These people may care about the profitability of the firm, but they care most about the direct pressures on them. The most immediate pressure on the personnel manager is to keep the industrial peace; on the line manager, to maintain production. For them it is a strike that hurts – what does concession cost mean to them? That's not their department – the bill lands on someone else's desk.

However, in some firms power is delegated not to *functions* like production or personnel, but to product divisions or 'profit centres' – their managers have to worry about costs as well as output. But even this type of manager will have a narrow perspective. It will be limited in time, for he is likely to be judged by this year's profits; and in the short run the impact of a strike is felt more than that of a concession, which increases costs indefinitely. It will also be limited in space: a concession may please *his* workers, and raise *their* productivity; if it leads to parity claims and jealousies in other divisions – that's not *his* problem.

How then are lower managers to be prevented from being too generous on wages? It is not enough to take away their formal authority to negotiate on wages. Line managers at least will still control the *hours* that are worked and paid – and a foreman can easily make an 'invisible' concession by agreeing to 'clock up' overtime hours which have not in fact been worked. Even if you could take that power away from him he would still control the *effort bargain* – the intensity of work put in, in return for the agreed wage. If workers become dissatisfied with their earnings, it is a natural response to work less hard.[9] If the foreman and production managers allow this to become customary, the workers will have won a pay rise, in terms of money per unit of effort, and be ready for the next step – to win more money per hour – by negotiating a 'productivity bargain' of harder work for more pay. (Even if senior management is not prepared to negotiate such a deal formally, the foreman can do it for them by 'clocking up' imaginary overtime in return for harder work during normal hours.)

It is impossible, then, to take away line managers' power: they have to be persuaded to use it in the interests of the firm – and that, with a well-organised labour force, may require constant vigilance and a good deal of personal unpleasantness. They are, as a recent report described them, the 'front-line' of management.[10] As such, you might expect them to be treated with a good deal of respect. In Britain, you would be wrong. Not unnaturally, a country which thinks little of industrial management thinks least of the most 'industrial' part of it, production management.[11] They have the lowest salaries and the least chance of promotion.[12] Not surprisingly, the best engineers prefer to go into research and development or, still better, the universities or civil service.[13] Below them, the foreman is even more neglected. He used to be a figure of authority and importance both inside and outside the factory, and to have fair prospects of climbing into management (as an 'NCO').[14] As the 'graduate trainee' has entered management, the foreman's chances of promotion have declined; so has the pay differential between him and manual workers, and his authority and prestige have been steadily eroded.[15] In short, line management in Britain has less and less reason to identify itself with top management or to do battle on its behalf.

Germany, of course, is different. A culture which honours industry, naturally honours production, and the production manager has a position of prestige and good prospects. The foreman (or *Meister*) is also much better off. The Meister has a relatively large number of workers under him, and even one or two assistants (*Vorarbeiter*), and as he has lost more and more responsibility for production (to engineers), he has had his 'man-management' responsibilities upgraded.[16] His position of privilege and power helps to keep him loyal to top management, and that loyalty makes him their ally in their 'almost obsessive' efforts to assert their authority throughout the firm.[17] Those efforts are helped also by social attitudes in general, and by the structure of their firms; it is easier to keep control over a few more-or-less uniform plants than over a baffling variety of plants with different products, techniques and traditions.

The Objectives and Organisation of American Firms

In the pressures upon them, American managers resemble the West Germans much more than the British. In the first place, they operate in a culture which has been dominated by 'business' values for more than a century. At a time when the British manufacturers were already on their way to being smothered by their aristocracy, their counterparts in the Northern States crushed the Southern squirearchy in a bitter civil war, and thereafter reigned supreme in society and politics. Later they easily held off the challenge from a labour movement which was never as strong as in Britain or Germany.[18] The great manufacturing families – Rockefellers, du Ponts, Mellons – thus never had any reason to abandon the principles that had made them rich: to get and keep control of large firms and to use it to make those firms as profitable as possible. They have held to them, as have the new rich who have fought their way up to join them in each generation. The great families have not needed majority shareholdings to keep effective control; as the Patman Report concluded, 5–10 per cent is enough, given determination and ingenuity.[19] Such qualities they have certainly shown. Rockefeller Family and Associates, for example, is a remarkable organisation, at the hub of a network of interlocking directorates which reaches across most of large-scale American industry, providing eyes and ears with which to direct the use of Rockefeller shares.[20] Such families are prepared to cooperate with other major shareholders in keeping management up to the mark[21] – where profitability is concerned they have the same interest. (Together, two or three family blocs can and do wield great power. Not only do the Fords control Ford, and the du Ponts control du Pont, but the Rockefellers, du Ponts and Morgans between them control General Motors, while the Rockefellers alone have a large minority holding in Chrysler, etc., etc.)[22] They also work closely with the banks.

The role of American banks has been quite similar to that of the German Grossbanken. They have always lent a great deal to domestic industry – in the early years it absorbed most of their funds – and have built up a lot of industrial expertise. Through their Trust Departments they deploy shares deposited with them much as the German banks do. And like the German banks they tend to work with, rather than against, the powerful families. (Chase Manhattan, one of the American Big Three, has David Rockefeller as President, and his family have $2\frac{1}{2}$ per cent of its shares.)[23]

In this perspective, the resemblances to Britain are superficial. In both, firms are controlled by one-tier, not two-tier boards of directors, but in the US, two thirds (in the UK only one third) of directors on average are non-executive, that is, not full-time employees of the firm:[24] it is they who provide the eyes and ears of such as the Rockefellers. In both, employers' associations are relatively weak – indeed in US manufacturing they scarcely exist.[25] But in the US this does not indicate any lack of cohesion. Firms find it possible, as we shall see, to get the upper hand over unions without resorting to such formal devices: where they need to cooperate they are quite capable of doing so informally.[26] In both, finally, foremen have a relatively humble place; their discretion is less and their numbers are greater in the US than (probably) anywhere else. Nonetheless, we shall see that American management induces them to serve its purposes in much the same way as it succeeds in controlling the rest of its labour force.[27]

Implications for the Bargaining Stance

Consider the effects of such differences in management's objectives on its bargaining stance. When a wage increase leads to a reduction in a firm's profits it implies a loss to the owners, now or in the future. When through emulative wage increases it reduces another firm's profits, it implies a loss to that firm's owners. Suppose that the owners are in full control, or management is acting as though they were; that the owners have a stake in the other firm, or they and management feel 'solidarity' towards it; then all these losses will be taken account of in management's bargaining stance, and make it tougher. This in essence has been the position and strength of West Germany, and almost equally, of the United States.

All the pecularities of British managers will tend to soften the bargaining stance of British management. 'Satisficing' makes their concession costs low if their profits seem more than satisfactory; their short-term view makes strike costs seem more important because they are mostly short-term; their lack of 'solidarity' means they ignore the cost of a concession to the other firms who may be forced to follow it. Their bargaining stance will be further weakened by the unimportance of employers' associations, since strike costs (relative to concession costs) are higher for firms bargaining alone; and by the importance of lower managers, who of all concerned have the least incentive to resist.

Recent Trends

It is the British situation that one looks to first for change, for it is clearly too bad to last. I scan the *Financial Times* daily for signs that my description is already out of date. The City institutions accumulate industrial shares, the government inherits bankrupt industries; both have the power, and (heaven knows) the incentive, to impose an effective system of control over industrial management. What they lack is the expertise (and perhaps also the will) for the task; and that task grows harder as firms grow bigger. There are some who understand: in the past decade the Bank of England has repeatedly tried, with little success, to spur the insurance companies into action.[28] Something has been done in the last decade by top managers themselves, to regain control over pay bargaining within their own firms;[29] but it is harder to regain power than to keep it, particularly in very large organisations. For the present, my description stands.

There is less reason to expect change in the other two countries. The US system of control is well tried and tested, and looks secure. The German system is rather more fragile, for it depends very much on the dominance, and vigilance, and omniscience of the Big Three banks. In the last twenty years big firms have become much bigger and more complex, and they depend much less on the Big Three for finance.[30] But so long as the banks keep the support of major shareholders, they will remain immensely powerful; so long as the *Unternehmer* sets the tone in industry and society, their pressure for maximisation will go with the managerial grain.

Whatever managers' attitudes and organisation, their policies will be affected by the pressures on them from their workers, and the economic circumstances in which they face those pressures. The prospect of a strike, for example, will disturb the management of a capital-intensive firm more than a labour-intensive one, for it is easy to see that strike cost for the former – with idle capital not earning its keep – will be higher than for the latter, which will save almost as much in wages as it losses in revenue. A wage increase which might prevent the strike, on the other hand, will be much more expensive for the labour-intensive firm. So the ratio of concession cost to resistance cost is higher for the labour-intensive firm, and its stance should be tougher. Differences in labour-intensity go far to explain wage differences between industries, but there is no clear trend, towards or away from greater labour-intensity, which would explain changes in whole countries over time. There *is*, however, a trend, long and slow, which has worked and will go on working to turn the balance of bargaining power against management wherever workers are organised to exploit it. I describe it in the next section.

2.2 GROWTH AND CHANGES IN THE PRODUCTION PROCESS

> To take an example . . . from a . . . manufacture . . . in which the division of labour has been very often taken notice of, the trade of the pin-maker, . . . in the way in which this business is now carried on, not only the whole work is a peculiar trade, but it is divided into a number of branches, of which the greater part are likewise peculiar trades. One man draws out the wire, another straights it, a third cuts it, a fourth points it, a fifth grinds it at the top for receiving the head; to make the head requires two or three distinct operations . . . and the important business of making a pin is, in this manner, divided into about eighteen distinct operations . . . though the same man will sometimes perform two or three of them. I have seen a small manufactory of this kind where ten men only were employed. . . . Those ten persons . . . could make among them upwards of forty-eight thousand pins in a day. But if they had all wrought separately and independently, and without any of them having been educated to this peculiar business, they certainly could not each of them have made twenty . . . in a day; that is, certainly, not the two hundred and fortieth . . . part of what they are at present capable of performing, in consequence of a proper division and combination of their different operations.
>
> Adam Smith, *Wealth of Nations*, ch. 1, p. 6.

Adam Smith's pin factory is the model for economic growth. To make something more efficiently, every action, each step in its manufacture must be more efficient, and usually that means separating this step from the others so that specific tools, machines, skills can be applied to it. As time goes on, ways are found to improve efficiency further by separating another step. So each 'stream' of production has more steps; but the production process for a good is not like *one* stream, so much as a whole river system, with a number of components ('intermediate goods') coming together at each step like rivers joining.

Take the car industry. Down one stream of the production process comes sheet steel, which is rolled in a rolling mill, then pressed in a body plant. In another stream the engine is assembled from a multitude of components in an engine plant. Glass for windscreen and windows comes in a number of steps from a quite separate industry, as do the tyres, which belong in principle to the rubber industry but use major components from the aluminium, steel and synthetic fibres industries. The various parts of the electrical system come from yet another industry. All these things, and many more, are joined together – in a long sequence of operations – at the final assembly plant, then tested, transported, and sold.

Economic growth means more rivers and tributaries in each system, as well as more steps. It is not only efficiency that requires this increasing complexity in the production process; the goods which are being made are more complex in character and as such need more steps and components.

So the cost of each individual step in the production process makes up a smaller and smaller proportion of the cost, and value, of the finished good(s) to which it contributes. In the rest of this section I propose to show that this simple fact has remarkable implications for inflation.

We must begin with some unrealistic, simplifying assumptions (bear with me, we return to realism soon): that each wage increase applies to all the workers at one step, and no-one else; that if these workers strike they all strike – and no-one else; and that such a strike halts the whole production process in which they work. (So for example, an increase affects only the windscreen workers, and if they strike the whole industry stops.) Further, I assume that management concession cost is equal to the increase in their wages bill, while its resistance cost includes all the damage the stoppage inflicts on the economy. It is then obvious that economic growth, as it subdivides production into more and more steps, will tilt the balance, making management's concession cost smaller and smaller relative to its resistance cost. Let us now see whether this conclusion survives the journey back to realism.

First, of course, the stoppage will not be so damaging if stocks of the item – of windscreens – are kept large enough to maintain supply till it is over (and if production of glass and plastic can go on upstream, for stock). But stocks are expensive, to build and to hold, and the more complex the production process the more expensive to hold stocks of all items. The conclusion is not much affected.

There are two more objections. A strike may *not* halt all production at that step, in which case the damage to the economy is reduced. And the concession and resistance costs to the managers making the decisions *may* be different from the costs to the whole economy. Do these changes in the assumptions change the conclusion? That depends on the organisation of workers and employers. This in turn has been much affected by the structure of markets.

The Importance of Market Forms

Take first the sort of market which existed for many products in the last century, one with dozens of competing firms, making products which were almost identical – and known to be;[31] the steel industry, for example. There would also be many rival steel-makers abroad, or in other regions, kept out of the market in normal times by transport costs and/or import duties. If one steel-maker was shut by a strike, the damage to the *rest* of the production process would be small: the firms which supplied its inputs could sell them to other steel-makers, at home or abroad, and its customers could get their steel from its many competitors. The strike cost to the firm involved would not be small, of course, but it would be related to the value of the firm's *net* output, and would not include the value of production upstream or downstream. The concession cost, on the other hand, would indeed be the full increase in the wage bill – because the firm would not be able to increase its price afterwards. So the firm's stance would be tough, and it would not be affected by Adam Smith's process of growth and subdivision.

As a result we would not be surprised to see the bargaining process move to a higher level – the whole industry. The workers would find it useful to organise at that level, so that *either* they could support those in one firm, during a long strike; *or* they could stop the whole industry and thus bring the entire production process to a halt. The users of steel, and the raw material suppliers, would then put pressure on the employers to make a concession, so that their resistance costs *would* reflect at least part of the value of production up- and downstream. And the employers would find it convenient to form an association. For then all could support any firm which the union tried to 'pick off': support it either by direct subsidy, or by 'locking out' their workers, thus using up the union's strike fund faster. They could also reduce their concession cost: since all increased wages together, all would be able to pass the increase on by raising prices together.

Such 'industry-wide' bargaining would suit the employers, but it would be a very mixed blessing for the workers. It is much easier to organise a hundred or so employers than their (say) ten thousand workers; one reason is that workers in some firms may be tempted to take a 'free ride' on the others' efforts, knowing that their employers as members of the association will pay the negotiated wage even if they neither join the union nor support the strike. Such 'free riding' will reduce the cost of a strike both to the EA and the economy. The EA or the customers can soften the blow to the economy even more by importing while the strike lasts. On the other hand, the prospect of foreign competition if prices go too high may inhibit the association – they may already be charging as much as this threat will permit, so that their concession costs remain high.

Compare this with the typical modern market;[32] perhaps a dozen firms, of various sizes, competing with one another, but not with interchangeable products: each 'make' will be different in the eyes of the buyer, either because there are real differences of quality or performance, or because advertising makes him think there are.[33] In this 'differentiated oligopoly' some of the firms will probably be foreign, competing like the others on the special qualities or image of their product. To unionise and strike in just one firm now looks a much better bet, for two reasons:

1. Its concession costs will be relatively low. Its customers are unlikely to be very price-sensitive, so it may be able to pass on at least part of a concession; and its domestic rivals may be linked to it by emulation, so that their workers press them to copy its concessions – that will reduce its concession costs further.
2. Its strike costs will be high. Its customers and suppliers may be tied to its product, in the short run (other makes being too different, or its market share too big to be replaced by other producers at short notice). So they will suffer through a strike; and since in the long run they may switch to its rivals, the firm itself will suffer.[34]

With 'differentiated oligopoly' the employers clearly have less incentive to insist on bargaining at the industry level. For that will have less effect on their concession costs: foreign competitors will not join in the wage increase anyway, and emulation may force home rivals to follow even if the firm bargains alone. Industry bargaining will also have less effect on resistance cost: if all home firms are shut they will still wince at the loss of sales to foreign rivals. (Imports in this situation are a menace, not a convenience, for you cannot count on tariffs and transport costs to shut them out of the market afterwards.)

See how much has changed. My initial assumptions, which did not hold for 19th-century industry, are now not far from the mark. In modern industry concession costs are lower than in the past, lower even than in the original assumption. Resistance costs are higher than they were, either because the whole production process *is* disturbed (as I assumed) or because from the firm's own selfish point of view the loss of customers is as bad. And for that same reason there is less incentive now to unite with other employers. Two conclusions follow. First, the employer's stance is likely to be softer, and employers' associations to be weaker, unless there is a strong sense of solidarity among them. Second, my 'long slow trend' will now begin to affect their stance, because the strike will now interfere with the whole production process, or hurt the firm as much as if it had.

These conclusions still depend on debatable assumptions, assumptions about the organisation not of employers but of workers. First, the union must be able to shut the whole firm down, or at least all its output of a particular product. The employer has two ways to escape. He may be able to confine the strike to one of his plants while output of the product goes on at others – for nowadays there are firms which make some of their products at more than one plant. He may also keep some production going at the 'strike-bound' plant, either by finding new workers quickly, or by persuading part of his workforce not to go out. I shall show in Chapter 3 that the unions are so weak in one country – the United States – that many employers do have either or both of these escape routes.

The second problem is one of structure rather than strength. Negotiations, strikes and concessions are not usually confined to the workers at one 'step', for in most firms there are several steps – that is, there is some *vertical integration* – and a wage increase for one group of workers usually has to be extended, sooner or later, to all. So the more steps there are within each firm, the higher its concession cost: if vertical integration increased fast enough, it would cancel out the other tendency, and there would be no shift in the balance of bargaining power. This may have happened, in effect, in Japan,[35] but not in Western industry;[36] still, it is interesting that Germany seems to have had more vertical integration than Britain. The British bias is to *horizontal integration* – i.e. towards monopoly – [37] which I shall show has quite the opposite effect.

I have had to discuss market forms in this section in order to show that my 'long, slow trend' is now at work (at least where unions are reasonably strong). In doing so, I have shown how important those forms are. In the next section I shall follow this up.

2.3 THE EFFECTS OF CHANGES IN MARKETS AND FIRMS

> We rarely hear . . . of the combinations of masters, though
> frequently of those of workmen. But whoever imagines, upon
> this account, that masters rarely combine is as ignorant of the
> world as of the subject. Masters are always and everywhere in
> a sort of tacit, but constant and uniform combination.[38]

It is as well to have Adam Smith's reminder that there never was a golden age of *perfect* competition. Such a market is acutely uncomfortable for all who have to operate in it, and they will use any means available to escape. What is necessary, to escape, is to have not too many competitors in any one market – to have oligopoly, 'high market concentration' – and then they can find some way, tacit or open, to cooperate. If there are too many to start with, the numbers will be brought down by mergers or bankruptcies (as Joan Robinson said, the chief cause of monopoly is competition). But in the 18th and 19th centuries, many industries where there were apparently a large number of competing firms in one country, were in fact broken up into quite cosy local or regional oligopolies; for transport costs were much more important than now, particularly over land, and the costs of marketing at a distance were also a deterrent to a small firm.

If oligopoly is the normal market situation, and always was, that does not mean nothing has changed. On the contrary, there are three great continuing changes in the oligopoly situation: in the geographic extent of the market, in the role of the State, and in the forms of competition.

Markets widen, and firms grow. Wider markets give firms the opportunity to grow, and the need to do so, to survive. Having grown, they press against the confines of the market, and extend it, if they can. The limits are transport costs, differences in consumers' requirements, and trade barriers. Since the 19th century, transport costs have fallen drastically, tastes and techniques have become more uniform, and trade barriers have been lowered (though with intervals of increased protection, like 1914–50). Markets for many products now are world-wide, and so are many of the firms that serve them. The two trends, which encourage one another, may also seem to cancel one another out: as concentration increases within countries – which would tend to reduce competition – the home industry becomes more and more exposed to foreign competition. Still, the market situation does change. There is a profound difference between x firms competing within a local, regional or national market, and x larger, perhaps multinational firms competing in a more or less open world market.

In the first case, protection, whether by transport costs or by tariffs, was not absolute. Often there was an important export trade, perhaps competing fiercely with another country's goods in a third market; or there was a threat of import penetration should domestic costs rise too high. In other words, there was an external market discipline which could override any cost and price increases the oligopolists might arrange among themselves. The discipline was particularly strong within countries, upon local and regional oligopolies, for their margin of protection would usually be small, and their employers' associations would be local too, responding to locally-organised unions.[39] A generous increase agreed by (say) Yorkshire employers would leave them uncompetitive if not followed by other British associations.

In the second case, there is a world-wide oligopoly. If the firms involved can learn to cooperate – and they have a strong incentive to do so – where is the external market discipline to come from?[40] Mars? True, the cooperation is more limited than with a national oligopoly – wage bargaining scarcely operates yet across frontiers – but it is also less necessary. In the wake of world-wide competition has come the system of flexible exchange rates (no coincidence, as I shall argue in Chapter 5). It doesn't much matter if the Ruritania Chemical Co. pays higher wage increases than Vulgärische Chimie AG, so long as both keep fairly close to their national averages. If Ruritania's inflation is faster, its pound will soon fall far enough against the V Mark to bring the RCC wage costs back into line.

But do not take this argument as implying that we have world-wide free trade in industry in general, or have even been moving toward it.[41] Tariff barriers may have been disappearing, but non-tariff barriers have not. The State in its role as customer is a particularly effective, and growing, barrier to trade. (It would be an odd State buyer who did not buy at home when he could; if his sense of national duty, to home industry and the balance of payments, is not enough, his home suppliers can no doubt put pressure on his Ministry.) Where such 'non-tariff' protection is at work, there is no counterbalance to increasing concentration – unless of course the State imposes its own discipline. Some hope! – when it sets out to regulate an industry, particularly a concentrated one, the agency set up to do so is soon regulated *by* the industry.[42] Yet it is still difficult to assess what the overall effects of structural changes have been. Every established world oligopoly, or industry under a State umbrella, makes concession costs lower – but every industry in which international competition has intensified, makes them higher. Which effect is the stronger? We cannot give one answer for all times and places.

With the changes in the *forms* of competition, a judgement is much easier. The argument here is similar to that in the last section and partly overlaps with it. Consumers have more money to spend and less time to decide how to spend it. More and more their choices are affected by advertising, and by whether a good is available, perhaps the only one of its kind available, when they have the whim to buy. Thus price competition counts less, non-price competition more.[43] On the one hand, then, a wage concession does less damage; on the other hand, a strike does more: by interrupting supplies it may disrupt a marketing campaign, or shake the inertia on which brand loyalty depends. That applies to consumer goods. The industrial buyer has changed in much the same way. The growing complexity of production makes a marginal rise in the cost of one item less important, compared to reliability of supply. The impact on the balance of bargaining power is clear.

The Effects of the Growth of Firms

It seems safe to conclude that the market changes I have been describing tend to tip the balance towards concession. True, employers' solidarity may be strong enough, as in Germany, to resist the growing temptation to bargain alone and selfishly; but strong employers' associations make it still easier to pass on a concession to the customer, so the union will lose little. The effect of changes within firms, on the other hand, is not nearly so clear-cut.

By growing, and diversifying, across the boundaries of industries and states, firms win a great opportunity to outflank the unions. Their strike costs will be lower unless all their plants are hit; the unions now have a bigger, stronger opponent.

Fortunately for the unions this opponent is unlikely to be able to punch his weight. The easiest way to run a huge enterprise efficiently is to decentralise most decisions to the managers on the spot. If you decentralise decisions on wages, you lose the advantages of size and indeed may be left with some of the disadvantages, for, as I showed in Chapter 2, Section 1, it is in the lower manager's interest to take a relatively soft stance.But if you insist on making all decisions on wages at the top, you cannnot operate a payment by results system (that has to be administered by lower management) and the financial incentive for effort is then absent. In order to get that effort the workers must then be very closely supervised by first-line management.[44] This solution is popular in the US – which has the highest ratio of supervisors to operatives, and the least use of payment by results, of any Western country – and it works there; but it requires loyal lower managers, facing weakly-organised workers. As we shall see, firms in the USA generally have both these advantages; firms in most of Europe do not.

US firms are also able to make more effective use of the tactic of divide and rule. The US is not so much a country as a subcontinent, and it is very unevenly unionised.[45] Large US firms are normally multiregional, and also multinational; from certain locations abroad they have the right to import duty-free. So they can site plants beyond the reach of US unions, then use their production to tide them over a strike. Matters are not arranged so conveniently in Europe. Trade is only free within Western Europe, and for all its diversity the old continent is more uniformly unionised than the new.[46] Nor, as we shall see, do the politics and public opinion of Western Europe allow such ruthless tactics as are normal in North America.

We can thus reach a tentative conclusion which will become firmer when we can take unions properly into account: in US firms greater size means greater strength in wage bargaining; in Western Europe it tends to mean greater weakness. So much for the remorseless laws of economics. Social differences count.

Market Forms and Prices

In the 'pattern case' of neoclassical economics, prices are fixed, and changed, every day by the forces of supply and demand. Firms do not choose what to charge, but what to produce, and then they sell it for whatever it will fetch: they are *price-takers* operating in a *flex-price* market. In the post-Keynesian pattern case, it is the firm which decides the price at which it will sell, and supplies, if it can, what the customer chooses to buy. It is a *price-maker* in a *fix-price* market.

This might not make a great deal of difference if sales were extremely sensitive to price, and firms in response were constantly adjusting their prices to what the market would bear. But sales rarely are, and firms rarely do. Whenever economists have ventured to ask businessmen how they set their prices (as Hall and Hitch did in Britain in the 1930s and Kaplan, Dirlam and Lanzilotti in the USA in the 1950s)[47] the reply has been much the same: they calculated their unit costs (usually on the assumption of 'normal' capacity utilisation) added the profit margin they thought appropriate, and that was their price. The sceptical economist asked how they decided what margin was appropriate. Hall and Hitch's British businessmen said, whatever was customary in that market. Kaplan's Americans were more sophisticated: their margin was what was required to yield a certain target return on capital invested, over the life of the project. Then how was that target rate of return chosen? Well, it was what seemed appropriate to that market[48]. . . .

Do not imagine that these people were either fools or liars; or even necessarily satisficers. If they had close rivals and the market was sensitive to differences in price, this would be the best way to keep prices in line and avoid cut-throat competition.[49] They would only change prices when costs changed, and their rivals' costs would usually change by much the same amount, for they would keep their wage increases in line, with or without an association.[50] If a firm had little competition, or that depended on other things than price – say on advertising, or quality, or service – then its main fear would be that in the further future, too high a margin might attract new rivals into its market. What would vary would not be so much the method of pricing, as the profit which seemed appropriate. If the firm had many close rivals and no secure understanding with them, it would tend to keep its margins low, for safety's sake.[51] Where it got on well with what rivals it had, and new firms would find it difficult to break into the market, then it would feel free to aim for a high profit.[52] As I pointed out in Chapter 1, Section 3, international competition makes a difference, if price is an important consideration, for you may have to keep in line with foreign rivals,[53] and their costs, particularly wages, may move differently at times. But as I showed, before long, exchange rates will move to cancel out most of the cost differences, and the usual margin can be restored.

And the level of demand – how does that affect margins?

The Effect of Demand on Prices

Economists have traditionally assumed that firms cut their prices when demand falls, and raise them when it rises – that they 'price cyclically'. Well, consider what will happen if they do. Costs per unit are a good deal higher in most firms if they are only operating at (say) three-quarters capacity, than if they are working flat out;[54] so a recession will mean a large loss of profit even if prices are unchanged. Any reduction in price will make the situation that much worse. And what do you achieve? Your price cut is intended to win customers from your rivals – at least, that is how they will see it – so they will retaliate; in that case, to gain anything you must cut again. Prices will have to fall a long way before it pays any firm to stop cutting, unilaterally. So, the result of a 'neoclassical' response to recession is so dire that firms make sure it doesn't happen.

It is not usually necessary to resort to formal agreements to avoid such 'disorder'. There is a strong sense in any oligopoly that one must maintain discipline, not break ranks, during recession. 'List' prices are maintained, and increased in the normal way, as costs increase; the only 'indiscipline' which is often shown in a recession is that large buyers manage to use their bargaining power to extract larger discounts below list prices than they normally get.[55] Very rarely, such indiscipline snowballs, and gets out of hand, as it has in the world steel industry during the very severe recession since 1975;[56] but the effects are so traumatic, that the industry involved takes whatever steps are necessary, legal or illegal, mergers, import restrictions, or cartels, to ensure that they are not repeated in the next recession.[57]

As a result, industrial markets show a range of responses to fluctuations in demand. More or less at the centre of the range are the 'average' oligopolies, which respond, if at all, by small increases in discounts. Further 'down' are those markets, perhaps less concentrated or more price-sensitive, which do break ranks – this time. (Price-cutting is much more common on exports than on home sales; the industries in which prices have fallen most in recent recessions have been those, like steel, which are only newly internationalised and haven't learnt how to cooperate yet.)[58] And at the other end of the range are those oligopolies (and monopolies) which are well enough organised and disciplined to price in the *rational* way – counter-cyclically. How much better sense it makes to raise your prices *more* in a recession, and thereby keep up a reasonable flow of profits. When the boom comes, you can then afford to hold your prices down, which will help to pacify the customers you have to keep waiting, and avoid making those very high profits which would tempt outsiders into your market.[59]

Taking the whole range of industrial markets together, the extremes seem roughly to cancel out. A number of recent studies for the UK have found no significant effect of domestic demand on prices, one way or the other.[60] Historical studies for the USA have found that pricing was on balance definitely cyclical between the wars, but that the effect of demand has gradually changed. By the 1970s the low point of price inflation was during the upturn, the high point during the downturn; for it was in the downturn that firms had to raise their profit margins if they were to make enough profit in spite of falling capacity utilisation to finance investment programmes launched in the boom.[61] In the 1940s most firms had had to accept that competition prevented them from increasing margins at such times; now, competition is less of a restraint.

A *world-wide* recession is different. It has some cyclical effects on industrial goods, because as I said restraint is weakest on export markets; and it has a strong effect on agricultural and mineral products. Not on all of them; Western farmers and miners have far too much political clout to allow *their* markets to be ruled by supply and demand. The benefits of free competition are given above all to the farmers and miners of the Third World: come boom, their prices soar, come slump, they plummet. (Any Third World government which joins a 'producer cartel' in the hope of interfering with this natural process is punished by the United States, which shuts out its exports.) It is mostly for this reason that price inflation does fall in a world-wide recession, and rise in a world-wide boom. Yet even such a recession does not reduce inflation in the long run. The powerless of the Third World find weapons in their very poverty: when prices are low they cannot afford to care properly for their land, or finance new mines, and so the seeds are sown for shortage, and more inflation.

A small country (like Britain) can do very little by itself to bring about a world-wide recession, or boom for that matter. It can only deflate its own home market, which will now do little or nothing to reduce its own producers' margins. Yet deflation has become a more and more effective way of reducing price inflation. This paradox is explained by the effect on the balance of payments. Crudely put, if you deflate the economy you reduce imports and increase exports, and that causes a balance of payments surplus. As a result your currency is revalued (or 'floats up'), making your imports cheaper and your industry less competitive – which raises firms' concession costs and helps to hold down wage inflation. This effect is becoming steadily stronger, as each country becomes less self-sufficient. For any increase in its demand is met less from its own resources, more by extra imports; any decrease means a larger saving in imports, and with flexible exchange rates this quickly leads to revaluation. And any revaluation has more effect on prices and wages because imports make up a larger part of costs, and because international competitiveness is more important in bargaining.

Unfortunately these effects are all short-term. The fall in demand means less investment and expansion of capacity (much of the saving in imports is in machinery and other investment goods); this leads to reduced exports and more dependence on imports in the future. So the balance of payments, the exchange rate, and inflation all in turn grow worse than before. But the benefits may last two or three years, and that is a long time for a politician.

Conclusion: Management's Part in the Inflationary Process

We have looked at managers from several points of view. I argued first that their *objectives and organisation* would affect their bargaining stance. If they were satisficers, risk-averse, and 'short-sighted', and if decision-taking on wages was decentralised, their stance would tend to be soft. With this we were some way already towards explaining *variations between countries*. Next, it appeared that the increasing complexity and subdivision of the process of production would make for a softer stance, if (a) markets were broadly of the 'differentiated oligopoly' type, (b) unions were strong enough to halt the firm's output of at least one product. As both conditions seemed to hold quite well for Europe, the *rising trend* of inflation became easier to understand there; this was not true in the US, where (b) was doubtful. Finally I dealt with prices. Home prices depended on productivity and wages, clearly, and on the exchange rate, which affected the cost of imports and the competitive pressure on home producers to hold down their profit margins. Those margins were affected too by the relationships among rival producers. And by demand? Not, *on average, directly*. Low domestic demand raised the exchange rate, for a time, which held down margins, and import prices. Low world demand cut import prices – for a time. Later, through lower productivity, the effect would be inflationary.

We shall now see that management can affect inflation indirectly, through its influence on unions.

3 The Union Side

3.1 UNIONISATION

Why do workers join unions? To improve their wages and working conditions; to reduce the employer's power, and to increase their own, over their working lives. These motives, which we can call economic and social, are not unrelated; they coexist, mingle, and reinforce one another. But it is convenient to discuss them separately. The economic motive is the simpler one, and I begin with it.

The Economic Motive

Workers can reasonably expect, in most cases, to be able to win better wages and conditions by unionising. The obvious exception is the firm which is already paying the 'union rate', or more; this is most likely where comparable firms are already unionised, and the firm is trying to prevent its workers following suit. Otherwise unionisation should pay. But how much?

To answer that we have to go back to our theory of wages. If the workers unionise they can strike (or ban overtime etc.),[1] and how much they gain by that depends first on the employer's strike cost, relative to his concession cost. An industry which is capital intensive, for example, will have relatively high strike costs, low concession costs, and so offers big gains from unionisation. This sort of information may not be directly known to workers, but if once one firm in such an industry is unionised, and concedes high wages, workers in the others will take the point. Still, the first concern will be with the wage increase the worker hopes to gain: how much is it worth to him or (in my language) what is his concession cost? That is surprisingly variable; it depends on

(a) How long he expects to stay in a job affected by the pay increase. A woman who, for example, expects to leave in six months to have a baby, will have far lower concession costs than a young man who thinks he will probably spend the rest of his working life there. The young man is likely to expect this if he is in a large plant which provides the only obvious opportunities for him – and if he has little hope of promotion (see below).

(b) The worker's wage target, or level of aspiration. Do workers feel the need for a high wage to support their families, or feel their self-respect threatened by a low wage? Then until they reach their level of aspiration their concession cost will be high, and they will be more ready to join a union to improve their wages (and more militant once in it – see Chapter 3, Section 3). If they feel, as many married women once did, 'I'm just here to get out of the house, and the pay's just "pin-money"', then their concession cost will be low.

Of course to gain from unionisation workers have to be ready to strike – in fact they may have to do so to get the union recognised. So *their* strike costs are important, too; I discuss how these may vary in Chapter 3, Section 3.

Whether workers want to join a union may be only half the story. In most cases they do not beat on the union's door – it has to recruit them, and once they have joined it has to keep in touch with them. That will be easiest in plants where the labour force is large and stable. (One industry where it is difficult, is the catering trade – restaurants tend to have only a few workers each, and these often change jobs.) Finally, the union has at some stage to win recognition from the employer. This brings us back to the employer's costs – if his concession costs are high he will have more to gain from keeping the union out; if his strike costs are low he will have less to lose by resisting demands for recognition. So, again, it is high-strike-cost, low-concession-cost employers who are most likely to be unionised. But we have also to take employers' *attitudes* into account. If they have some particular objection to unions they may make a special effort to keep them out, even perhaps by paying 'over the odds'. Such hostility is more common in the USA and Germany than in Britain. In large firms it is the lower managers who are in the 'front line' of any anti-union policy, and so their attitudes count too. They too are more friendly in Britain (see below).

The Social Motive

It seems natural to prefer to be one's own master at work, as elsewhere; or, failing that, to accept the authority of immediate workmates. After all, that is broadly the situation outside the workplace, and in pre-industrial societies it is normally the situation at work. It is an ironic aspect of the Industrial Revolution that it removed all kinds of restrictions on personal liberty at the same time as it imposed a much tighter discipline inside the workplace itself. Nowadays most people have to work within a hierarchy of authority, in which they are somewhere near the bottom, obeying orders from above.

Subordination is normal; how workers react to it depends largely on the nature of the hierarchy. Most people learn at school and elsewhere to accept authority more or less easily; but even the most docile seem to be much happier with the authority of an identifiable person, who can deal with problems and redress grievances, and makes decisions in a predictable manner according to recognised rules. Authority which is impersonal, arbitrary, unresponsive, unpredictable, always seems to create discontent, and usually that discontent leads to resistance.[2]

The wish to resist managerial authority, or at least the abuse of it, is the essence of the social motive for unionisation.[3] It is likely to be much stronger in larger plants and firms, which lack a 'boss' whom one knows and can talk to. (As the economic motive is also stronger there, and it is harder to crack down on individual union militants, it is not surprising to find that unionisation is much stronger in large firms and, above all, large plants.)[4] There are of course other reasons for resisting authority. However accessible your boss is, if the work he is asking you to do is unsatisfying, or worse, you are more likely to feel the need for a union to help improve matters. Much also depends on the worker's attitude to managerial authority, as such. Women, for example, have traditionally been loath to unionise, partly because they did not resent at work the male authority they had been taught to put up with everywhere else. The more they challenge their traditional inferior role, the more inclined they are to unionise.

Sociopolitical Attitudes

Unionisation uses horizontal links to weaken vertical ones. That is, people at a similar social level, inside and outside the factory, act together to be able to resist the orders which come down to them from a higher level. So their attitude to unionisation is likely to be affected by their attitude to horizontal relationships – with other workers, and to vertical ones – with employers and 'superiors' in general. If workers merely see society as divided into distinct social classes to which people belong mainly by the chance of birth or environment; if they think one has most in common with others within one's own class; then they are *socio-politically* pro-union. If they see society as divided on other lines – racial, religious, linguistic, sexual – more than by class; if they think a person's socio-economic position depends above all on his own individual efforts; then they are socio-politically anti-union.

The Escalator Process

When an economy, or its industrial sector, is growing rapidly, and its labour force is expanding, its workers at all levels tend to find themselves in an enviable position. There are more and more managerial and skilled jobs every year, and one of the easiest ways of filling them is to recruit from the grade below. So unskilled become semi-skilled, semi-skilled become skilled, skilled become foremen; foremen and clerks become managers; and for managers, the sky's the limit. Nor need a man make his way only within the firm, or by moving to another: there will be many opportunities for skilled craftsmen, technicians, lower managers to set up on their own to exploit a new opportunity they have spotted in their work. Those who move out of the lower positions will be replaced by new recruits from outside, who will, if young and energetic, have great hopes of following them up.

The escalator has a deep effect on industrial relations. It is the best possible argument against 'horizontal' organisation: why should the activist help to organise his fellow-workers, when he could use his energy to rise above them? And who better to avoid the arbitrary, im-personal, unresponsive style of management which provokes un-ionisation, and worse, than a man who knows workers' problems from personal experience and their attitudes from living among them? Those who have risen are grateful to the firm for the promotion, those who have not yet done so, look forward to it; and the gap between Management and the Workers is bridged by the links between friends and relations.[5]

In any economy there will almost always be some escalator effect; – the question is, how strong? The most common cause of a strong escalator is the one I assumed to begin with: rapid expansion of the labour force, in the whole economy or the industrial sector; the extra labour may come from agriculture, domestic service, or housewives, from a high birth rate, or immigration. There may also in some periods be a rise in the proportion of skilled and managerial jobs in the labour force, so that there is room for workers to move up from grade to grade without any increase in the total. But neither this nor rapid expansion has ever gone on for very long, except in a 'new land' like 19th-century North America. There is, however, a factor which can increase the effect of a weak escalator: the division of the labour force between what I shall call a privileged group and a downtrodden group (or groups). If whatever chances for promotion there are, go mostly to the privileged group, that gives it what can be described as a *boosted* escalator – at the expense of the downtrodden group. The privileged then have less reason to unionise; but the downtrodden have more.

The split will be effective in preventing unionisation, or at least weakening it, only if the privileged think they deserve their position, and so do not make common cause with the downtrodden; if the latter also accept their position, so much the better. In modern Western civilisation there are only two sets of beliefs which have this effect, racism and sexism, the one justifying discrimination by race, the other justifying it by sex. (Sexism is in fact the more successful prejudice, for it is strongly held not only by the privileged group – men – but also largely by the downtrodden one – women; racism, on the other hand, is only general among the privileged group, whites – few blacks accept that discrimination against them is fair.)[6] A downtrodden group which rejects its position can still be prevented from successful organisation if the privileged (and perhaps other downtrodden groups) take management's side. Thus strikes by black workers have often been broken because the whites, who had most of the strategic skilled jobs, refused to join them.

The situation is worst of all, for the unions, when there is a strong natural escalator (because of expansion) which is boosted by new downtrodden groups coming into the labour force. For not only do racial and sexual discrimination make the escalator more effective, but the escalator in turn helps to entrench the discrimination. A fast escalator gives the most energetic (and co-operative) blacks and women reasonable prospects, while others, new to the labour force, are not resentful because their previous situation was worse. So these groups may stay quite acquiescent, while the white males who gain from discrimination will be contentedly racist and sexist. If the escalator slows down, the latter's prejudice may well grow fiercer at first, as they try to increase their share of a smaller cake; but in time they may wonder whether they could not do better by making common cause with the downtrodden, who by now are beginning to put up a fight. Unless strongly entrenched and encouraged, prejudice may gradually give way to a sense of 'solidarity'.

We may expect, then, that where an escalator is 'natural', without much division into privileged and downtrodden groups, unionisation will be weak, but grow stronger soon after the process slows down. Where there is 'boosting' by division and prejudice, unionisation will be still weaker, and may not rise for a long time after the escalator slows down.

Short-Run Effects

The escalator argument implies that booms tend to decrease unionisation, recession to increase it, which will seem odd to anyone who knows that most theorists say the opposite.[7] In the short run, they are right: the escalator effect works mostly through attitudes, and is therefore slow – it may take five years or so to work through. The immediate effects of an upturn certainly favour the union, as I shall show in Chapter 4, Section 2. It will be easier to win a strike for union recognition – or indeed any strike; and union victories on any issue will encourage workers to join. At the same time growing labour shortage will make it easier for union militants to get into firms and stay in: a blacklist of 'troublemakers' can work very well in a recession, much less well when firms are inclined to hire first and ask questions afterwards. So in the short run – two, three, maybe even five years – booms will tend to increase unionisation, recessions to reduce it.[8] These short run effects will be strongest in countries like the USA, where employers are most anti-union and inclined to take advantage of any shift of the economic breeze in their favour.

Another economic effect which will work quickly, is that of prices. When prices are rising fast unions will be regularly claiming and winning large increases, and thus reminding their members how useful they are – even if they are doing no more than keep up with prices. When prices are falling – to take the other extreme – a union which can prevent wages being cut has achieved a great deal – but will its members feel as grateful? And it does make some sense to think a union more useful in a time of fast inflation – a careless employer is likely to need more pressure to raise wages in line with prices, than he is to refrain from cutting them too fast when prices are falling.

Until recently, prices tended to rise in upturns and fall in recessions, so that the two short-run effects worked together, and reinforced one another. Nowadays, as I explained in the last chapter, the link is looser. At all events, we can say that the economic situation most favourable to the unions is an upturn with high inflation, following a long period of low demand; least favourable, is a recession, with falling prices (or at least low inflation) after a long boom.

The Role of the State

Governments, laws, the courts, the police, can separately or together do a great deal to help or hinder unionisation. By fixing (and enforcing) minimum wages, for example, they can reduce the economic motive for unionisation;[9] by providing for works councils which open a channel of communication between workers and top management they can reduce the social motive; by limiting the right to strike (and picket) they can reduce both motives. They can have a more direct effect by upholding the right to belong to a union – or the right not to (banning the closed shop).[10] More directly still, the state as employer (at national or local level) can refuse to recognise unions; or encourage them, even grant them a closed shop. State policy towards racial and sexual discrimination is also relevant: if it practises, encourages or merely ignores it, it indirectly hinders unionisation; if it bans it, and tries to enforce the ban, and gives security to immigrant workers, it helps the unions.

While laws, and the state's policy as employer, can be shown to make a good deal of difference to union density, the relationship is not just one way: union strength in turn affects laws and policies. For politicians respond to pressure; and there may be an element of shrewd calculation in the pro-union policies of employers, whether public or private. Henry Ford stopped at absolutely nothing in his long struggle to keep unions out of his plants, but when he gave in he gave the United Auto Workers every help in getting 100 per cent membership throughout Ford. Governments and employers alike may well decide, like Ford, that if the unions are going to be strong anyway you have a better chance of making them moderate if you do not force them to fight all the way.

The Analysis Applied

The meagre set of analytical tools I have just described can explain much of the differences in union density, between countries, and the changes in each country over time. The increase in unionisation which has taken place in every Western country over the last 100 years can be explained largely by the increase in size of plants and firms which has also taken place everywhere; as I have already shown, this was bound to strengthen both economic and social motives for unionisation. For more detail, I will take countries individually, concentrating on the chosen trio, the US and UK, and Germany, but dealing also with France, Italy, Sweden and the Netherlands.

The United States

The USA is the escalator country *par excellence*. Almost throughout its history, until the 1930s, there was a strong escalator process of one sort or another, and that fact explains as much about industrial relations as it does about the rest of American life. The American Dream – log cabin to White House – is really the Escalator Dream. Because the escalator gave most (white) people the chance to rise if they worked hard enough for themselves, it helped to entrench individualism as an American belief; because it was powerfully boosted by racial discrimination it helped to entrench racism almost as firmly. Both individualism and racism, as I have shown, are anti-union values.[11]

The early escalator – until the First World War – was fuelled mostly by white immigration from Europe. Where and when this immigration was heavy, there was little unionisation except among skilled craftsmen, who were of course mostly native, white, and male. (The unions they set up, which came together into the American Federation of Labour (AFL), showed little interest then or since in organisating outside the privileged group.) The new white immigrants were not only downtrodden, and thus in a weak position to unionise; they also had good hopes of moving up in due course, to join earlier arrivals in the privileged groups; or they planned to go home again before long. Either way they would have less inclination to unionise or form pro-union attitudes.

Even during the 1920s only a small minority of the labour force was unionised, far less than in the industrialised countries of Europe (see Fig.3.1); by this time the escalator was being boosted, for whites, by large-scale migration of Southern blacks to the industry of the Northern states. But then came the Slump. For the best part of a decade the escalator was effectively stopped, even reversed. It had been long, and strong, and boosted, so attitudes did not change quickly; and laws and employers were hostile, and the AFL sat on its hands. It was 1937 before the upsurge in unionisation started, with the help of new legislation, and the new Congress of Industrial Organisations (CIO), but it was all the

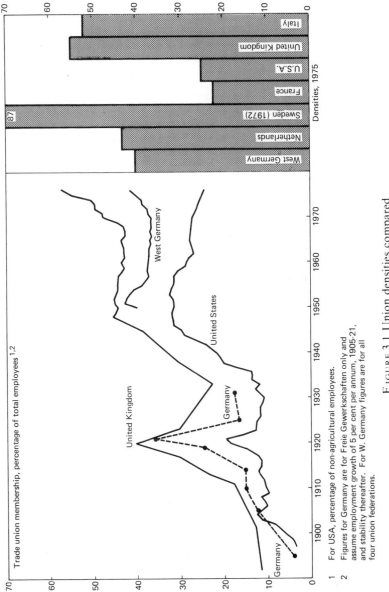

Trade union membership, percentage of total employees [1,2]

Densities, 1975

1 For USA, percentage of non-agricultural employees.

2 Figures for Germany are for Freie Gewerkschaften only and assume employment growth of 5 per cent per annum, 1905-21, and stability thereafter. For W. Germany figures are for all four union federations.

FIGURE 3.1 Union densities compared

stronger when it came. By 1947 nearly a third of non-agricultural workers were union members, and the more militant unions of the CIO had grown the most.[12]

Then the tide ebbed again. The most obvious cause was the Taft-Hartley Act and other anti-union legislation, and the anti-communist witch-hunt in the late 1940s and early 1950s which discredited and divided many of the CIO unions. But more important, in the long run, was the effect of wartime expansion: the escalator restarted, and with a vengeance, for from now on it was boosted not only by blacks but by women. Women's share of the labour force rocketed during the war, dipped when the soldiers returned, then rose steadily thereafter.[13] Discrimination seemed the more natural (even to them) because a large and increasing proportion were either married, with families, or soon expected to be:[14] many were part-time workers, few permanent, and they depended less than men (or even unmarried women) on their jobs for either money or status.

It was not until the mid-1960s that there was a halt – this time only a pause – to the decline in unionisation.[15] Again, it was partly due to a political change: the Democratic Administration of 1961–9 was mildly friendly to the unions and encouraged the organisation of federal employees (from 1962);[16] but the check to the escalator in the recession of the late 1950s was probably more important. That also had implications for racial and sexual discrimination. Blacks and women who had perhaps once felt lucky to be away from Southern farms, or the kitchen sink, now grew more resentful – particularly the blacks. In 1963 they gave white America, as the Lord gave Noah,

> . . . . the rainbow sign:
> No more water – the fire next time.

and before long the cities of the North burned. The Vietnam War must also have had an effect, as the soldiers came home. All conscripts on active service learn to despise their officers and detest their NCOs, and when they get home are in no mood to be ordered around by managers either.[17]

Yet it was no more than a pause, and soon the retreat resumed. First, some long-term trends were working against the unions. For about twenty years plants in manufacturing industry have no longer been growing larger, and the manufacturing sector, the stronghold of US unions, has been shrinking. What new employment there is in it, is mostly for white-collar workers, the least unionised. The main expansion is in the service sector, which is hard to unionise, because most workers are white-collar, and units are small. In Europe the state-controlled part of the service sector – administration, education, etc. – has in fact high union density, but this reflects the friendly attitude of the state, and the large centralised organisations involved. In the United States, the majority of public sector workers are divided up among a vast number of state and local authorities, mostly under the control of anti-union businessmen. As a result, even in the public sector, density is low.

The unions were also hurt by a new aspect of the escalator. With the boom of the sixties it had picked up speed again, and turned even more against the unions than ever. For the pattern of migration had changed again. The black who moved north during the forties had probably had a grade school education; he found himself in a black community which had some notion of union organisation; and he had all the legal rights of a citizen. Now more and more of the new entrants to the American labour force came from Mexico. They were likely to be neither literate nor English-speaking; they had no tradition of industrial labour or unionisation either at home or in the US; and most of them were illegal immigrants, in terror of *la migra*, the Immigration Service.[18] Worst of all, they were not migrating into the relatively unionised and liberal North – they were going where the new expansion was, in the swathe of land from Los Angeles through Texas to Atlanta: the Sunbelt.[19] In most of the Sunbelt, state and local authorities were and are allied with employers in bitter hostility to unions in general and the organisation of blacks and Mexicans in particular.[20]

So the Mexicans, foreigners in a country which had once been theirs, were forced to take the place allotted them – at the very bottom of the heap.[21] This may have reduced black resentment; it certainly reduced black power to do anything about it;[22] and the white male workers who might once have seen themselves as the victims of exploitation, had now at least *five* distinct downtrodden groups below them: white women, black men, Spanish-speaking men, black women, and Spanish-speaking women. These groups made up nearly half the labour force (more in the Sunbelt) and the proportion was increasing. There was little prospect of union recovery in the United States until they learnt to resist effectively.

West Germany

There was rapid expansion during the industrialisation of Germany, but the German escalator was not so hard on the unions as the American one, for most of the new industrial workers were Germans, and men. Workers' attitudes were equally different. It was only the employers' determination and solidarity (explained in the last section) which kept the unions weak until the First World War. The war, then defeat, then its aftermath, brought the country politically very close to revolution, and the loosening of managerial authority (like every other kind) let unionisation grow enormously. Both political and industrial threats were contained under Weimar in the early 1920s, but not without large concessions (see next section).

The economic crisis of 1929–33 which brought the Nazis to power did not much weaken industrial workers' loyalty to the unions or to the working class parties – few of *them* supported Hitler. The Nazis crushed both unions and parties, but after their defeat, the unions were free to start again, and they began to grow rapidly in numbers and militancy.[23] This pleased neither the employers nor their friends the Christian Democrats, then in power, and they responded with some ingenious legislation, which seems to have had two ends in view. The social motive for unionisation was to be diverted as far as possible into other forms of organisation (I show how in the next section). At the same time a great deal was done to weaken the economic motive. Many forms of strike action were outlawed: sympathy strikes, unofficial strikes, and strikes without authorisation by secret ballot. While unionised workers would thus find it harder to profit from their organisation, the unorganised were to lose less by the lack of it, for even those few employers who stayed outside their association could be legally obliged to pay the wage it negotiated. But there was no frontal attack on the unions: although the constitution gave the right to stay out of them, thus banning the closed shop, it also protected the right to join.

The unions soon had to face another handicap: the post-war 'economic miracle' created a strong escalator. At first it was at any rate not boosted, for most of the new recruits to industry were unemployed or refugees from the East, many from union strongholds like Brandenburg and Upper Saxony. The proportion of women was at first quite high, but even they were not the most docile, being almost all widows or single, forced by the loss of men in the war to fend for themselves.[24] But soon industry began to recruit from the (conservative) countryside; many firms even moved there, so that new workers need not leave their smallholdings. During the 1960s married women began to come into the industrial labour force in large numbers, for the first time in German industry.[25] And then there were the 'guest workers', the foreign immigrants.

From the late 1950s, as other streams dried up, the Southern tap was opened, and new immigrants flooded in. In the industries where they were concentrated, their arrival split the workforce between privileged natives, increasingly confined to skilled jobs, and foreigners, mostly unskilled, who had few rights, and could not afford to displease their employers.

On the face of it the outlook now looked as bleak for unions in Germany as in America. But a few years of a boosted escalator, and unfavourable laws, cannot get rid of pro-union attitudes formed over more than a century. German workers were quite racist and sexist, of course, but all the same they and their leaders made a considerable effort to bring the new groups into the unions, and many of the immigrants, if not the women, joined.[26] (Fortunately most immigrants were not very different physically; cultural differences can quickly fade, but a black skin stays black.) The unions held on, density falling only slowly in manufacturing and rising still in their public sector strongholds; and then after 1965 help arrived.

With the deep recession of 1966–7 the escalator stopped, picked up again after 1968, then came in 1974 to a standstill from which it has not yet really recovered. From 1973 immigration was virtually stopped, and the number of foreign workers actually fell, while the influx of women slowed down. Union density rose among women and immigrants and they became less acquiescent; by 1978 politicians were seriously discussing banning sex discrimination.[27] (And these were politicians in power, for since 1969 there had been a social democrat/liberal coalition, not unfriendly to the unions.) In Germany, more than the United States, the unions were now entrenched, politically, socially and economically, and the pressures against them were balanced by the demands of their members.

Britain

For a hundred years, till the end of the 19th century, the industrial revolution in Britain produced a fairly fast escalator, fuelled by farmworkers, and even boosted by Irish immigrants who were not absorbed for a generation or so. Plants and firms were smaller than they were in the US or Germany at the same stage of growth, and employers and the state were almost equally hostile; so until 1900 the unions were very weak outside the skilled crafts. Around the turn of the century, however, a period of economic stagnation began which lasted almost until the outbreak of war. The escalator almost stopped; the electorate swung left and in 1906 elected a strong Liberal Government which was friendly to the unions; the growth of the unions speeded up. After 1914, as in Germany, wartime disruption and inflation, and the mushrooming of large munitions plants, helped them even more; and though after the war there was a period of ebb as government and employers tried to get back to the *status quo ante*, density stayed much higher than before the war. It was higher, too, than in Germany, and this may reflect a difference on the employers' side which was now becoming clear (see Chapter 2, Section 1): Unternehmer were determined to maintain their authority; sleepy British owners let managers choose their own *modus vivendi* with the unions. The Slump and the Second World War had the effect one would expect; in 1945 a government came in which was the friendliest yet; and by 1950 union density was not far short of half the labour force.

Then the British unions met another boosted escalator. For twenty years after 1945 the economy expanded fast enough to draw in new labour. Female participation, which had shot up during the war, then dipped, rose steadily from about 1950, and most of the increase was among married women, the most 'docile'. There was immigration from the non-white Commonwealth (mostly in the late 1950s and early 1960s). It was probably the women who did the unions most damage: the coloured immigrants were relatively few, there was less intense prejudice against them than against non-whites in America, and the large majority of them arrived legally, with full civil rights, unlike the Mexicans in the US or even the foreign workers in Germany.[28]

Density did fall, but not far. Pro-union attitudes were by now far too strong to be seriously eroded by two decades of a mild boosted escalator, nor did the employers or their friends in the Conservative government (1951–64) counter-attack, for by now the owners of British industry had almost stopped trying to control it. Since the mid-1960s almost everything has made for growth of union density. The industrial labour force has been shrinking, and employers have chosen to add insult to injury on the shop floor by hiring ignorant young graduates rather than foremen and technicians, for management jobs; the 'NCO' was at least good for industrial relations.[29] Immigration has been cut to a trickle (although racism seems to have been increasing, and the laws against discrimination are flouted). In the public sector, which has been expanding fast, management is friendly. The influx of married women has continued, but women are less and less content with their inferior status, and more and more aware that they will work for most of their lives: the unions are there to be joined (unlike the US) and women are joining them. So are white-collar workers, remoter now from top management, employed in larger units, and hurt most by the advent of the 'graduate trainee'. Density has now passed 50 per cent, and is still rising. British unions are as much stronger than German, as German are stronger than American.

France

France has a strong left and yet the lowest union density in Western Europe. The paradox can be explained historically. Until the 1950s France was essentially a peasant (and artisan) country, and most of the peasantry had radical anti-clerical traditions going back to the Revolution and beyond: they, not industrial workers, made up most of the left-wing voters. Plants and firms in the industrial sector were a good deal smaller in general than in Britain, Germany or the United States, and much of the heavy industry which should have provided the core of union strength was located in the most conservative, clerical area, Alsace-Lorraine. As in Germany, most of the top managers were owners determined to assert their authority. With so much against them, the trade unions got little help even from the mildly left-wing governments which came and went under the Third and Fourth Republics: the politicians gave the radical peasantry what they wanted – cheap credit from state banks, anti-clerical teachers in their schools, and brave speeches; to the workers they gave only benefits which help to keep the unions weak – works councils and minimum wages. Isolation and the hostility of the employers helped to push the unionised minority to the left, and the Communists came to dominate the union movement – which only antagonised the employers more, deterred moderate workers, and divided what there was of the unions.

Post-war changes did nothing to help. The rapid industrial expansion which began at last in the 1940s produced a fast escalator, and a boosted one: the abler blue-collar worker was helped up the ladder of promotion by the best system of technical further education in Europe, and his place at the bottom was taken by heavy immigration from Southern Europe, Africa and the West Indies.[30] Much new industry was sited in the other clerical stronghold, the West. All these handicaps to unionisation persisted into the 1970s, although (as I shall show in the next two sections) a right-wing government brought on itself the crisis of 1968 by taking too crude advantage of them.

Italy

Until little more than a decade ago the position of trade unionism in Italy was similar to that in France. Italy too was a country of peasants and artisans with most of its industry in the traditionally more clerical, conservative provinces (Piedmont, Lombardy, Veneto) and run by anti-union owners. In a divided union movement, the Communists were as dominant as in France, plants and firms were still smaller, the State (until the 1960s) more hostile. From the early 1950s, Italy even had an escalator, which ran very fast during the 'Italian miracle' (about 1955–65)–but it was the escalator which in the end let the Italian employer down, for it was not properly boosted. The new recruits to Northern industry were not foreigners, nor (for the most part) women, but Southern men. The Sicilian in Turin had full civil rights, and a language in common (more or less) with the locals and with other Southern immigrants; when he settled down he was by no means as isolated or helpless as the Algerian, assorted with Portuguese and Africans, was in France. As plants and firms had grown bigger during the 'miracle', all the unions needed was that the escalator should slow down. After the mid-1960s, as Italy slid into a spiral of declining growth, it did. An upsurge of militancy began in 1968 which within five years had forced the employers and the state to drop almost all resistance to negotiation, whether at plant or at industry level.[31] Between 1968 and 1974 union density rose by nearly half.

The Netherlands

Until 1940 the Netherlands was an essentially commercial and agricultural society, in which social attitudes and structures had persisted which could not long survive industrialisation. The most important of these, for us, is the vertical division of Dutch society into 'pillars', to use Kruijt's expression (*verzuiling*).[32] Almost all the Dutchman's social relationships were within his pillar. There were the religious pillars, the Catholics and the Protestants (the latter themselves divided) and then an anti-clerical pillar, which had split into liberals and socialists.[33]

As a result, the unions were divided into Socialist, Catholic and Protestant federations (in that order of strength). As *vertical* structures, the pillars clearly made for union weakness, which was increased by the small scale of most of Dutch industry. But they made for moderation too, wherever workers *were* unionised (see next section), so neither employers nor state had reason to make union recruitment and recognition particularly difficult. And though they split the workforce, the pillars did not split it into definite privileged and downtrodden groups, as racism and sexism do. There was, by the way, not much scope for *those* prejudices. At first there was little immigration, except for a wave of Indonesian refugees in the late 1940s, who were generally treated extremely well; and Dutch women kept their traditional role as housewives. The escalator, which was quite brisk, was 'naturally' fuelled by a high birth rate and workers (*not* downtrodden) from agriculture.[34] In the 1960s a considerable influx of Mediterranean immigrants and married women did begin, but both female and foreign participation remained very low by Western European standards. (See Figures 3.2 and 3.3.)

Pillarisation was also less durable than other divisions. In an industrialised society it began to look absurd, and by the 1960s was crumbling quite rapidly. Union density began to rise; when after the mid-1960s the escalator slowed down somewhat, and the size of plants and firms grew, density rose further, and touched 40 per cent in the late 1960s. At this point the industrial relations crisis (see next section) brought some intelligent responses from the state and the employers: first, a minimum wage was introduced in 1969 and steadily raised until by 1977 it stood at about three quarters of average earnings, and applied to 15 per cent of the workforce. Second, the works councils were made more effective, through changes both in the law and in employer attitudes. At the same time, new natural gas riches made possible a currency revaluation which restrained price inflation and made possible rapid rises in living standards.[35] These things combined to reduce the incentive to unionise, and density stabilised, and even fell for a time.

Sweden

Swedish industrialisation began quite late, at the end of the 19th century, but when it did, the trade unions were lucky. Industry was mostly in the North and Centre and recruited from provinces like Dalecarlia where the peasantry had long radical traditions; and the main industries – iron-mining and steel, lumbering and paper – are known everywhere for strong unions. The Slump, which hit Sweden very hard, produced a second leap forward. It stopped the escalator for several years, and helped to weld the political alliance of unionised workers and radical peasants which brought the Social Democrats to power. From that time,

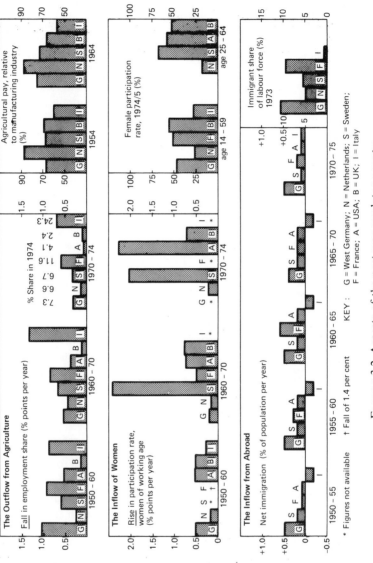

FIGURE 3.2 Aspects of the post-war escalator process

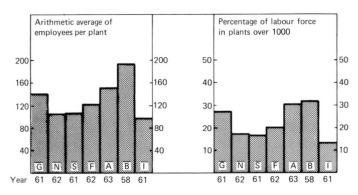

F IGURE 3.3 Plant size in manufacturing in the early 1960s

the state was the unions' friend.[36] This gave them enormous advantages – for example, an Act of 1936 *obliged* employers to negotiate with unions representing white-collar workers. The employers soon gave up any real attempt to prevent union organisation, and concentrated on perfecting their own. By 1950, outside the smallest plants, Sweden was a unionised country.

The Swedish unions were thus ready for the more and more severe tests they faced in the 1950s and 1960s. As expansion used up the reserves of male labour in the industrial areas, it was fuelled by new workers – Norwegians, conservative peasants, Finns, South Europeans – who were successively less pro-union, more distinct from native workers, or both. There was also an enormous influx of married women – female participation shot up between 1960 and 1970 from 34.7 to 59.4 per cent (Figure 3.2). But unions *and state* went to great lengths to avoid the formation of downtrodden groups – banning discrimination, giving immigrants security, civil rights, and education – and to a large extent they succeeded. The Swedish escalator stayed relatively 'natural' and as a result, when it paused (in the 1967–8 and 1972–3 recessions) the response was rapid – density rose further, where possible, and unions became more militant.

Conclusion

I have shown, very briefly, how my theory can explain the levels and changes in unionisation in seven important countries. The graphs and charts in this section will help to confirm my arguments by giving hard data on many of what I call causes of unionisation, as well as some very rough figures on union density itself. Density data is always hard to assess – what is a 'trade union' (does the term include 'staff associations'?) – what is a union *member* (only someone who has paid his subscription?) – what is the relevant 'population' (is density the proportion in the whole labour force, the full-time labour force, the industrial labour force . . . ?). Reliable data can also be hard to come by; in France and Italy, for example, the unions' own figures are the crudest (over-) estimates and the true figures have to be guessed; so Fig. 3.1 provides only a general indication of relative densities.

In any case, sheer numbers are not the only measure of unionisation we need, to explain wage inflation. We have to know also about unions' *structure*, and their behaviour – their *degree of militancy*. As I have hinted at various points already, the same basic theory which explains density can explain structure and militancy too. I deal with these questions in the next two sections.

3.2   UNION STRUCTURE

Three aspects of unions' structure are most relevant to inflation: *territory*, that is how the workforce is divided between unions; *democracy*, how much control members have over their union's actions; and *centralisation*, at what level in the union structure decisions are taken. The last is crucial for my purpose, and I will concentrate upon it.

There are two ways of judging the degree of centralisation or decentralisation of a union. You may ask first, *by* which level a decision is taken – is a wage increase negotiated by the central leadership, or a 'shop steward' elected directly by his own work-group? and you may ask second, *for* which level the decision is taken: is the increase to be made for one small work group, or for a whole industry? The first question relates to the *people who* take the decision, the second to the *people for whom* it is taken, so we can talk first of 'who' centralisation, second of 'whom' centralisation. We might have a wage increase for one individual work group negotiated by the central leadership (or someone responsible only to them), in which case there would be 'who' centralisation and 'whom' decentralisation; or a negotiation for all the workers in a giant firm might be carried through by a committee of shop stewards, and approved or rejected by a vote of the whole labour force, in which case there would be a large measure of 'whom' centralisation, not much of 'who'. But 'who' is clearly affected by 'whom': it is difficult to centralise decision-making for small work-groups, still more so for the rank and file to control a negotiation for a whole industry.

So we can begin by asking, 'for whom'? That depends partly on what bargaining is about. If it is economic, that is about wages, hours, etc., it can be at any level – one worker's 'piece rate' or a whole industry's wage per hour. It will depend then on the level at which management is willing to negotiate (which the union of course may influence). But if the bargaining is 'social' in the sense I used in the last section – if it concerns the workers' right to challenge orders, to get redress for grievances – then 'whom' must be highly decentralised; it is then essential for union power to be decentralised too. By one definition, the job of the British shop steward (the unpaid elected representative of a small group of workers) is to make it possible to say 'why?' to management, and then – failing a good answer – to say 'no'.[37] No outside official could do that job. So if the union is to respond well to the social motive for its existence, there must (formally or informally) be a good deal of power at the lowest level, in the hands of shop stewards, or similar representatives of the rank and file.

We can now work out what conditions will make shop stewards (or other elected workplace representatives) strong. Management, union leaders and the state all play a part. Management, as ever, comes first. Managerial authority, where it is particularly remote, arbitrary, unresponsive, harsh, creates a need for stewards' services, by making the social motive strong. I have already argued that this motive will be strongest in large plants and firms; so too will the 'economic' need for stewards, for it is in large units that management most requires some kind of payment-by-results (PBR) to give the incentive for effort which in a small firm comes simply from the nearness of the Boss. A large firm may get by without PBR by using a lot of supervisors (this is normal in the US – see Chapter 2, Section 3) but they will then have to enforce rather rigid rules about working practices and effort rates which will be a continual irritant and make the social motive even stronger (Huw Beynon in *Working for Ford*, Chapter 6, describes an epic battle in Ford's Halewood plant over the speed of the assembly line, which brings out this aspect of the steward's role).[38]

Such firms, though they create a need for strong stewards, may not willingly accept them, for the steward challenges management's authority within its own walls. This is bound to be hard to stomach; how hard depends on how much managers value their authority. That in turn depends largely on what they want to do with it. The grim maximiser must keep complete control, not only to hold down his costs, but also to be able to respond flexibly to any new opportunity for profit. The mild satisficer is not so shocked by obstruction to change, being inclined to obstruct it himself; in any case, that is usually a problem for the long term, which does not interest him much; in the short term, what *he* looks for in industrial relations is peace and quiet so that production can go smoothly on, and the surest way to get that is to deal with shop stewards, for they know better than anyone else what the ordinary worker will stand for. So a satisficing top manager will be inclined to recognise stewards, to make agreements with them, and allow his subordinates a good deal of latitude to do the same.[39] The maximiser will be hostile to stewards, and refuse to build up their authority by negotiating with them; he may be able to weaken them by 'hard' tactics – sacking stewards and their supporters in 'unofficial' strikes, and/or by 'soft' ones – providing other channels of communication between management and workers (see below).

Both ways of keeping stewards weak depend very much on the foreman, or 'first-line supervisor'. He above all can give managerial authority a human, responsive face on the shop floor; he above all can resist workers' encroachment on managerial authority. As I showed in Chapter 2, Section 1, the German *Meister* is well placed, and motivated, to do this. US foremen are much less fortunate, having little scope beyond the grim task of enforcing rules and keeping up the work-rate.[40] Their position gives them little reason to feel loyal to management, and they began to unionise rapidly as soon as the law gave them the chance (in 1941); but in 1947 the Taft-Hartley Act withdrew the protection of the National Labor Relations Board, and the employers crushed the Foreman's Association of America, quickly and for good.[41] Since then, in getting foremen to vent their frustrations on those below them, rather than their superiors,[42] employers have had the great advantage that the supervisor is usually white and male, and the supervised, increasingly, either black or female. The British foremen, as I said in Chapter 2, Section 1, is as miserably placed as the American, but the pressures on him are different: weaker from above, stronger from below; and he is less likely to feel distinct from the workers he is supervising.[43] He is now almost as much inclined to unionise as they are,[44] and he has become as ineffective in resisting workers as in conciliating them.

One alternative to stewards as go-between between workers and management, is of course the union leadership and its full-time officials. They can be most useful where most of the membership is concentrated in a small area, so that officials are close to the workplace. (In Britain, most shoe workers used to be in or near Northampton, cotton textile workers in South-East Lancashire, wool textile workers in West Yorkshire; but the tendency in every country is for industries to become more dispersed.) Clearly it helps them too if the country itself is small, and also if the *territory* of a union is one industry (industrial unionism), rather than one occupation in whatever industry it is practised (craft unionism) or just anywhere it can recruit members (general unionism). Democracy helps too. The more democratic is the union, the more likely the members are to be satisfied with the union leadership, and the less they will feel they need representatives directly responsible to them. The strength of the steward is also much affected by the leadership's attitude to him. If it backs him – trains him, supports the strikes he calls, protects him from victimisation – he will be in a far stronger position than if it disowns him and encourages hostile managements to do their worst. Either policy is possible, as I shall show.

The state, as ever, has an influence too. It will normally aim to weaken or at least moderate stewards, and here, like employers, it has 'hard' and 'soft' tactics open to it. The 'soft' tactic is to try to reduce the need for the steward as go-between by encouraging, or even compelling, the employer to provide other channels, usually through some sort of *works council* (see below). The 'hard' tactic is to make strikes led by stewards illegal; this can often be done indirectly by outlawing strikes which breach agreements, for as I shall show, 'unofficial' strikes are almost always in breach of whatever agreement has been made. It will also be effective to ban 'sympathy' action by workers outside the dispute, for a strike without official union backing may well only succeed if, for example, transport workers ban deliveries to or from the plant. But laws and edicts are clumsy ways of influencing industrial relations; they are unlikely to work unless management, and preferably also the union, really want them to. In fact, there is one state policy which may unintentionally help the steward more than all the others hinder him: 'incomes policy', that is, wage restraint. For if a government cramps the union leadership by imposing a statutory incomes policy on it – or by negotiating a voluntary one with it – it leaves the field clear to the stewards, who as I shall show in Chapter 4, Section 1, may find it temptingly easy to win pay rises for their members by evading rules which leaders cannot or will not break. No law can give back to the central leadership what it lost to the stewards because they showed that they alone could protect workers' interests.

How effectively the stewards can protect their members' interests without strong central support will depend, of course, on management's stance; that in turn is affected by the firm's market situation. Though a recession weakens unions in general, it weakens stewards more, for the lower manager with whom they normally deal is no longer under pressure from above to *produce*, never mind how. He may even be encouraged to seize the chance to take the stewards down a peg or two; and if that means a strike, well, there is output in stock (one of the Ford stewards was quoted by Beynon as saying you could expect a strike at Halewood whenever the car park was full).[45] The stewards' handiest weapon, a ban on overtime, is useless when there is no overtime to ban. To hurt the firm in a recession you may need to stay out a long time, and to bring out many others too; such a struggle calls for central backing, central funds. When the cold winds blow, the shop floor looks again to the leaders it ignored in the summertime of the boom.

I have left till last the most important factor: history. Union power is not simply decentralised when circumstances suit, then all taken back when the wheel turns. The conditions I have described make for the growth, or decline, of 'steward' power, but in each period one starts with no blank sheet, but with institutions, with habits of action and thought inherited from the past, and formed by past conditions. To understand the power structure of each country's unions, we must know something of their history.

Britain

I begin with Britain because here it stands at one extreme: its union movement has been throughout the twentieth century the most decentralised in the world. This decentralisation grew out of the long tradition of workplace organisation by the skilled workers in the heavy engineering industries. These workers, split among a number of craft unions, demanded a high standard of 'social' and 'economic' service which stewards were best able to supply, and management unable – or too 'soft' – to prevent.[46] The first great upsurge came in the First World War. The demand for munitions transformed the engineering industry: huge new plants appeared, and old ones changed their production methods drastically.[47] Every industry was affected by the rapid price inflation which soon began. The new situation put enormous strain on relations between management and men, management and unions, unions and rank and file, at just the moment when the union leaders were least able to cope, because they had bound themselves to help the war effort by restraining wages and keeping the industrial peace.[48] Had shop stewards not existed, they would have been promptly invented; as it was, they were merely copied, almost throughout engineering. At the same time their role was transformed. They ceased to be the defenders of the privileges of a skilled elite, and set out to represent also the many semi-skilled workers who had flowed into the industry.[49] Their new egalitarian basis combined with political ferment outside the factory to create a shop stewards' *movement* of a revolutionary character.[50]

By 1918 the stewards movement was so strong and militant that it was feared that they might soon lead a revolution.[51] The employers now saw threatened not just their authority, nor yet their profits, but the whole social system. The end of the war, reversing the balance of bargaining power in the munitions industry, gave the employers their chance to strike a first blow against the movement, by widespread dismissals.[52] The movement was further weakened by divisions among the workers, as skilled workers saw the chance to restore their previous privileges, and by the release of the union leaders from wartime constraints.[53] The Engineering Employers' Federation waited until massive deflation had 'broken' the post-war boom before striking its final blow, the great lock-out of March–April 1922.[54] Afterwards, the shop stewards still survived in the better-organised parts of engineering, but weaker, more defensive, much more dependent on the union leaders. So they stayed till the next war. Then another upsurge began, this time more controlled, for the whole war effort was more controlled, and the union leaders got a much better bargain for their cooperation.[55] After the war, on the other hand, there was (this time) no recession and no counter-offensive from the employers: with a Labour government, the talk was more of compromise than of combat.[56] If the stewards now showed restraint, it was from deference to the new prestige of the leadership, not from weakness.

Since the war the stewards have had a great deal in their favour. In 1948–50, in 1966–9, in 1972–4 and again in 1975–7, there were incomes policies, either voluntary or statutory (or both) in which the initiative on wages passed to the stewards while their leaders were hobbled. The employers grew more and more soft during the 1950s and 1960s,[57] and the economic situation was usually quite favourable. Finally, the stewards got crucial help in spreading within and beyond engineering, from the policy of the most powerful union in Britain, the Transport and General Workers' Union (T&G). The T&G changed in the early 1950s from right-wing to left-wing control.[58] For its new leadership, support for shop stewards in wage demands and other activities suited both their natural inclinations and their interests in competition for members against other unions.[59] Others followed the T&G's example.

As union membership increased after the mid 1960s, the stewards movement grew faster, in both strength and numbers.[60] They coped well with management's increasing insistence in the 1970s on bargaining at plant or firm rather than 'shop' level;[61] they simply formed plant or firm 'joint shop stewards committees' and this prevented 'whom' centralisation from leading to 'who' centralisation. By the mid-1970s, in most British industries, the shop stewards had come to dominate the union side of the bargaining table.[62]

The United States

The United States was always far too large for union power to be concentrated at the centre. From the beginning, the local branches (called just 'locals') had and kept a considerable independence from the national leadership. Even within one local the membership could be quite widely scattered (the more so since the AFL's skilled 'craft' unions each organised a separate occupational group) and so there was always a role for stewards in the AFL unions, if only to keep liaison between officials and rank-and-file. But against 'tough' US employers – while the unions were so weak that only by the tightest discipline could they even hold their ground – the stewards' role could not develop far. Their chance should have come in the 1940s, when the unions recruited most of the manual workers in large manufacturing plants; yet neither then nor since have American stewards won half the strength or independence of their British counterparts. Odd; the social motive should certainly be there, in industries such as autos, given the size of plants and the nature of the work (American plants are large by international standards,[63] and there is no channel for consultation and communication like the European works councils I shall be describing).

We can perhaps explain stewards' weakness partly by workers' attitudes. Most manual workers in mass production industries were until recently first generation immigrants, and had something of the immigrant attitude to work in America – it was something to be suffered in the course of making money; their motives for unionisation, as I argued in Chapter 3, Section 1, were more purely economic than those of Europeans at home, or indeed 'native' Americans.[64] That attitude may survive in their descendants. But more important is management policy. US firms minimise the economic incentive for strong workplace organisation by insisting on payments systems which are highly centralised, and exclude payment-by-results.[65] Wage contracts, negotiated with the union leadership, specify wages and terms of employment in detail, last for two or three years, and bind the union not to strike until the contract expires.[66] In the haggling over the details of these legally-enforceable agreements, lawyers are in their element, stewards out of their depth. Once the ink is dry, tightly controlled lower managers – including the numerous, non-unionised, foremen – will make no concessions to shop floor pressure. The steward is reduced to little more than a whistle-blower who complains to the union about breaches by management, who are then taken to court or to arbitration[67] . . . and in the meantime, the workers must do as they are told. There *are* unofficial strikes, of course – many, by international standards[68] – but they reflect not shop floor power but rather management deafness to shop floor grievances. In the United States, employers have the upper hand over the union leaders, and both have the upper hand over the shop floor.[69]

Sweden

If Britain shows what happens when strong unions face weak managers, and the USA illustrates the opposite situation, Sweden shows strength against strength.

Strong Swedish unions developed workplace organisations (the works clubs), and forced the employers to negotiate with them over a wide range of matters, including pay.[70] (The clubs bargain mostly over piece-rates, which are normal in Swedish industry, unlike American;[71] this is as much a consequence as a cause of strong workplace organisation, for where sticks cannot be used, managers must resort to carrots.) But the Swedish employers are strong too. In their cultural tradition and also in their tight control by owners and bankers, they have been very like the German *Unternehmer*.[72] Weaker at the political level than German or American employers, they have been quite as strongly organised and determined in industrial matters. Workplace bargaining is confined within limits set by industrial agreements between EAs and unions, and those in turn are set within 'frame' agreements between the 'peak' organisations of employers and unions, the SAF and LO.[73] Employers insist, with the support of the courts, on keeping 'managerial prerogative' in the workplace, and the SAF provides compensation for losses suffered through unofficial strikes (which are, moreover, illegal).[74] Inevitably, the toughness of Swedish employers has made the 'clubs' more dependent on the central unions than shop stewards are in Britain.[75] At the same time the unions are well organised (by industry) to help the clubs. As a result, the clubs are more closely integrated into the union than stewards are in Britain, and the scope for workplace bargaining is more restricted.[76] In the 1950s this was perfectly acceptable to workers, but during the 1960s, with plant size increasing and mergers becoming much more frequent,[77] it led to increasing frustration, and a wave of unofficial strikes.[78]

France

The three countries I have discussed so far, for all their differences, have one thing in common: inside strongly unionised plants there are usually elected representatives of the workers who are both officials of the union and recognised by the employer as representatives of the shop floor; the three vary mainly in the degree of independence of these 'stewards' from the outside leadership, and the readiness of management, in practice, to negotiate with them. The other four countries are quite different: in all of them, employers have traditionally set their faces against 'letting the unions inside the plant'.[79] Where they have recognised unions, it has been as negotiating partners of employers' associations; where they have accepted 'consultations' (not negotiations, if you please) within the plant, it has been in works councils, with people elected by union members and non-members alike. A good arrangement, clearly, if you can get it, for besides defending the 'managerial prerogative' it gives workers as little incentive as possible to join the union; but for just those reasons it will be bitterly resisted by the unions, and perhaps also by the workers.

In France the unions have been so weak that it hardly mattered that they disliked the arrangement. In fact in many French industries the employers have not felt obliged to negotiate regularly with the unions at any level, and although after the crises of 1936, the liberation, and 1968, the State set up and extended works councils (*comités d'entreprise*) for consultation within the plant, employers rarely treated them with respect; there seemed no need.[80] Where in Britain there is a day-to-day routine of industrial relations, in France there has been an institutional vacuum which is eerie even by Swedish and American standards, and became more unnatural as plants and firms grew rapidly larger in the 1960s. Not surprisingly, a study in 1967 found that French workers, compared with Swedes and Americans, had a strong feeling of powerlessness.[81] Note the date: in the next section I shall pick up the story at this point.

Italy

Until the 1960s Italian employers had almost as little to do with the unions as the French did, and for much the same reason – they could be safely ignored, or at worst kept at arm's length in industry-level negotiations. There were works councils, set up by law to help calm the turbulence after the war and the fall of fascism, but nobody took much notice of them.[82] Then Italy began to diverge from France, in union structure as much as in union strength. As plants grew larger and the escalator slowed down, workers felt more need for organisation within the plant; the unions however, politically divided, weak in numbers, and opposed by the employers, were slow to provide it. In Italy, shop stewards did not exist, and something like them had therefore to be invented – by the workers themselves. What they produced were the *consiglii di fabrica*, the factory councils.[83] These councils are much like British shop steward committees, except in one respect: they are still more independent of the union leadership. Shop stewards are union officials, of a sort, and even where the shop steward committee has members from a number of unions, it is still linked to union officials outside. Members of an Italian factory council are elected by work-groups in which some pay dues to the Communist, some to the Socialist, some to the Catholic union federations, some to none; as council members they have no allegiance to any outside body.[84] In the late 1960s and early 1970s the factory councils spread quickly through large and even medium-scale industry, and soon forced employers to negotiate with them, in earnest. I say more about this period in the next section.[85]

The Netherlands

The weak and moderate Dutch unions have, not surprisingly, been highly centralised as well, and so, until very recently, was the bargaining system. What representation workers had within the plant was provided by works councils set up under a law of 1950 with the usual very restricted powers. As plants grew rapidly larger in the 1950s and 1960s, and incomes policies produced tensions between what was allowed and what could easily be won, unofficial strikes increased; there was a wave of them in 1963 which brought one incomes policy to an end.[86] Unions began to press for more decentralisation in the *for whom* of bargaining, and one even tried to establish a shop steward system; but employers resisted both.[87] However, a new wave of unofficial strikes in 1970 (again against an incomes policy) led to renewed union pressure and reduced

employer resistance.[88] Unions, employers and government saw the need
to satisfy the growing demand for workplace representation and
negotiation. In a law of 1971 the government extended and improved the
works council system, and employers helped by taking them much more
seriously than before.[89] At the same time, large employers and unions
began to negotiate increasingly at company and plant level;[90] and
unions rapidly improved their organisation at the workplace.[91] But
works councils are not allowed to negotiate, still less call strikes, and
workplace negotiations are the prerogative of local union officials rather
than workplace representatives.[92] Thus the vacuum which was developing within the Dutch workplace was filled before it could engender
independent workplace organisation on the British or Italian model. In
the larger plants and firms, the new workplace organisations have been
growing in strength and independence, but not quickly, for the
employers have resisted the new trend: on the one hand, they have
nurtured the works councils,[93] on the other, they have developed

> a more professional, disciplined, employer organisational system
> ready to resist trade union demands in open social combat, a striking
> innovation in the Dutch industrial relations system.[94]

The problem was not resolved, only contained: union representatives
within large plants and firms were bound to seek more power over
negotiations *about* those plants and firms, and as they got it would
increasingly overshadow, or take over, works councils without power.

West Germany

The history of workplace organisation in Germany goes back at least to
the early years of this century, when industry was already on a large
scale. On the one side, workers rebelled against the oppressive discipline
of large plants; on the other, *Unternehmer* insisted on full authority.[95] In
the First World War, as I said in the last section, the Unternehmer lost
their grip. The workers' response was rather like that in Britain, but
more sudden, because they had been more suppressed, and more far-
reaching, because defeat discredited all old authority. The *workers'
councils* they set up threatened for a time to take complete control of
German industry.[96] In reasserting their control, it was pointless for the
employers to try to go back to 1914, as if the workers' councils had never
existed; instead, they had to be replaced by institutions which rather

resembled them, and gave the workers something of what they wanted, without detracting from the employer's authority. At the same time one could exploit the fact that the councils were separate from the unions. The new *works councils* were designed to do all this, and they worked quite well, until they were destroyed by the Nazis.[97] After the Second World War, as the unions recovered, the Christian Democrat government prudently decided to restore and extend the old system. It brought back the works councils, much as they had been,[98] and it let the unions at last, if not into the plant, at least into the firm – not to dispute management's authority, by negotiation, but to share, and thus (it was hoped) reinforce it. This was to be done in most of industry by giving worker and union representatives a third of the seats on the supervisory board. In the coal and steel industries, where the employers were particularly hard pressed, the share was half, and the union was even given a post on the Management Board, that of 'labour director', with responsibilities for labour relations and personnel.[99]

For a decade and more the new system seemed to work well; machinery which had been designed and used to satisfy militant workers was ample when their militancy waned. Then in the 1960s faults began to show. The representatives on the supervisory board were too remote to be visible to the worker on the shop floor; they were bound by statute to put the shareholders' interests first and leave management to the management board; and anyway they could be outvoted. (The 'labour director', where he existed, was in much the same position.)[100] As for the works council, its rights were so limited that it could only have real influence on important decisions if there was a close relationship between workers and councillors, on the one side, and between councillors and top managers, on the other. During the 1960s this became more difficult to maintain. Plants and firms were growing larger and more complex; a whole new stratum of middle management, not recruited from the shop floor, was inserted between the *Meister* and the board, and the board itself might be replaced by strangers in one of the mergers which became common in the 1960s.[101]

As the social motive for workplace organisation became stronger, so did the economic. Although wage rates were negotiated between the union and the employers' association for a whole industry, they were only *minima*: large firms have always paid well above the negotiated rates.[102] In the 'fat' years of the late 1950s and early 1960s, large firms let actual earnings rise a good deal faster than 'union rates';[103] one of their motives was to keep their workers loyal and content, but it was a dangerous way of doing so, for the worker now faced the insecurity of having earnings so much higher than the negotiated rate that management could effectively reduce them at its discretion.[104] In the deep recession of 1966–7, some large firms made the mistake of using that discretion, and they found, to their surprise, that their workers had quietly built up a workplace organisation which was capable of protecting their 'supplementary' earnings.[105]

The new workplace organisation was built out of two recognised institutions. One was the works council, discussed already; the other was the *Vertrauensmann*, the 'trust man', or union steward.[106] The engineering and chemical unions (IG Metall and IG Chimie) had made particular efforts to train and support their stewards as their only representatives inside the workplace;[107] although they were not officially recognised by the employer, the works council was, and in well-organised firms the worker side of the council would be dominated by union stewards.[108] Potentially, the workplace representatives could act like a British shop steward committee, if they were prepared to ignore the legal restrictions upon them; if it was a question of getting attention for a grievance, or protecting earnings, they were.[109]

There were serious obstacles to the new form of organisation. As we shall see, the state cannot prevent 'unofficial' strikes, but it can stack the cards against them, and the German state had certainly tried to do that. The union leaders were ambivalent towards potential rivals, and top managers were bound to resist shop floor power. It was only in boom years, like 1969 and 1973, when management resistance costs were high, that the workplace representatives could afford to be aggressive; at other times they concentrated on defending past gains, and left it to the leadership to make the running.[110] When the latter held back, in the period of voluntary wage restraint between 1966 and 1969, shop floor power quickly increased; the wave of unofficial action in the 'September strikes' of 1969 taught the leaders their mistake. It also spurred the new centre-left government into improving the works council system and extending its powers (without removing the 'peace obligation') in a law of 1971.[111] The employers too, shaken by the September strikes, were ready to do more to make the works councils effective within the rules – but at the same time, as they showed in the strike wave of 1973, they took a much harder line against action outside them.[112] For most of the period since 1973 economic conditions have helped make that hard line effective. As a result, unofficial strikes have been few, and the militants have been on the defensive in the workplace; the union leaders, by way of compensation, have become more militant. But workplace organisation is still much stronger than before 1969.[113]

As a result, the structure of German unions, and of German industrial relations, is now strangely and delicately balanced. The upper level, of union leaders and their negotiations with employers' associations, is in principle all-powerful; in practice it is still (or again) dominant, but will remain so only so long as the leaders bargain assertively and/or the lower, 'unofficial' bargainers are kept weak by adverse economic conditions. This balance reflects the indecision of the employers. A large and complex modern firm must have some discretion over its own wages: detailed regulation of pay levels by an association is only possible when firms are small and their circumstances are similar. But if big firms are to set their own wages in negotiation with the unions, this must lead to strong workplace organisation (British or Swedish style) unless lower management is kept under tight, US-style discipline. German employers fear the 'English disease', and they would find the US solution scarcely more attractive, since it might disrupt their pattern of management, infuriate their workers, and reduce their capacity for growth and innovation. So they stand between the devil and the deep sea; an acceptable position only until the next wave of militancy. Is such a wave imminent, in Germany or elsewhere? We shall have a clearer idea after the next section.

3.3 THE CAUSES OF MILITANCY

I have spoken of militancy, and moderation as its opposite, without explaining what I meant. I might use the same excuse for that as was once used for not defining an elephant, that everybody would recognise one if they met it in the street; but union militancy is too emotive a term for loose handling. I shall generally use the term in an 'economic' sense: workers are militant if they press for high wage increases and are prepared to strike to get them. So militancy affects the union's bargaining stance; but we must remember that a union's stance depends on the militancy of its leaders as well as its members, and on the balance of power between them. I begin, however, by looking at the militancy of the rank and file, for they are the base on which the superstructure of union authority rests.

We can use much the same analysis to explain militancy as to explain unionisation. With the economic motive the link is obvious: if people join a union in order to improve their wages, then once in it, that is what they set out to do. Even when the motive for unionisation is social, the strong workplace organisation this leads to, will encourage workers to press higher wage claims; what is more, strikes which had mainly social causes can have economic effects. A recent French study found that 62 per cent of demands for wage increases were admitted by union militants to be linked to frustrations over hierarchical relationships, and alienation due to working conditions.[114] (The main difference between unionisation and militancy is that the former persists after the reasons for it have receded; militancy fades quickly. So periods of militancy tend to be periods of fast union growth; when workers are non-militant – 'moderate' – unions tend to decline.) Still, some of the causes of unionisation affect militancy more than others. I shall concentrate here on three which are particularly important, or thought to be: emulation, the level of real wages, and the cost to workers of striking.

Emulation (Wage Comparisons)

Emulation is dynamite. A group of workers who are convinced that they are entitled to 'parity' with another group, may be ready to fight for it with sacrifices they would not otherwise dream of making. That seems irrational, but in a society where people judge themselves and others by how much they are paid, 'unfair' pay is a standing insult.[115] There is nothing irrational in going to some trouble to wipe out such a slur; and even if they fail to wipe it out, or are too weak even to try, the employer will suffer all the same, as their sense of grievance affects their productivity.[116]

Emulation is important also for the effects I described in Chapter 1, Section 3, the effects on workers who are emulated, or can expect to be. Their employer has lower concession costs if his rivals are among those who are forced to follow; and if 'linkage' in general is strong it tends to cancel out the effect of the original increase and make the workers who won it come back for more.

The normal and less explosive type of emulation can be called *conservative*: traditional 'relativities' are regarded as right, so that if group X is emulating group Y it will be satisfied by getting the same pay *increase*.[117] There is nothing in itself inflationary about this sort of emulation – in principle parity could be maintained with 10 per cent *reductions* all round! – but it does mean that if for whatever reason, group Y gets a big increase, it will have a tendency to spread. (It goes without saying that an unusually small increase is less likely to be copied.) This will be a particular problem when Y's increase was meant to be a relative increase, so that when copied they may be given another increase.

There is also the possibility of disagreement about what relativities *are* traditional. Take an example from Britain. The wages of workers at the Ford plant near London fell behind those in the Midlands car firms over a period of years in the 1950s and 1960s. When they woke up to this they pressed for big increases to restore traditional relativities, and after a stiff struggle made up much of the lost ground.[118] It seems that the Midlands and other workers thought of the existing rather than past relativities as fair, and proceeded to emulate the Ford *increases*. (The miners' strikes of 1972 and 1974 had similar reasons, and their success had similar effects.)[119]

The real explosive force is *reformative* emulation: group X decides that its pay relative to group Y's is too low, never mind how long it has been that way. But if X's claim is granted, it is likely that Y will notice and resent the change, and then counter-claim for 'restoration of differentials' in the normal 'conservative' way. If emulation in both directions is strong enough, and based on these two conflicting principles, then the sky is the limit.

The crucial question is, why and when does reformative emulation arise? It is easy enough to understand the conservative kind: it seems *fair* that things should stay the way they are, or at least not change to your own disadvantage, and what is more that seems a *feasible* target to aim at. But why should you decide that you want (and deserve) the same level as a group which till now has been ahead of you – reformative emulation?

To understand this we need to look briefly at the sociological theory of *comparative reference groups*, which explains emulation. Surveys have found that workers tend to make extremely modest choices of comparative groups. The first choice will be those they have (or have had) personal contact with at work. Second are others within the same workplace. Third are those in a similar work situation: the same firm, the same occupation, the same union.[120]

Towards the closest comparative group, their 'nearest neighbours', workers will have strong feelings about *equity*. Any difference in pay, or in any other respect, needs a justification, though there is a wide range of reasons – responsibility, skill, hard conditions, etc. – that may serve to defend the status quo. The more distant the reference group the easier the status quo is to defend, first because the worker is less inclined to make the comparison, second because he is not so well equipped to judge whether the difference is justified.[121]

We find, then, that reformative emulation is applied only to the 'nearest neighbours', and there only when it seems clear that there is no difference between the groups important enough to justify the existing wage differential (or alternatively, the existing differential is too small to match the difference). Conservative emulation is applied to near neighbours with whom present relativities seem fair, and to more distant ones, with whom relativities are usually assumed to be fair. So the range of emulation of pay increases, which involves conservative emulation, is much wider than emulation of levels, which is inherently reformative. Fitter X in one part of a plant may not know, or much care, that grinder Y in another part gets £10 a week more than him, but if that grinder and his mates get a bigger *increase* than him, the fitter will probably hear about it, and will want to know the reason why.

It follows that conservative emulation will change into reformative emulation if:

(a) reference groups come closer, and no justification is then found for the existing differential;
(b) social values change, so a differential between near neighbours which was previously accepted, is now rejected.

To take (b) first, the most striking case of reformative emulation resulting from a change in values is women's drive for equal pay. Women who for years accepted that men working alongside them on much the same job should be paid anything up to double, now reject any difference. (Changes in British and American law have only expressed, and encouraged, underlying changes in attitudes.)[122]

What is likely to bring a reference group closer, or create a comparison where there was none before? Social trends like more travel and better communications, and more uniformity of culture, will have an effect in broadening people's horizons. Nowadays a British car worker in Linwood does not see that a Ryton car worker is 'different' just because he lives 300 miles or so away, and it will be increasingly easy to find out how much the Ryton worker is paid or at least what increase he got this year. Both of them are probably beginning to take an interest in French and German car workers' pay.[123] As people travel further to work, networks of friends, neighbours and relatives connect factories which used to have quite seperate work forces.

For the closest comparisons it is probably organisational changes which are most important. Mergers are the most drastic: groups of workers who might never have heard of one another before, wake up one fine day to find they are doing the same job for the same firm. Any differences between the jobs are likely to diminish as 'rationalisation' proceeds, and the fellow-feeling between plants will grow as employees (managers at least) are moved around from one to another. Large differences in wage levels for similar jobs are then unlikely to be accepted, and 'reformative' emulation by the lower paid will begin.[124] (Union mergers will have a similar but lesser effect.)

Organisational developments within an existing firm or union will also be important. Often these take place in response to emulation. If group X is determined to copy group Y's levels or increases, and *vice-versa*, then the best way to avoid the disruption of jealousy and 'leapfrogging', which is almost as unpleasant for the union as it is for the employer, is to have joint negotiations for both groups at once, and settle the proper relativities there and then.[125] Unfortunately the attempt to bring order into this relationship, even if it succeeds, is likely to increase awareness of the wider disorder. The more centralised a pay structure and bargaining system is, the more formal it will have to be, and the more visible to groups outside it. So there will be more emulation from them, which may create problems for other firms. Within the firms, the crystallisation of the pay relationships between X and Y leaves the new X/Y group without a focus for emulation. That may not necessarily bother the individual workers, but it is likely to concern their representatives more. Their job is to make a 'fair' bargain which they can justify to their members. Emulation provides a clear-cut target. 'Group Z got 10 per cent, and we want 10 per cent – at least': that they can say to their members beforehand, to unite them in their claim, and afterwards they can triumphantly announce their 10, or $10\frac{1}{2}$ per cent. (They *hope*: the art is to pick a reference group which *can* be successfully emulated; that is, which will lead to claims which management can and will agree to. Another firm in the same industry may be suitable, since both firms will then have similar cost increases which they can then pass on in prices.)

This practice may suit both sides, but from the point of view of the economy as a whole what is happening is an extension, and tightening, of the network of emulation. Even if it is only a 'conservative' network it works, as I said, to transmit and generalise increases, and at any point it can erupt into 'reformative' emulation if values change or groups come closer.

Emulation and Union Structure

The union structure plays an important part in channelling emulation, and either stimulating or controlling it. Unions as well as employers generally have an interest in avoiding emulation which would lead to uncomfortably ambitious claims. A centralised 'industrial' union (one representing all the workers in one industry) is best placed to restrain and channel it. For other things being equal, emulation is most likely within the industry, that is within its domain.[126] Each group involved, emulated, emulating or both, is to some extent under the union leadership's control. It can avoid or at least discourage the selection of the 'wrong' target, it can affect the bargaining structure which develops, and it can restrain increases which with the existing network of emulation would lead to 'over-ambitious' claims by other groups. Disagreements over proper relativities can be settled within the union structure, rather than by competitive claims.

We can see that Britain is furthest of the three from this happy state. For *territorially*, the British union movement is divided up not so much by industry, as by 'craft' or occupation, or by the accidents of the growth and mergers of large 'general' unions. The craft unions, and the tradition of occupational 'solidarity' they represent, tend to encourage emulation between firms, and even between industries where the same skill is involved (there are for example electricians in almost every large industry). The general unions must also encourage emulation among the different industries they organise. And within a given industry, or even firm, there is likely to be rivalry between two or more unions, organising different groups which emulate each other: the division will make it harder to establish a single bargaining structure which can keep jealousies under control. Worst of all, the decentralisation of British unions gives more power to the representatives of small groups, who may have no interest in limiting the scope of a network of emulation, or holding back an increase which would cause jealousy within the network.

The other organisation with both motive and opportunity to hold emulation in check is a strong employers' association. If a rise in one firm will lead to pressure on all, then the employers collectively have more interest in preventing it than the firm has alone. If a wage rise for one group in a firm (perhaps through piecework drift) has disturbed internal relativities, the firm alone may find it more convenient to allow a wage rise for everyone else. Since that would disturb *external* relativities, a strong EA should press the firm to take the harder course of holding back the first group. Similarly, a tightly managed firm will not allow lower managers the autonomy which might lead to the disturbance of relativities in the first place.

On all these counts Britain has been the worst placed, but it is quite hard to decide whether (of the other two in my triangle) the US or Germany is the better off. The US employer, bargaining alone, may seem worse placed to control emulation than a strong German employers' association, but as we have seen, the German associations do not really try to control the emulation which results from informal concessions by member firms. In principle such concessions should not be made, or copied, because there are no negotiating rights at this level – but in practice there are.[127] Better to face facts: disciplined American firm faces disciplined American union and between them they keep emulation in check. German employers can do as well only when economic conditions keep the works councillors weak; once lift that lid, and one works council is likely to compete with another, and all with the central leadership, in a game of inflationary leapfrog.

Emulation and the Non-Union Sector

It is not only unionised firms which copy wage settlements elsewhere: non-union firms do too. This is of course partly in order to recruit and keep enough workers of the right quality, but there are two other reasons which are at least as important:

1. the 'morale effect'; it has been shown that workers' productivity is rather sensitive to their rate of pay relative to 'comparable' groups;[128]
2. the 'threat effect'; the more discontented they are over (relative) pay, the more likely workers are to unionise.[129]

Where a large majority of workers are unionised already, and/or unionisation is spreading, the 'threat effect' will naturally be strong, and all three pressures – market, morale and threat – will work to keep non-union firms closely in line with the union sector, at least on pay *increases* (see Chapter 1, Section 3). However, the link will be weaker where non-union workers are psychologically isolated from the rest of the labour force – as women and recent immigrants have tended to be. We can see again the vital role of these two groups in the labour force: by working hard for low pay they will certainly help to keep prices down for other workers; they may help make 'privileged' groups feel content, and put competitive pressure on the employers of 'privileged' workers to keep their wages down. Compare the United States, which has a non-union majority many of whom are 'downtrodden', with millions of illegal immigrants at the bottom – compare the US with Britain and Germany, where the non-union sector is much smaller[130] and women and immigrants neither so numerous nor so 'downtrodden'. The evidence for the US suggests that the union sector is not dominant and that much of the non-union sector pays little attention to its wage rises.[131]

A weak union sector may be reinforced by the existence of a legal minimum wage which is regularly raised in line with union wages, providing a rising floor under the non-union sector, so that its employers are pushed from below as well as pulled from above. Such legal minima do not exist in Germany, and in Britain only apply to certain industries individually. In France and the Netherlands, as I have already said, they are important. The US stands between: the minimum wage was introduced in 1938 but initially applied to only a fraction of the low-paid. Its coverage was increased in 1961, and greatly in 1967; [132] since over the same period its level was raised relative to average earnings,[133] it became in the late 1960s, for the first time, an important factor underpinning the wage structure and increasing wage inflation.[134] But during the 1970s, as its relative level was allowed to fall again, and employers found that it was feebly enforced,[135] its effect waned again.

Emulation of the Rich

Among the reference groups workers may choose to emulate, I have not mentioned their managers, directors, or shareholders, or the more affluent in general, because there is no evidence that they make such lofty comparisons *directly*. But that is not to say that they are not vaguely aware, and envious, of the affluence above them; if they are, it will tend to raise their aspirations and increase their militancy. This inflationary pressure will grow if the gap widens (as it did in France before 1968) or if for some reason workers grow more resentful of it.[136] They would grow the more resentful, the less they believed in the fairness, the efficiency, the *legitimacy* of the existing social order. At the end of that road lies revolution; along the way, increasing inflation. I see no reason to think that any of the countries discussed here has gone far along it.[137]

Real Wages and Wage Aspirations

One school of thought sees dissatisfaction with living standards as the main force behind wage inflation.[138] In its view, workers come to regard a certain standard of living as the least they need or deserve. They compare it with what they actually have, and set their level of aspiration for wage increases accordingly. If a large proportion of the work force feels much dissatisfied with its standard of living, the level of aspiration will be high, and so, as a result, will the settlements negotiated. Higher wage inflation will lead to higher price inflation, and the dissatisfaction will continue: next time the money wage increase aspired to will be higher still; and so on up, until some way is found either to improve the standard of living or to clamp down on the pressure.

But do low living standards raise the level of aspiration? It may seem that they must; but remember, that consumer aspirations are not something *given*, which can be satisfied if national income grows fast enough. The late Fred Hirsch argued in his last book (Hirsch (1976)) that most of what we spend goes on what he called positional goods: goods which are always scarce, except for the relatively rich, however rich the country. Some of these goods are material things like houses in beauty spots – if more people had houses there, they would no longer be beauty spots; others require personal service – only a limited number of people can be waited on hand and foot, others must do the waiting. There are also intangible satisfactions that come from having something enjoyed by few – expensive perfumes would lose much of their fragrance if every woman could wear them. Other goods, which seem at least partly to be valued for their usefulness, behave all the same very like positional goods. For example, social habits in the West are now so much adapted to television and the motor car, that whereas twenty years ago those who had them felt rich, now those who do not, feel poor. And yet other goods, like video cassette recorders, had not been invented then, so that no one could want them, but now exist and are well known through advertising, so that many people covet them.

If one accepts this argument, as I do, it follows that a society which sets out to bring even material contentment to its people by making them all richer, is only chasing its own tail. True, people who become suddenly richer, as many Western Europeans did in the fifties, may be content for a while, until they get over the surprise. But they may then get used not only to being rich but to becoming richer, until mere stagnation would seem like hardship.[139] As countries draw closer together, the time may come when the richer feel content by comparison with their neighbours, particularly if the neighbours provide cheap labour and holidays; but for every gainer there will be an equal loser.

At all events there will be times and places of more contentment, and of less. Probably the worst effect of a feeling of poverty will be to sharpen resentments which have their roots in wage comparisons. Even that effect may not last. In the end, it may very well be that the most dangerous expectations to disappoint are not for money but for position. During the 1960s German boys grew up expecting to get skilled jobs, while immigrants and women did the rest. Those who now have to take unskilled jobs may feel frustration and resentment for the rest of their lives. That reminds us again how important is the escalator.

The Cost of Striking

I take this last because it seems likely that workers do too: you decide first if you have a good reason for striking, and only then ask if you can afford to. Indeed it has been argued that workers take very little notice of the cost of striking; but I think this is going too far.[140] Even if they do *not* calculate the cost of striking beforehand, they will have a general idea of it from their own experiences, and their friends'; and if they are involved in a long strike, they will find out the truth soon enough for it to affect their stance. Even if the union stance is decided mostly by emulation and price increases (as Daniel found)[141] this does not mean that strike costs are unimportant – wherever they cause, say, a 1 per cent rise in one settlement, that leads, via emulation and price increases, to rises in many others. Cumulatively, invisibly, the effect may be very large.

There have been great changes in strike costs almost everywhere, over the decades. Everywhere manual workers have more savings than they used to, which can be drawn on during a strike.[142] More and more married women have jobs which can provide income while their husbands are on strike (or, conversely, they can strike while he is at work!). An increasing proportion of income goes on what can loosely be described as 'investment': on buying durable goods of various kinds, such as clothing, household goods, cars, housing, and on saving. The beauty of investment, for the striker, is that it can easily be put off. More and more of the rest goes on things which are not necessarily thought of as luxuries, but which can quite easily be economised for a while – drinks, convenience foods, entertainment. More and more manual workers, almost everywhere, own their homes,[143] or have considerable security of tenure.

In short: the striker can nowadays stay out longer before he feels the pinch, and far longer before he or his family run short of food, clothing or shelter.[144] Does this not affect workers' willingness to strike?

The greatest differences between countries are in the costs of *unofficial* strikes. In Germany a worker who goes on strike without official union support, and strike pay, is more or less from that moment uninsured (so that a serious illness in the family could ruin him). Neither he nor his family can expect any support from the State. He is in breach of his contract with his employer. Sympathy strikes by one group in support of another – which can be very effective – are illegal. An unofficial striker in the USA is not much better off. But in Britain, a striker loses none of his protection against sickness, etc. His family is entitled, in case of need, to social security benefits. Within two or three weeks he can look forward to a steady flow of rebates on tax paid in that financial year. He has done nothing illegal or even unconventional, nor (usually) has any one who strikes in sympathy with him.[145]

Some of these differences – in tax rebates and social security benefits – are still relevant when the decision to strike is taken centrally and the strikers are backed by union funds. Union strike pay is not a panacea – it is rarely more than a pittance,[146] and even at that it puts a great financial strain on the union, the more so because this sort of strike is likely to be large-scale. The long British miners' strikes of 1972 and 1974 were successful partly because the union was able to keep its meagre reserves as a 'hardship fund' without giving any general strike pay.[147]

But the differences should be seen in perspective. Nowadays, in every country, most strikers have very large resources potentially available to them: besides their own savings, they can look for help (gifts or loans) from friends and members of their family, who could easily provide the minimum necessary to tide them over a strike; in the rare cases where many friends and relatives are also involved in the strike, it will almost certainly be an official one; and then their union can look for support to the rest of the union movement, at home and abroad.[148]

The crucial question is, will this help be offered? In a strongly unionised country, at a militant time, for a popular strike, it will; the strikers will find it much easier to bear what hardship they have, if they are treated almost like heroes. In Britain in 1972, in the first of the great miners' strikes, there was that sort of atmosphere, and the miners held out without any sign of weakening for six winter weeks, until power shortages forced the government, their employer, into complete surrender.[149] Yet barely a year before, the power workers' union which could have done the same damage in a few hours had been forced to give up its own disruptive action with no concession on the government's part.[150]

The difference was summed up in the pubs: in December 1970 a power worker who was known as such could think himself lucky to be served, and risked being beaten up; in January 1972 the only difficulty a miner had was in being allowed to pay for his drinks.[151] It is no longer possible, as it was in 1926, simply to starve strikers into submission – you must use subtler methods now.

The Militancy of the Leadership

Union leaders are essentially politicians. That is, they may have their own views, but their instinct is to respond to those of others – they would not otherwise have got to the top. Once there, there are many pressures on them for moderation – from employers, government, even from other union leaders, as I shall show in the next section. Pressure for militancy can only come from below; unless it is strong, their policy is unlikely to be militant – only their rhetoric.

Pressure from below can take two forms, direct and indirect. Direct pressure uses the democratic rules of union government; if the leadership's policy is unpopular, either the policy or the leaders themselves are voted out. All unions are democratic in theory; some are more democratic than others in practice. In this, circumstances count more than constitutions: a small union in a small country with strong unions (e.g. Sweden) is likely to be much more democratic, in practice, than a large one in a large country with weak unions (e.g. the US, and notably its largest union, the Teamsters)[152] – for the members will find it easier to make the constitution work.

Indirect pressure uses the simple democracy of the workplace to win by decentralised action what the central leadership choose not to fight for. There is little problem of getting democracy here – a shop steward can hardly help responding to the wishes of his workgroup – but can he respond effectively, without central support and approval? I have answered that question briefly for each of our seven countries in the last section. As I showed in the last section, the answer varies a great deal among countries: from 'quite effectively' for Britain to 'no' for the US.

The more successful is workplace militancy without central help, the more will the centre feel obliged to be militant too. Unless it is, some groups within each union, and some unions, will do better than the rest. Those who have done worse will then have the strongest possible motive to use the democratic rules to throw the leadership out, or – almost as bad – to build up strong and independent workplace organisations; those who have already got them, and gained by them, will rely more on them than ever, less on the leadership.

In some countries we can expect a regular alternation between moderation and militancy. Suppose we start with the union leadership firmly in the saddle and responding to government's and employers' pleas for restraint. This is Phase 1 – Centralised Moderation. But this frustrates the aspirations of the rank and file, who, led by stewards or works councillors, press forward on their own: Phase 2 – Decentralised Militancy. The leadership then takes fright at being overtaken, and rushes to put itself at the head of its troops (or is defeated and replaced by others who will): Phase 3 – Centralised Militancy. In this last phase the militancy is most effective, because stewards and leadership are pushing together, but it will fade: the rank and file will regain confidence in the leadership, who will then make use of it to return gradually to Phase 1.

It is clear that this 'three-phase militancy cycle' will not start turning in the first place without stewards or works councillors who are capable, if their members demand it, of winning wage increases without central help. Thus it is hard to pick out any such cycle in the US. (The most we can expect then is a *two*-stage cycle, in which frustrated workers resort to democratic pressure on the centre, and there is then a milder alternation between Centralised Moderation and Centralised Militancy.) But why, in other countries, should leaders make the mistake of letting the cycle start turning in the first place? In some cases, where workplace organisation has been weak or non-existent, they may be simply unaware that it is now stronger, or can become so in response to rank-and-file frustration. In others, the leaders see the need to keep a careful balance, but are thrown off it by forces beyond their control. One such force is incomes policy, which I discuss in the next section. Another is the business cycle.

In a deep recession, frustrations accumulate, as the stewards are too weak to win what workers want, and the leaders cannot either, or will not. If there is a sudden boom, the leaders may be slow to react, or have to wait till contracts expire, and the stewards may strike first – literally. The great growth of workplace organisation in Continental Europe – in Belgium, Holland, Italy and West Germany in the late 1960s and early 1970s – can be partly explained by the sequence of unusually deep recession (1966–7) followed by strong boom. Those events help to make another point about the militancy cycle: each is bound to differ from the one before, if only because people learn. Workers may learn, and have better workplace organisation ready, for the next Phase 1; leaders may learn, and take more care not to overdo Phase 1; employers may learn, and prepare better to resist Phases 2 and 3.

The Events of May and their Aftermath

I shall end this section by looking at two examples of militancy which reveal much about its causes and effects, because they show them in an extreme form. The first is very well known; it took place in France just over ten years ago, as I write, and it is usually called, simply, the events of May.

I have treated strong union organisation – above all, strong workplace organisation – as a disadvantage for the employer; and so it must be, if it challenges his authority and forces up his wage costs. Yet it serves a purpose for him: it keeps his managers on their toes, both to redress grievances, and to resist pressure. It also creates a structure of power on the workers' side in which the leaders – in the workplace as well as outside – learn to look for limited solutions to small conflicts, and to see management's point of view. Without a union there may be nothing to vent workers' discontent, and when it builds up, nothing to moderate and channel it. This normally poses no problem, for as the discontent grows, so do the unions; if they are weak, it is because workers are more-or-less contented or (like the Mexicans in the US, till now) so profoundly weak and isolated that management has nothing to fear from *their* anger.

So it looked in France in the mid-1960s: most French workers seemed satisfied by the escalator and dramatic rises in purchasing power over the past decade; there were immigrant workers at the bottom, as weak and isolated as the Mexicans.[153] Yet there *was* a great deal of discontent – the sense of powerlessness Seeman found in 1967 is a sign of it.[154] It was bound to arise as management kept up its old authoritarian style in the new large plants. Workers should have built up the organisation to express it – but they needed something to build *on*. The unions were remote and divided, the works councils ineffective; and management obstinately refused to bargain with either about the issues that mattered. And they needed some group to give a lead. Everywhere else, it has been the skilled blue collar workers who have led; but it was precisely this group which gained most from the French variety of the escalator. Unskilled manual workers, and white collar workers, felt more frustration but had a less strategic position and thus less power to express it.[155] So they were all, in the mid-1960s, below the 'flash point' of militant action. It was, in the end, the policies of de Gaulle's government which brought them up to this point, together.

De Gaulle, in power since 1958, had followed policies which had been economically successful, but socially unscrupulous. The legal minimum wage, which under the Fourth Republic had been used to make up for union weakness, was allowed to lag far behind the average wage (between 1955 and 1967 it rose only 71 per cent while salaries of middle management ('cadres') rose 190 per cent); differentials, wide already, became easily the widest in Europe.[156] That policy could be tolerated only so long as it was mainly immigrants who suffered, while Frenchmen were able to climb up the lengthening ladder. During the 1966–7 recession the escalator stopped, and many Frenchmen felt the unfairness of their society at first hand.

What made the situation particularly explosive was the lack of the normal distinction between industrial and political grievances. The government was known to own much of industry and have wide powers over the rest; industry (through business links with the Gaullists) was assumed to have great influence over government; and the revolutionary tradition still strong in the French working class made many workers think in terms of one capitalist ruling class.[157] If anything, this made them less militant at work – what hope or point was there in taking on the little boss, when the big boss sat in the Elysée, out of reach, helping the little ones? But by the same token, when they did strike, they would strike against big and little boss together; by the spring of 1968, all they needed was a lead. A group with grievances of its own, the students, sniffed the wind from Vietnam and Prague, and gave it.

The strikes and occupations of May 1968 were not primarily for higher wages – in fact it is hard to say what they were for, easier to say what they were against – the arrogance of power at all levels from de Gaulle to the foreman.[158] But neither President nor foreman were ready to give up their power, least of all at such a moment. The President flew to Germany to make sure of his tank units' loyalty; the Prime Minister, Pompidou, negotiated with the union leaders at the Palais Matignon;[159] they came away with the promise of massive wage increases, including a one-third increase in the minimum wage.[160] (It is a paradox of militancy, that the less interested strikers are in money, the more money they are likely to get, for the more important it is to buy them off; and the concession is made if possible to leaders who did not call the strike, to help them regain their authority.)[161]

The strategy succeeded: the strikers went back, richer but not stronger, and the government set to work to ensure that they never became so militant again. It committed itself to raising the minimum wage faster than average earnings (between 1970 and 1976 the minimum rose 144 per cent, while 'Cadres' earnings rose only 86 per cent); and it revived the escalator with five consecutive years of high demand.

Employers responded by taking a good deal more notice of the works councils, though they still set their faces against any negotiation at plant or firm level. Government and employers alike seemed to understand that they could only keep their authority in future if they made less blatant use of it. There is still scarcely any effective workplace organisation in French industry, and union density, though higher than in the 1960s, remains the lowest in Europe (Fig. 3.1).

Within two years the French crisis had been followed by waves of unofficial strikes in most of Continental Europe. I will look here only at the Italian case. The militancy in Italy resembled that in France in the revolutionary tradition of the workers involved;[162] on the other hand, the Italian government was a byword for feebleness rather than arrogance, and the conditions for union organisation (see Chapter 3, Section 1) were better. Perhaps in consequence, the workers concentrated on power at the workplace rather than threatening the state, and built up permanent workplace organisations, but the first effect was the same as in France: the outbreak of *decentralised militancy*[163] spurred the unions into *centralised militancy* and made the employers particularly generous to them in an attempt to turn the workers away from the factory councils.[164] But the councils won recognition, and henceforth the unions (and employers) had to reckon with their power: moderation was only possible whenever recession clipped the councils' wings. Even that proved unwise for the unions in the lasting recession after 1974: counting too long on its members' loyalty, the Communist federation found itself outflanked by new 'extremist' unions closely linked to the factory councils – and with that, the leaders' room for moderation grew even less.[165]

Italy provides an example of a point made already in this section: wage inflation will normally be slower while the union leadership is moderate, and also during recession. Governments have noted these facts too. Not unreasonably, they have concluded that if they could induce such moderation, or recession – or both – they could reduce inflation. It is a very reasonable conclusion; still, I think both parts of it, in the long term, entirely wrong. But I will not dismiss the bases of all western counter-inflation policy, and the views of almost all of my profession, in one sentence. They deserve more respect. I will give them the next chapter.

Conclusion

There were three strands which ran right through this chapter. The first was the role of management and the structure of the firm. The way in which industry is organised and run, affects the incentive and the opportunity, (a) to unionise, (b) to decentralise union power, (c) to emulate other groups' wages, (d) to be militant – in effect, to strike. The second strand was the effect on all these things of workers' attitudes, values, beliefs. How far are they individualist, how far collectivist? How important do class differences seem, as compared with racial, sexual, etc.? Attitudes are inherited, but can be changed: by facts like the escalator, or immigration; by pressures from 'above' – like the mass media or the law. The third strand was the role of the State. It can make it easier or harder to unionise and strike. As employer it can affect management policy and structure directly. Its policy on minimum wages and works councils can help to reduce grievances; its policy on immigration and discrimination can affect attitudes.

The implications are important. For strong unions raise employers' resistance cost, and reduce their own. Decentralised unions can put pressure on that level of management whose stance will be softest. A large union sector, and a wide, tight network of emulation, increase the *linkage* between employers, and thus reduce the concession cost of each. Militancy increases the concession cost of the union, and the resistance cost of the employer. So union strength, decentralisation, emulation and militancy are all inflationary – other things being equal. (Where union-isation is held down by minimum wage laws, as in France and now Holland, other things are not equal – the wage minima are inflationary too.) We are now a long step further towards understanding the rising trend of inflation, and international differences in it.

4 Medicines and Quacks

4.1 INCOMES POLICIES

Voluntary Incomes Policy

The simplest way to reduce wage inflation is for unions to accept lower wage increases. But can the unions be persuaded? That will depend on the structure of wage bargaining, and the objectives of those who take the bargaining decisions on the union side. Let us look at them in turn.

The Bargaining Structure

Suppose one group of workers – say a few hundred men in one plant – win a wage increase of perhaps 10 per cent. How does that affect the economy? Their firm puts up its prices a little more than it otherwise would, but the effect on the Retail Price Index is insignificant. A few neighbouring groups of workers put in parity claims and get slightly higher increases as a result. And that is all. The result is that (apart from tax effects) our group is very nearly 10 per cent better off than it would have been without any increase. That is still true even if there is in fact price inflation of 10 per cent; this simply means that without the increase they would have been 10 per cent *worse* off. So, to use my bargaining language, the group's concession costs are high.

For the trade unions collectively it is different. Suppose all of them win 10 per cent for all their members, and that non-unionised workers will follow the union increase very closely. Then no union members will have improved their relative position. How they will do in absolute terms depends on how much prices and taxes are affected by the general level of wages. If there is a close link, then the union movement as a whole will have rather little to gain from an increase, certainly much less than one small group. If the government and perhaps the employers hold down taxes and prices in return for union wage restraint, then restraint may cost union members nothing – they may even gain by it, as everyone gains from lower inflation. So for the unions' members as a whole, concession costs may be zero, even negative.

This is the case for 'voluntary incomes policy' that governments put to the trade unions, and it is very persuasive, in principle. Whether union negotiators are persuaded in practice depends on who they are, and who they are responsible to. If they are top officials negotiating for the whole membership of their union, they can hold down their own settlements, and keep an eye on the other unions. If all toe the line, none loses by it, and assuming inflation is held in check, as a result, their restraint will be seen to make very good sense.

If you put the same case to an individual shop steward, or the shop stewards' committee of a works, they may find it equally convincing, but they are unlikely to believe that it is in *their* members' interests to restrain *their* wage demands. From their own selfish point of view, the bigger their increase the better. To appeal to them for restraint, *on grounds of self-interest*, will be futile.

The Bargainers' Objectives

By concerted restraint union leaders can keep their members' concession costs low. Their own may be still lower. To recall the last section, if the pressure from below is weak they may be sensitive to pressures from government and employers, and glad to make a (short-run) sacrifice of their members' living standards in the interests of 'national prosperity'; that is, to accept voluntary restraint of wages. Shop stewards, on the other hand, are likely to reflect rank and file workers' attitudes more or less directly, and not be able or willing to come to their own view of what is in their constituents' best interests, or the nation's. As for the rank and file themselves, they are not necessarily selfish. They too can understand and accept the arguments for wage restraint, if they are put across forcefully enough in the mass media. If the situation is dramatised as an economic crisis, they may willingly accept sacrifices, but normally on one strict condition: *equality* of sacrifice. It must appear that all alike are affected: other workers, salary-earners, and even shareholders. Otherwise anyone who holds back is seen not as a saint but as a mug.

Conditions for Success

We can now see that a voluntary incomes policy will be most effective where, first, the bargaining system is centralised, second, the rank and file support restraint. For the union leaders should then be able to keep increases down right across the board. (The non-union sector is not likely to get provocatively out of line unless demand is unusually high.) This in turn will help to keep the policy popular, for there will be no high increases to emulate, and presumably price inflation will soon be low. This is the sort of system which operated successfully in Sweden and Holland for most of the 1950s and 1960s.[1]

In a more or less decentralised bargaining system, one with some workplace independence, a policy of restraint is much harder to operate. Even if the shop stewards and their members accept the policy in principle – to begin with – they have not the same incentive, as we have seen, to observe it in practice. Most people can think of some reason why *their* group – *this* time – should get an exceptional increase. One of the best justifications is that some other group already has; so any exceptional increase – any which is even *regarded* as exceptional – is like the hole in the dyke, which lets the water through, and as it does, gets larger. Once the breach in the policy is large, it begins to have a significant effect on prices too; and so we move from Phase 1 of the union cycle, Centralised Moderation, to Phase 2, Decentralised Militancy. The voluntary policy will only survive, then, if employers cooperate by refusing to give exceptional increases – but if employers had been so tough, we would not have a decentralised system.

Statutory Incomes Policy

If a government cannot persuade unions to restrain their wage claims, it may set out to force them to. In the public sector it is the employer, and can simply decide to take a tough stance, and hope this sets the private sector an example. Public settlements do influence the private sector, certainly, but the effect is not one-for-one, so that such a policy cuts the relative wages of public sector workers, who will resist with militancy before long, as the British miners did in 1972. (If there is a minimum wage, that can be held down too; but de Gaulle did that, and we saw what happened to him.) Somehow the private sector has to be brought into line; if persuasion fails, then by compulsion.

Statutory incomes policy is a last resort. Each time it has been used in Britain – 1966–9, 1972–4, and 1975–8 – it has followed a failed attempt at voluntary restraint.[2] In the US it has only been used once in peacetime, in 1971–3.[3] In West Germany it has never been used at all. It is easy to understand the reluctance of governments, for what is involved is the extension of law and administration into a vast and complex area. Employers as well as unions are bound to resent the loss of their freedom to bargain, and state authority is exposed to dangerous confrontation with organised labour, which could go so far as a general strike.

To reduce these risks, governments have done their best to get popular support and union consent or at least acquiescence. This requires much the same policy as voluntary restraint does: public opinion must be cultivated, and prices must be held down. (Price restraint must now be statutory too, to seem fair.) In one way consent is harder to get for a statutory policy: it is natural to resent being *forced* to do something. On the other hand, union leaders who wanted, but did not dare, to hold back before, can now do so, pleading compulsion. Above all, it may be possible, by holding all pay down, to avoid the strongest reason for discontent with restraint – resentment of those who break the rules.

The vital thing, as with voluntary incomes policy, is that the rules should be obeyed, and seen to be obeyed. But how can the authorities find out whether the rules are being obeyed, how can they enforce them – and what are the rules to be?

There is a cruel dilemma here. The easiest policy to monitor is the simplest. A complete freeze is ideal, but unacceptable if prices are rising fast. Next best is an £x per week or x per cent 'ceiling'. Monitoring such a policy seems straightforward: all wage settlements must be reported by the employer to a Pay Board or some such agency. Further, regular data on actual earnings in the firm must be supplied. Inaccurate reporting will carry a stiff penalty. But now suppose a firm pays by results (PBR). Pay goes up above the permitted, negotiated increase, because productivity has risen. Is that to be allowed? It cannot be generally allowed, or the policy cannot stick; the PBR workers' negotiated settlements must be reduced accordingly, so that their earnings increase stays within the limit. That will require very close monitoring, and it will probably cause a great deal of discontent among those affected. Worse, what do we mean by earnings? It is surely out of the question to fix *total* weekly earnings – if workers do overtime they must be allowed to earn extra. That opens a loophole: overtime can be clocked up that wasn't worked.

Such simplicity involves dangerous rigidity. There are all kinds of good reasons for changing the wage structure within and between firms – anomalies which have cropped up, the need to attract labour, perhaps the need to offer a *quid pro quo* for some change in working methods or increase in effort ('productivity bargaining'). Prevent such changes, and you make for increasing discontent and inefficiency. Permit them, and you make an administrator's nightmare. For in a decentralised system there are tens or hundreds of thousands of wage settlements every year. It will be extremely difficult simply to check that every group's earnings have stayed within the limit. To check that thousands, perhaps tens of thousands of increases *beyond* the limit are justified under the policy rules, will be virtually impossible; certainly many such decisions will be arbitrary, or seem so. It will be tempting to make a practice of giving the benefit of the doubt, but that will encourage evasion of the policy.

The extent of evasion will depend to some extent on how the policy is enforced. It is the workers who clearly stand to gain from breaking the rules, so that it seems logical that the legal coercion should be applied to them, through fines or jail for those who strike in support of an excessive claim, or negotiate an excessive settlement; alternatively excessive increases can be taxed away. Under the 1966–9 system it was on the union side that the weight of enforcement fell.[4] But since then British governments have found it less politically embarrassing to lay the penalties on the employers. Either they were legally compelled to stay within the limit (1972–4), or, more indirectly, they were to be punished by having price increases disallowed (a back-up provision in the 1972 legislation and the only statutory prop of the 1975–8 policy).[5]

The difficulty in working through the employer is that you already depend on him to report settlements and earnings accurately and complain about union pressure to breach the policy. If he reports an excessive increase he is to be punished; if he complains about union pressure he is to be told that he must not let it succeed. It does seem a little hard, and not likely to make him any keener to stick to the rules.

This brings us back to the crucial question about any incomes policy, voluntary or statutory. The union leadership may have some incentive, and ability, to see that the rules are kept, but the employers have much more. *Are the employers, at every level, committed to making the policy work?* If they connive at evasion the whole enterprise is hopeless: through non-existent overtime, loose incentive systems, bogus productivity deals, and even unreported increases, the policy can be quickly sabotaged. But why on earth should they behave like this – surely an income policy, voluntary or statutory, is a godsend for them?

Unfortunately this is not true for all managers. The problem, as on the union side, is individual self-interest in a decentralised system. Most employers' associations will be delighted to have government and /or TUC[6] support in resisting a large pay claim; even if enforcement is applied to them, that will help them to say convincingly, sorry, we *cannot* concede the increase. An individual firm may be less enthusiastic. It may have some damaging anomaly in its pay structure that it would like to get rid of by paying some part of its work force more than the rules allow, or need skilled labour which it hopes to recruit by raising wages.

Least of all can lower management be relied on. As I showed in Chapter 2, Section 1 their concession costs are particularly low, their strike costs high. What is the hapless foreman or works manager to do if a shop steward approaches him quietly and says, 'Look here, the lads are very angry about not getting that increase. . . . I think you should know, as things stand you haven't a chance in hell of meeting your production target and getting that big order off on time. But if they saw their earnings rise by a couple of quid in the next week or two . . .' . Does he warn Head Office, complain to the TUC, alert the Department of Employment, call the police? Not if he has any sense. He sees to it that a piece rate is loosened here, more overtime is recorded there, perhaps presses his superiors to be generous with that productivity deal or regrading exercise. No one but himself and the shop steward need ever know what is going on; his boss will be happy that the work has been done, and not too curious to know how.

Such workplace pressures, together with labour shortages, kill incomes policies. Where firms are small, workplace pressure will be weaker, but small firms operate in more-or-less competitive labour markets, in which any shortage of labour will tempt them to break the rules. Large firms have less reason to respond in this way to a labour shortage (see next section) but it is they whose workers will have independent workplace organisations. Each firm, small or large, which breaks the rules, increases the pressure on the others.

How fast will the policy die? Where firms and plants are mostly small, as in the Netherlands in the late 1940s and 1950s, it will depend on the state of the labour market. Dutch incomes policies of that period collapsed when the economy 'overheated'.[7] Where the pressure comes from workplace organisation, the level of demand will still count (as I show in the next section), but less. Strict rules, and popular support for restraint, will help to keep the policy alive. But most important is the organisational strength of employers and workers at the workplace. As we have seen, where firms are large it is unwise to count on workers' weakness, unless there is something like a boosted escalator to keep them crippled; otherwise, as in Germany and Holland in the late 1960s, and in Britain in every incomes policy, they will rise to the occasion and improve their organisation to the point where it can break the policy. The organisations they build will then be available to break the next incomes policy quicker. That in fact is the most important difference between the early Dutch policies, and those tried anywhere in the 1970s: the Dutch could see one policy destroyed by economic overheating; wait till the wage structure had settled again, and the economy had cooled; then start again, fresh. Now each attempt at wage restraint – in the Netherlands as in Britain – shortens the life of the next.

The best hope lies in the large employers. If they are disciplined and firm, workplace pressure can be resisted, and will not spread. From that point of view the US might well seem suited to an incomes policy; but the US firm, unlike the West German, is accustomed to imposing its own discipline rather than conforming to one imposed from outside, and the size and diversity of the US economy makes the problems of enforcement and equity all the more serious. (The one serious attempt at statutory incomes policy, Nixon's, was dropped after barely a year and a half, before these problems could come to a head.)

There is perhaps another, still better reason for the American aversion to incomes policy. The whole structure of US industrial relations, seen from Europe, depends on the tacit acceptance of the law of the jungle – the principle expressed by W. C. Fields' famous gag, 'never give a sucker an even break'. The market, or rather, economic power, rules. If you don't like the wages in your job, your first thought is, I must go some place else, or get promoted, or set up on my own. You *may* use collective muscle instead, and strike, but you do so without any great sense of righteousness – you don't see your low pay as particularly *unfair*. Once introduce incomes policy, and that attitude may change, for the moral and political rationale of incomes policy cannot be the law of the jungle, but the principles of social democracy. Argue that people should not be allowed to exploit their power in the market or the negotiating process for their own selfish ends, and they will ask, 'If power is not to dictate wages and prices, what is to take its place?' Only one answer will satisfy them – 'Social justice'. A very dangerous answer, for it is the appeal to justice, to fairness, that is the root of wage emulation, and the moral basis of unionisation itself. Workers in Alabama or South-West Texas may start asking what is fair in being paid a third or a half less than north-eastern workers in a similar job, even in the same firm, and the old answer will not do – that economics is not fair. Next thing, they may be organising to *make* it fair.

So the United States has most to lose by incomes policy, being the country which starts furthest from social democracy. But those which are nearer must also lose. Everywhere, emulation is based on a desire for fairness, and on the supply of information; incomes policy increases both. Justice here, as elsewhere, must be seen to be done; the curiosity which already existed about other workers' wages and wage increases now becomes almost a craving for information, which the mass media are glad to satisfy. Better information is also required by the policy's enforcers, in government, or unions, who can hardly stop it being made public. Knowing more about others' wages, people will naturally take more account of them.

If people come to care more about wage comparisons, and are in a better position to make them, this must have inflationary effects, as I have already shown. These will be weakest, and least obvious, in the earliest stages of an incomes policy, when there is some crude but simple rule – say, x per cent all round; for then emulation, so long as it is 'conservative', agrees with the policy. But already 'reformative' emulation will make for tension, and once evasion becomes common and/or the rules are made more complex and flexible, the strains are bound to increase. The effect of increased emulation will be clearest and strongest when 'free collective bargaining' returns: there will be more of the 'linkage' of Chapter 1, Section 3, and of the 'leapfrogging' of Chapter 3, Section 3.

And thus another force which helped make incomes policy seem necessary, is strengthened by it; strengthened, helps to destroy it; and having destroyed it, worsens the sickness the policy was meant to cure.

4.2 THE FALL OF THE PHILLIPS CURVE

In the Introduction I explained the Phillips Curve, and how it was *augmented* by *expectations*. (It is summed up, rather cruelly, in Fig.4.1.) The Curve states that some increase in unemployment will lead to some decrease in wage inflation. The *augmented* Curve states that *expectations of price inflation* also affect wage inflation. A sufficient rise in unemployment will in due course bring price expectations down and thus, in the long term, reduce wage inflation much further.

A glance at the statistics suggests that inflation has *not* responded in this way. Whenever unemployment has risen sharply, inflation has fallen, during the next year or so (see Chapter 5, Section 3); so far so good. But in the longer term – comparing late 1970s with late 1960s, or late 1960s with late 1950s – a rise in unemployment seems to go with a *rise* in inflation. If you choose your theories by how well they fit the facts, you must then prefer one which explains and predicts just this: that the effect of deflation , in the short term, is to reduce inflation, but in the long term is to raise it. In that case, as I am about to show, you must prefer mine.

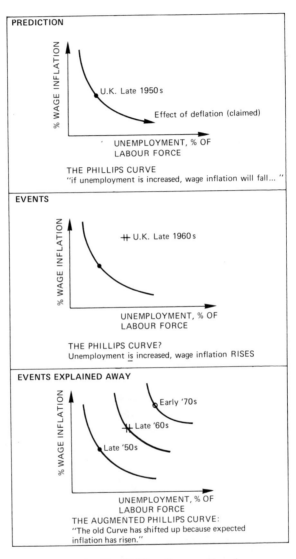

FIGURE 4.1 The Phillips Curve, old and new

Wage Inflation and the Business Cycle

We need to start off with a definition of the business cycle, and its various parts, upturn, downturn, recession, boom. It can hardly be in terms of unemployment. Unemployment does vary cyclically, but it shows other variations too. In Britain it has never been so low since 1970 as the highest point it reached during the 1950s, but we would not wish to say that the 1950s were a period of continuous boom and the 1970s of continuous recession. Instead I shall use the concept of *capacity utilisation*: the proportion of available productive capacity which is actually in use. When this is low we have a recession, when it is high we have a boom; the downturn is a period of falling, the upturn of rising capacity utilisation. (Note that to be realistic we must think in terms of human capacity as well as physical. A firm is in effect working at full capacity if *either* its plants or its men are at full stretch. It may take as long to train or find more skilled labour as it does to get new machines, and because of that it will keep spare capacity of both kinds through the recession.)

Let us consider the effect of the downturn – falling capacity utilisation – on management's strike and concession costs. It usually begins with a fall in sales; as a result, stocks of finished goods increase, without planning by the firm and probably against its wishes. Then production is cut back: first by reducing working hours, and only later by the less easily reversible step of laying off workers.

Although the unplanned build-up of stocks, and spare physical and human capacity, will be unprofitable and unwelcome to the firm, it will clearly reduce its strike costs a great deal. Until a strike has lasted long enough to exhaust the 'buffer' of stocks, no sales need be lost. Even after that point, the firm can work off any backlog of orders soon after the strike is over, by temporarily increasing its capacity utilisation – putting workers back on overtime, perhaps even rehiring workers recently laid off. This will repair much of any damage done to profits and goodwill.

Thus we can expect management strike costs to decrease in the downturn, so that wage inflation will slow down. (In the upturn the opposite can be expected: stocks of finished goods will be reduced, human and physical capacity fully stretched, so strike costs will be high and wage inflation will speed up.) But these are not lasting effects, because the downturn does not last. The unplanned stocks will be run down, men will be laid off, training schemes pruned, investment cut back, as the firm adjusts to the lower level of demand. So first the stock/output ratio will fall, then the rate of overtime will rise, finally the rate of capacity utilisation will rise as the investment cuts take effect; and back goes the strike/concession cost ratio towards its previous level. (And in the upturn it goes back down.) Capacity may take some years to adjust fully in either direction. At the beginning of a recession, machinery may remain available, for use if required, even though not normally in action; similarly, men recently dismissed may well be available when needed. But sooner or later the machinery will be scrapped or become totally obsolete, and the men will find jobs elsewhere, leave the area or simply fail to acquire newly needed skills.

The cycle has a similar effect on the union side. The downturn affects workers' incomes by cutting overtime. They run down their savings for a while until spending has been cut enough to match the lower level of income.[8] (Hire purchase commitments will help to delay this adjustment.) This raises their strike costs, for as stocks of output cushion management during a strike, so do savings cushion workers. But workers, like managers, do adjust: as the HP debts are repaid, and savings brought back into balance with consumption, their strike costs will fall again. An upturn, by increasing overtime, will of course have an opposite effect: until he has had time to adjust his habits and commitments the worker is flush with funds, and well placed to sit out a strike.

These arguments show how a recession can reduce wage inflation, but they do not imply that deflation, government action to reduce demand, can have a *long – run* effect. What goes down, as it were, must come up. We have no reason to expect a deflationary policy to lead to lower capacity utilisation and overtime and a higher stock/output ratio, in the *long term*; by making management more cautious it will probably have the reverse effect. A firm which has been caught repeatedly with excess capacity, labour and stocks is likely to try to make sure in future that it operates with high capacity utilisation, high overtime, and low stocks, even if that means turning customers away in a boom; what is worse, it is cautious firms which best survive deflation, while the optimists are crippled or wiped out.

It is, on the other hand, possible to raise unemployment permanently. It has been done. What effect, then, does high unemployment have on the bargaining stances of unions and employers?

Wage Inflation and Unemployment

I shall begin, as usual, with the management side. Will unemployment reduce their concession costs, their strike costs, or their indirect resistance costs? I can see no effect on concession costs. It might reduce their strike costs by making it easier to get 'blacklegs' from among the unemployed, but such tactics are rare in Britain and Germany nowadays, so the point is hardly relevant there. (In the US, however, it cannot be ignored.) But it will reduce indirect resistance costs, on two conditions: that it makes it easier to recruit and keep the labour they require, and that this reduces the incentive to concede a wage increase.

The first is true only briefly. The labour that counts most is skilled – production is rarely held back by shortages of unskilled labour – and high unemployment only improves the supply of skilled labour in the short term. In the long term it makes it worse. I will explain how. During 1977 and 1978, with unemployment at its highest for more than forty years, British industry began to complain more and more loudly about shortages of skilled labour, and a writer for the *Financial Times* set out to find out why these had arisen.[9]

The most obvious reason was that firms had pruned their training, like their investment programmes, during the slump. But many workers already *in* skilled trades had left them. Interviewing such workers, he found that two reasons were most commonly offered for the decision: lack of job security, and poor prospects of promotion. Both, of course, had been made much worse by the recession. If these problems drive men already trained away, how much more must they put others off training? Some have argued (without much support from this survey) that people leave, or are put off training, by the narrowing of 'differentials' between skilled and unskilled pay. But this narrowing has taken place since unemployment began to rise,[10] and very possibly as a result of it: it is known that unskilled workers resent skill differentials much more when they have little chance of getting skilled jobs. So as promotion prospects have dwindled, the unskilled have fought successfully to narrow the gap.

At least there should be a better supply of unskilled labour? Certainly there will be larger numbers of unemployed, looking for jobs – but what about quality? The ideal unskilled worker, from the employer's point of view, is the immigrant – usually young and strong, ready to go anywhere, and to work hard in bad conditions, to do shiftwork . . . and after all that, still grateful for his job. Adieu to *him* – when unemployment rises, tight control of immigration becomes politically inevitable, at least in a social democracy. In Britain in the 1960s, in Germany in the 1970s, as the natives began to fear for their own jobs, the inflow of new workers was cut to a trickle. (The United States, with a long border with Mexico and a different social climate, has been less responsive.)[11] The immigrants are hard to replace. Native workers have high expectations and feel frustrated and humiliated by unskilled work, when they cannot expect to move up out of it. More and more of them arrive depressed by periods of unemployment;[12] young blacks in particular become so demoralised or alienated by injustice that many grow almost unemployable.[13] So *good* unskilled workers grow harder to find than ever.[14]

Thus lower demand leads to lower supply, and today's surplus becomes tomorrow's shortage. But at least in the short term – for a year or so – labour shortages will ease. While this lasts, it will surely toughen the employer's stance? Yes – but less than it used to. When there were many firms in each labour market, we had something near 'perfect' competition: each firm, by raising its wages a little, could expect to attract labour from the others. When labour was short, a process of bidding and counter-bidding would drive wages up. But when there are only a few large firms in each market, as is increasingly true, each faces a quite different situation. Its needs are large relative to the size of the market, so that it would have to raise its wages more to attract the number it requires. Worse, wage comparisons are stronger now: if you raise the pay of a group in short supply, the rise is emulated by others within the firm (making it more expensive) and outside the firm, by rivals' workers (making it less effective).

So large firms come to prefer another strategy: to step up training programmes (probably promoting existing workers and taking on unskilled at the bottom), meanwhile holding the line by increasing overtime and taking on any more-or-less suitable worker they can find at existing rates.[15] (They will try to keep their wages competitive, sure; but then they would do that anyway, to avoid discontent which would reduce productivity.)[16] So shortages do less to drive wages up; and surpluses less, to hold them down.[17]

In unionised firms, there is also the union's stance to consider. If unemployment is high workers may be more afraid of any action, like an excessive wage rise (or a strike to win one), which might put their jobs at risk. That will raise their indirect resistance costs; so, other things being equal, it should decrease their militancy. But other things will not be equal, because in a number of ways the rise in unemployment will work to *increase* militancy:

1. Living standards will fall. Many still employed will find their incomes reduced because other members of their household are out of work. Those who have been unemployed will want to make up for lost earnings after they return to work. The deflationary policy which leads to the rise in unemployment will also reduce living standards, by raising taxation, reducing the 'social wage', and in the longer term reducing the growth of national income. As I argued in the last section, people adjust their expectations in a few years, so the cut in living standards will not increase militancy for very long – but the rise in unemployment will not ease labour shortages for very long, either.

2. The escalator slows down, or stops. Chapter 3, Section 1 showed how expanding employment and labour shortage drew shop floor workers (and foremen) up the ladder of promotion, and new entrants to the industrial labour force took over unskilled jobs. In various ways this worked to weaken unionisation. By stopping the escalator, high unemployment strengthens unionisation and encourages militancy. (A militant response can be entirely rational: if there is less prospect of moving to a better job you have more incentive to take action to improve your pay where you are: your concession costs are higher.)

And the 'Facts'?

It is impossible to settle the matter by arguing deductively, upward from first principles. All we can *deduce* is that the inflationary effects of unemployment will be relatively strong nowadays, and in the longer term, with the disinflationary effects relatively strong in the past, and in the shorter term; perhaps also that unemployment will be more disinflationary (or less inflationary) in the US than in Britain or Germany.

That is all. But it is a great deal, for it fits the facts I mentioned at the beginning: that unemployment seemed to reduce inflation in the short term, and raise it in the long term. This is what one would expect, from my reasoning, for in the short term one would have not only the more 'conventional' effects of unemployment, but also low capacity utilisation which is definitely disinflationary. As unemployment persisted, the excess capacity would disappear, and we would see the less conventional effects of unemployment. We would also see the inflationary effects of the slow growth of productivity which results from deflation. I have confirmed that my reasoning fits the facts by using classic econometric methods (multiple regression analysis of time series data) to explain British wage inflation. (See Appendix. The measure of wage inflation used is increases in average hourly earnings, adjusted for overtime, of male manual workers in manufacturing industry, 1959–75.) In order to measure the effect of unemployment one must allow for the effect of the other determinants; if one leaves any out the effect of the others is disturbed. My results comfortably passed the two standard tests for checking that all important determinants are in. They showed (looking now only at the factors directly affected by deflation) that excess capacity (of men and machines) had the expected large disinflationary effect; unemployment, after a *lag* of a year, had a definite *inflationary* effect, which was rather stronger in the later part of the period.

These results prove nothing: time series regression analysis, even when (like mine) it obeys the rules and passes the standard tests, is notoriously unreliable, as I will explain in the next section. But at least I have confirmed that my theory is perfectly consistent with the evidence in this area. (Work by others on Germany and the US gives some support for it too.)[18] And my results are a great deal better, on the normal criteria, than those of econometric tests of various forms of the Phillips Curve theories – those which predict that the main determinants of wages are unemployment or some other aspect of the labour market, plus prices or some other index of inflationary expectations.[19] But no statistical result, however depressing, ever crushed a theory in the social sciences. There is always some reformulation of the theory which can explain away the result; and great theories in their decline seem to attract expert reformulators and reinterpreters, deft with the wet sponge after a bad round. One recent reformulation seems particularly promising. It argues that unemployment only has the conventional effect to the extent that it is *involuntary*, that is, the unemployed really want jobs, and are not choosy about *what* job. A man who is taking his time looking for a job that will suit him, or who is not prepared to move to a place where there are vacancies, or who really prefers to stay on the dole, does not count as *involuntarily* unemployed, and does not tend to hold down wages.[20]

Used with a little imagination, this principle has a magical effect on what one naively thought was mass unemployment. The short-term unemployed are just 'between' jobs, taking a leisurely look around the labour market. The long-term unemployed, if they are in some particularly depressed area, are obstinately refusing to move where the work is – so they are voluntarily unemployed; if they have some characteristic which makes them unattractive to employers (being old, or handicapped, or without a history of steady work – or black) they are not really fit for work, therefore not really unemployed at all. Or they are fit for work, but don't want it.

This approach can not only show that there are very few real, involuntary unemployed; it can also explain why. The dole, relative to wages after tax, is too high.[21] More and more people, as a result, are content with unemployment, or at least not in a hurry to escape from it. And indeed it has been shown, for Britain at least, that the maximum benefits available to an unemployed person and his family have risen a lot in the last twenty years, relative to average take-home pay.[22] So that is the answer: the Phillips Curve still lives. Deflate *further*, or better still cut the dole, so that there will be more people *involuntarily* unemployed, and unemployment will be above the 'natural level'; then wage inflation *will* fall.[23]

But *is* the level of benefit available 'neutralising' the effect of unemployment? Cold neoclassical reason says it must be, but cold reason assumes cold calculation by the unemployed. The Tavistock Institute, who took the trouble of *asking* the unemployed what they felt about their position, found them less concerned with its financial effects than with its social and psychological implications, and it turned out that these had changed little in forty years.[24] To be out of a job is to be labelled a failure, a layabout, a sponger on the taxpayer – to lose the respect of others, and soon self-respect too. So far from taking advantage of welfare benefits to avoid having to work, a large proportion of those out of work are so ashamed of it, or so averse to accepting charity, that they do not even register as unemployed. Thus the UK Census of Population of 1971 found that a full third of those seeking work were not registered, and thus could not have been receiving benefit.[25] Of the two-thirds who were, various surveys since have found that:

> there are many benefits for which only a minority of them were eligible;
> they did not tend to apply for all the benefits for which they were eligible;
> many of these were *discretionary* rather than an automatic entitlement.[26]

As a result, in fact, it turns out that benefits actually *paid out* to the unemployed, as a percentage of average after-tax earnings, peaked in 1967, and have since gone down.[27]

The argument that the unemployed tend nowadays to be in the wrong place, or not really fit for employment, is equally unconvincing. Whenever there has been mass unemployment it has been much worse in some places than others. If the neoclassical approach held water, wage inflation in these places would be drastically reduced, balancing the effect of shortages elsewhere. And, of course, when there has been high unemployment for some time, most of the unemployed are people who are unattractive to employers – they are the ones who don't get what jobs are going. (And not getting jobs demoralises them and makes them less attractive.) Where were all these people in the 1940s and 1950s – where were they in 1955, when Britain had a bare 200,000 registered unemployed? In work, because employers had to take them, and the 'shiftless' among them had no excuse not to take the work. 'But,'complains the employer, 'there seem to be more and more of such people, fewer good skilled and unskilled workers – if it were not for the generous benefits the unemployed would be better and more willing to work.' No – the benefits are rarely generous; as I explained earlier, it is mass unemployment itself which causes the steady deterioration of the labour force.

Conclusion

I do not want to stand the Phillips Curve on its head, and argue that higher unemployment always and everywhere leads to higher inflation. On the contrary, I have tried to show that its effect depends on institutions and attitudes; that with these as they are *nowadays*, particularly in Germany and Britain, unemployment will be, on balance and in the long term, inflationary.[28] The Phillips Curve theorists take no such trouble to argue from assumptions based on observation of particular places at particular times. They assert that higher unemployment makes for lower wage inflation regardless of country, of industry, of time; whether all, some or none of the workers belong to unions; whether the firms they face are small or large, oligopolistic or classically competitive. As the Curve's assumptions and predictions drift ever further from the facts of observation, its defenders reinterpret the evidence and reformulate the theory, rather than abandon it. Market theories of wages came to dominate the economics of Adam Smith and his successors, two hundred years ago, because they explained the facts of the time quite well. Now the Phillips Curve, which is descended from them, has become an intellectual tyrant, for which the facts of our time have to be explained away.

Sic semper tyrannis: may all such tyrants perish.

4.3 THE MONETARIST MYSTIFICATION

In the last section I tried to attack the neoclassical explanation at its heart. All neoclassical economists agree that wage and price inflation are ultimately due to excess demand, for labour or goods or both, and can therefore be cured by cutting demand (and perhaps increasing supply, as when the unemployed are forced to take any work they can get). In Chapter 2, Section 3 (for prices) and Chapter 4, Section 2 (for wages) I have argued that this is quite wrong, and I am on my way to erecting an alternative explanation.

But neoclassicism is not so easily disposed of. There is one variant of it which still flourishes precisely because (I believe) its heart is hard to find. *Monetarism* is apparently simple: it holds that 'money matters': that the only fundamental cause of inflation is an excess *supply of money* which pushes up prices and wages by creating excess demand.[29] It might seem easy to tackle: never mind how important the money supply is in causing any excess demand – leave the monetarists and 'Keynesians' to argue *that* out.[30] Let us simply ask whether excess demand, once created, is *the* cause of inflation. To this I have already answered, no. But on the way to that answer I have used measures of demand which the monetarist rejects; unemployment, for example. For the monetarist, governments are not guiltless of creating excess demand for labour merely because they have presided over the greatest increase in unemployment since the Slump. As I explained in the last section, they are accused of causing this unemployment not by deflation – by reducing demand – but by making life out of work too attractive: the unemployment is, in effect, voluntary leisure, a reduction in supply of labour.

The monetarist does not depend or insist on this explanation; show him that the vast majority of the unemployed would be delighted to get a job, and he will shift his ground: he will argue that the unemployed, glad as they would be to get a job, are not allowed by the trade unions to offer their services for less than existing rates; employers, on the other hand, though they would be delighted to employ all those who wish to work, are not prepared to do so at present inflated rates. So it is the unions who are to blame for the reduction in labour supply, and thus for mass unemployment.[31]

Though the monetarist is inclined to blame the unions for unemployment, he does not hold them responsible for inflation. However they abuse their monopoly power, they can only raise their members' wage levels so far, before (like any other monopolist) they are brought to a halt by customers' resistance, and competition from non-union workers.[32] There the process will stop. Similarly with prices – what firms can charge will depend on what buyers can afford to pay; and both demand for goods, and demand for labour, will depend on the supply of money.[33]

So it is the government, and the central bank, the controllers of the supply of money, who are responsible for the inflation of wages and prices; but unions play a role indirectly, because when their actions increase unemployment, the government tries to remedy the situation – which it thinks it has itself created – by increasing the money supply. This only briefly reduces unemployment, by raising demand, for soon the unions raise their price in response, and thus restore the original level of unemployment at a higher level of wages and prices. The beneficial effect of this injection of excess demand grows weaker and briefer, as time goes on, for people grow accustomed to it, as to a drug. Any attempt to soften the effect of unemployment by a higher 'dole', or to restrain the inflation by other interference with the market mechanism (prices and incomes policy) will produce further distortions and make unemployment still worse.[34]

Even in the market for goods it is not easy to get the monetarist to agree on a measure of demand. Output, for example, will not do. If one shows him that fluctuations in output do not appear to lead to similar fluctuations in the rate of price inflation,[35] he will reply that he never had any strong reason to suppose they would. In his perfectly competitive markets the effect of increased demand on output is very variable: it may lead to a big rise in output and a small rise in price, or a big rise in price with little or no increase in output (as at a vegetable market where everything has to be sold whatever price it will fetch). [36]

So output is a poor guide to demand. . . . No, says the monetarist with weary patience to the man in the dole queue, I know it doesn't look as though we had excess demand, it doesn't feel as though we had excess demand, but we have, old chap, we have – how else could prices and wages be rising so fast?

You begin to see how difficult it is to deal with a theory like this. Whenever one thinks one has a hold on it, it slips away. The monetarist argument I have just quoted is based on the old neoclassical assumption of competitive, flexible-price markets, where prices respond to changes in demand quite as sensitively as output does. But it is of no use to say, or even show, that modern industry simply doesn't work like this – that its prices are normally fixed in the short run and may not ever respond to demand in the conventional way. For Friedman and other monetarists, as I pointed out in the Introduction, theories are not to be judged by the realism of their assumptions – unrealistic 'as if' assumptions are quite acceptable, so long as the predictions of the theory agree with the relevant facts of the real world.

The Theory and its Predictions

Let us then try to come to grips with the monetarists at the point where they believe theories should be judged – on the accuracy of their predictions. These boil down in the end to a single assertion: that increases in the money supply will be followed by increases in prices and wages:

> There is perhaps no empirical regularity among economic phenomena that is based on so much evidence for so wide a range of circumstances as the connection between substantial changes in the stock of money and in the level of prices. (Friedman, 1958).[37]

The first question one would like answered, about this 'empirical regularity', is the length of time which elapses between cause and effect: between increase in money supply and increase in price. How long are the *lags* in the system? Naive, enthusiastic monetarists are regularly trying to tell us. William Rees-Mogg, then Editor of the Times and devout apostle of Friedman, informed the world in 1976 that the time lag was two years, for he had found a high correlation (0.848) between yearly increases in the UK money supply and price increases two years later.[38] Other, still more naive monetarists took this as virtual proof of the monetarist theory; which stung two Cambridge economists, G. E. J. Llewellyn and R. M. Witcomb, to point out that on such reasoning the cause of UK inflation was in fact Scottish dysentery, since they had found that the correlation coefficient between cases of dysentery in Scotland and the rate of increase in prices in the UK one year later, was even higher.[39]

In fact more experienced monetarists avoid specific predictions about lags; Friedman himself has said many times that he does not know how fast the effect of increases in money supply work through, and that lags are likely to vary a great deal between different places and times.[40] What makes their predictions still vaguer is that the 'supply of money' is not a precise concept; it can be defined and measured in a breathtaking variety of ways, and at least four different measures (M_1, M_2, M_3 and Domestic Credit Expansion) are commonly used by monetarists (and others).[41]

There is an equal variety of measures of inflation which monetarists have found acceptable at different places and times.[42] Now it may be very fashionable to admit the limits of one's knowledge – it can be taken to show an open mind and freedom from dogmatism; but this 'freedom from dogmatism' makes it much easier than it otherwise would be to find some apparent confirmation of the theory. Just find *some* measure of money supply which is correlated with *some* measure of inflation, inflation following money supply with any lag you like. With a research assistant or two, a good library and a powerful computer it will be no great task to try hundreds, even thousands of permutations and combinations until you find some correlation which is reasonably high; and you can always say it would have been higher if at some time during your period the lags hadn't changed or inflation hadn't been temporarily 'suppressed' by government intervention. . . . Such methods are called 'data mining' by econometricians and are regarded as 'cheating', but they are marvellously easy to use in time-series regression analysis – as long as one is 'free from dogmatism'!

'Data-mining' may not even be necessary, in order to find Friedman's 'empirical regularity' between changes in the supply of money and subsequent changes in inflation; for there is undoubtedly a causal connection. First, there is a connection between money supply and the conventional measures of demand – output, for example. An increase in money supply stimulates demand, to some extent, and (at least as important) an increase in demand stimulates the supply of money. How? The supply of money rises in response to an increase in demand for goods because this increases the demand for money, and that in turn, (a) has usually led central banks to create more money, (b) has led others – particularly commercial banks – to create more money themselves. So increases in the supply of money are likely to be associated with increases in output.[43]

The second causal connection, which completes the chain, is between changes in output and changes in inflation. As I have shown, in the short term there is nothing controversial about this: increases in output work on wages by tipping the balance of bargaining power towards the unions, and on prices by causing a fall in the exchange rate – which tips the balance of bargaining power further.

It is not only monetarists, then, who would expect an increase in inflation to follow an increase in the money supply – so would almost everyone else. If it does, so what? – it does not imply anything about the *effect* of the increase in money supply.

So I must finally admit defeat. There is no way in which anyone who accepts the monetarists' criteria for judging theories can judge how far their theory is true; for the only procedure they accept is 'reasoning forwards', testing predictions against observed facts, and their predictions are too vague for such tests to be useful.[44] The linguistic philosopher A. J. Ayer once proposed a test to confirm that a statement was meaningful: it had to be possible to *conceive* of some set of evidence which would prove the statement to be false.[45] In Ayer's sense, then, the key propositions of monetarism are meaningless: if you follow the monetarists' methodology you cannot conceivably prove their statements to be false. But it has been recognised that Ayer went too far: he overlooked one category of statement which can have meaning although it is not 'falsifiable'. This is the type of statement which is intended as some kind of guide to action; which states or implies not that something *is*, but that something should be *done*.[46] Such statements, when they relate to action in society or politics, can be described as ideological. In practice, monetarism is ideology masquerading as theory.[47]

Monetarism as Ideology

> There is no hope of Great Britain maintaining her position in international trade . . . unless the unions are deprived of their coercive powers
> Friedrich von Hayek (1978), *The Times*, 10 October.

Let us judge monetarism, then, as ideology. The task of ideology is to guide and justify political action. This, monetarism does rather well: its prescriptions are far clearer than its predictions. Almost any 'credit squeeze', through restriction of the money supply, and almost any reduction of government expenditure, particularly any which increases the 'incentive to work', can be justified by monetarism. It can justify, too, any attack on trade unions, as 'monopolists' responsible not for inflation but for unemployment. This anti-union aspect of monetarism is seldom stressed by monetarists in West European social democracies, but it follows from the logic of their arguments, and one of their two Nobel Laureates, Professor Friedrich von Hayek, was indiscreet enough to call, in a recent article in *The Times*, for a drastic reduction of union rights.[48]

There is only one area where their ideological logic is a little hard to follow. If collective bargaining and unemployment benefit are damaging and wrong because they distort the working of the market mechanism, then what of the market power of large firms – should not that also be eliminated or at least drastically reduced? Apparently not. Few monetarists show much enthusiasm for government anti-trust activities. Professor Harberger, an old colleague of Friedman at Chicago, argued in a famous article more than twenty years ago that the 'distorting' effects of monopoly in the USA were small, small enough to be ignored;[49] and Professor von Hayek has claimed that large firms which appear to have monopoly positions are rarely, if ever, in any real sense monopolistic, for if they even try to abuse their position there are a multitude of firms elsewhere which may invade their market.[50] So in this area their prescription is to leave well alone.

Since monetarism is so clear a guide for government policy it seems appropriate to end this section by considering what would happen if the policies it recommends were implemented in full. The quickest to take effect would probably be the most typically monetarist: restriction of the money supply. In a serious inflation, shock treatment would probably be prescribed, with the hope of bringing down price expectations quickly; so the real value of the money supply would be sharply reduced. The shortage of credit and rise in interest rates this would induce would make it more difficult and expensive to finance investment, and spending on consumer durables; this would reduce demand, and so too would the cuts in government spending which would be taking place at the same time.

In the short run, a reduction in demand would (as I have shown) certainly tend to reduce inflation; but tight money does not only reduce demand; it has a wide range of side effects as well.[51] If credit is more expensive then that is an increase in firms' costs, which most will pass on to their customers; if credit is *more difficult to get* then they will have to finance more of their investment out of retained profit, and the quickest way to provide the extra profit required is to raise prices further. There will now be no price controls to stop them – the new policy-makers will have made sure of that; in the more 'secure' oligopolies and monopolies the only restraint will be the fear of rivals breaking into their markets if they push prices up too high. But 'new entry' needs a lot of finance, and since that is now harder to come by, the restraint on prices is weaker.

In the more competitive industries the squabbling over shrunken markets will be check enough on prices in the short run. But as I pointed out in Chapter 2, Section 3, any deflation leads soon to an increase in concentration, and then in due course a decrease in competition, as smaller firms merge, are taken over, or collapse. A monetary deflation hits small firms doubly hard. For the role of the financial system is to channel resources from areas where there is a surplus – profits greater than desired investment and dividends – to areas where there is a shortage – profits smaller than desired investment and dividends. Most large firms are diversified enough to have a reasonable balance of surplus and shortage areas at most times, which makes them financially fairly self-sufficient, with their head offices playing much of the 'resource-channelling' role. But the small firm is less diversified, and in periods of difficulty (or of rapid expansion) it is likely to have a particular need for external finance. A deflationary monetary policy which restricts the activity of the financial system is therefore bound to hurt small firms more. (Worse, small firms, in Britain at least, are used by their larger customers during credit squeezes as helpless providers of free trade credit: big firms delay payment of their bills, but woe betide the small firm if it is late.)[52]

Tight money will lead, then, to an increase in concentration which will soon give the once-competitive industries the chance to make the price increases they had had at first to forego. This increase will also, as I have shown in Chapter 2, tend to soften their bargaining stance. So, with wicked irony, will tight money itself. For since the costs of a strike are more-or-less immediate, while the costs of concession take effect gradually, a tough stance is in effect an investment; and it is more difficult to make investments when one is short of cash.[53]

On balance, then, the effects of *monetary* deflation are likely to be even worse than those of any other kind. As this becomes apparent, with inflation and unemployment both tending to rise, the trade unions will inevitably be made the scapegoat, and there will now be drastic anti-union and anti-strike legislation – if it has not been passed already. This will collide with an opposing current of increasing union strength and militancy, induced by frustration and the increase in firm size and concentration. Society and politics will polarise sharply into pro- and anti-union camps. Even if the anti-union camp keeps political power it cannot now succeed in making the unions weaker than before, without taking the most drastic measures. . . .

I shall certainly be accused of trying to frighten the reader with the nightmare of an imaginary situation. Guilty; though the nightmare will remain imaginary only so long as monetarist policies are not fully implemented. But it is better to do one's frightening with hard facts. There is a country where the monetarist 'medicine' has been swallowed, to the last drop. The only difference between the real nightmare which followed, and the imaginary one I have just described, is that the social polarisation which I predicted as a result of monetarism had already taken place before it was implemented. Monetarism *was* implemented, to the letter, by ex-pupils of Friedman and Harberger (called the Chicago Boys) with whom Harberger had kept in close touch. Price, profit, import controls were all abandoned; the money supply was tightly controlled; government spending was cut and welfare benefits virtually abolished. The government watched with apparent unconcern over the resulting slump and massive increase in concentration. As unemployment soared, so did inflation – both to record levels. But, it must be admitted, inflation has now come down to levels which in that country are regarded as respectable. This may perhaps be connected with the methods used to curb 'union monopoly'. Strikes were banned, most unions dissolved, their leaders and militants (the lucky ones) jailed. This, not surprisingly, strengthened management bargaining power, and before long wage increases trailed far behind price inflation; in due course, that too came down. (Oddly enough, this cut in real wages brought no increase in the demand for labour. Unemployment remained high, industrial investment and output, low.) Insult followed injury: Professor von Hayek visited the country and pronounced that its policies were generally healthy and that liberty in any meaningful sense was as well respected there as anywhere else in South America. And so, as the Gallic chieftain said of the conquering Romans, they made a desolation, and called it peace. Chile.[54]

I do not cite the Chilean example in order to cast suspicion on monetarist motives. Those of Professors Friedman and von Hayek, at least, are above suspicion. They are, like Brutus, honourable men. Their commitment is to their own peculiar vision of (economic) freedom. When a violent and dictatorial Cassius is required to implement it, they regret that sincerely. It may be, of course, that even academic economists are not immune to the distortions of ideology. Monetarists' beliefs about the laws of economics may be affected by what they would like to believe, which in turn may reflect their interests, and their friends' interests. But they are honourable men, all honourable men. Like the doctors of old as they clapped their leeches to a sick man's neck, they do believe, God help us, that they will do us good. We cannot, however, be so charitable towards their remedy. It will certainly discredit itself if we once wholeheartedly try it – but can we afford to give it any further trial? If we do, the monetarists may one day have to admit, as did one of those whom Hayek served in the First World War,

We were bound to fall. All we could choose was the manner of our falling. We chose the most horrible.[55]

Let us choose another for them – before we lose the right to choose at all.

Conclusion

There is some irony in my verdicts on the 'remedies' most popular with economists and governments. The monetarists are right, it seems, in their attack on incomes policy as a short-term 'fix' which in the long term worsens the disease – but right for the wrong reasons. Its advocates are mistaken not because they are too 'institutionalist' and neglect the forces of supply and demand, but rather because they are not 'institutionalist' *enough* and neglect the decentralisation, actual or potential, of the bargaining process. The irony grows when we consider the monetarists' own prescription. 'Not for us the quick, easy remedy. We know you must be cruel to be kind; and patient too, for our cure takes time.' In fact, in the short term their deflation works rather well. By raising the exchange rate (see Chapter 2) it makes imports cheaper and puts more competitive pressure on domestic prices; this increases employers' concession costs. Low capacity utilisation, etc., reduces their resistance costs, while union resistance costs rise. All these effects are disinflationary, but none of them is lasting. The *long-term* effects are all inflationary, and they are all due precisely to the cruelty of monetarism. The deflation which throws people out of work, reduces investment in skills and plant. That brings down productivity growth; it also worsens the balance of payments, thus in the end *lowering* the exchange rate. Deflation hurts small firms, and makes for higher concentration. It brings the escalator to a halt, and increases frustration over living standards. . . .

There is an old story about the sun and the wind. They saw a traveller one day, on the road below them, and each bet the other he could get the man's cloak off. First the wind tried: it became a gale, and tore at the traveller; but he only held his cloak tighter to him. Then the sun tried, and shone his warmest – and soon the man had his cloak off.

Moral: kindness pays.

5 The Analysis Applied

5.1 LEADERS AND LAGGARDS IN INTERNATIONAL COMPETITION

Neoclassical and Post-Keynesian Views of International Trade

I am now going to open another front in this war of the intellectual worlds. It is one I would rather not have fought on, for I can only spare it a few pages, while the other side is as strong here as anywhere. However, I believe that intellectual schools should be judged, and ultimately are judged, on their ability to answer *all* the important questions in their subject area, without inconsistency, starting from the same set of basic assumptions and propositions. The question here is important enough to be worth answering even if only briefly. Further, by sketching a 'post-Keynesian' view in this area too, I shall make the explanation of inflation more complete. But there is no need to stake everything on an argument which stands, after all, apart from the main analysis. The more sceptical reader can compromise. The first half of this section explains how one may expect international competition under free trade to result in certain trends in economic structure and performance. If the reader rejects the explanation, never mind; for the trends themselves there is independent evidence, and if he accepts that, he has no reason to reject the next stage in the argument.

The neoclassical view of trade starts from the principle of Comparative Advantage: countries should, and generally do, export what they produce relatively efficiently, and import what they produce relatively inefficiently. That is mild enough; but the next step is to assume that trade (and the movement of capital) tends not to make these differences in relative costs greater, but rather to reduce them. Thus (neoclassicists argue) Hongkong can produce shirts more cheaply than Western Europe because it has more abundant labour but is short of capital, and so is suited to this labour-intensive industry. If it is allowed to export shirts freely, then labour in Hongkong will become rather more scarce (and elsewhere, less so, as other shirt industries contract). If

126

there is free movement of capital then some will flow into Hongkong and relieve the scarcity there. With labour more scarce, and capital less so, the relative cost differences decrease; QED.[1]

Post-Keynesians take a cooler view. It is best illustrated by the example of an industry like computers. If, say, the US develops a computer industry first, then it is bound initially to have relatively low costs. Unless other countries' computer industries are protected, they will be unable to compete with US computers, and will not be successfully established. US firms will then continue to dominate the computer market. This may be because they continue to have relatively low costs; but that advantage does not stem from (say) low capital costs, but from superior know-how in making computers, and a large scale of production. Now this difference is very important.[2] If you make more of something that is capital-intensive you then have less capital; if you make more of something which requires know-how and large scale you then have *more* know-how and a *larger* scale; so trade and competition increase the initial differences rather than reduce them.[3]

And what of the 'factors of production' which by moving from where they are abundant to where they are scarce, tend to make countries more alike? The post-Keynesian sees movements of capital and labour as less important than the movement of know-how, through direct investment by multinational firms.[4] This ought to lead to a higher level of technology in the host country, and in the short run it no doubt does; but in the long run the existence of multinational subsidiaries is likely to impede the development of an industry under native control. The know-how on which such a native industry depended would be available within the country, to be drawn on for new ventures; much of the multinational's know-how, on the other hand, is kept in its home country and is not available to the 'host'.[5] Thus again the 'host' may end up with less know-how than it would otherwise have got.[6]

It is increasingly important to decide which view one prefers of the effects of freedom of trade and capital movements; for free trade increasingly prevails. Ever since the beginning of the Industrial Revolution the world economy has been moving towards one unified market. It has not been a continuous tendency – it was interrupted by twenty years of general protectionism in the 1930s and 1940s, and by revolutions in the East – but it has been *based* on continuous trends: falling transport costs, growing uniformity of tastes and technology, the increasing ability of firms to sell and produce on a world scale. Since 1950 this has been reinforced by a rapid dismantling of artificial barriers to the free movement of goods and capital. In Western Europe this has gone fastest and farthest, with the formation of the EEC and EFTA, and then what amounts to the merger of the two, and it is here that the effects of free trade show most clearly.

The Effects of Free Trade

Free trade and capital movement means more competition between firms, but only for a time, for they adapt. There are bankruptcies, closures, market-sharing agreements, mergers, product differentiation. Gradually the separate national oligopolies are replaced by European, even world oligopolies. The process makes the individual national economies more specialised – they withdraw from, or never enter, some industries, and grow stronger in others.

This specialisation is unequal, in an ominous sense. Certain countries tend to win a disproportionate share of the advanced technology industries. The factors which help a country on to the 'high ground' include:

   (i) being, for historical reasons, 'in possession' when trade is liberalised;

   (ii) having rapid economic growth which requires heavy capital investment, which in turn gives home capital goods manufacturers the first chance to introduce a new product or process on a large scale;

   (iii) having high consumer income which provides a market for a new product;

   (iv) paying high wage rates which make it profitable to introduce a new labour-saving process;

   (v) having managers and financiers better organised and equipped to seize new opportunities (see for example Chapter 2, Section 1).

The first four of these advantages are cumulative: they tend to make a successful economy more successful.[7]

By themselves, they are not necessarily decisive. A relatively backward economy, which is handicapped by (i), (iii) and (iv), may by intelligently imitating the production methods of the leaders, get a fast growth rate, and thus gain by factor (ii). Free trade, however, makes the catching-up process more difficult: in order to imitate their production methods it must set up the leaders' industries, and this may not be easy if the 'infant' industry is exposed to competition. Likewise, if it does grow fast, the backward country's need for capital goods may be met by imports rather than stimulate home industry. Still, 'free' trade is never perfectly free, since there are costs of transport and communication, bias towards native producers, and a state which is usually ready to weight the dice. The effect of free trade would not be so serious if it were not combined with the spread of multinationals.[8]

Multinationals Under Free Trade

Typically, the multinational manufacturing company starts as a success-ful firm in a 'leading' country which finds the growth of home demand for its products tailing off. It wins new markets abroad, where it has a lead over the native firms, and at a certain stage it decides to produce as well as sell abroad. The reason may be to avoid transport costs, tariffs, or other 'barriers to trade', or to take advantage of lower wages or other production costs abroad. The presence of the multinational is likely to exclude native firms from the new market even more effectively than its competition from outside.[9]

As trade becomes freer the character of the multinational changes. Its plants in different countries, which under protection had to be to some extent independent operations, become increasingly interdependent, as trade *within the firm* grows easier. There is specialisation, which usually follows a particular pattern. New products are kept near headquarters; for development and the early stages of production need close super-vision, and the initial market is likely to be largest at home (in a 'leading' country), as are the supplies of skilled manpower.[10] As the product (or component) gets 'older', production moves to the more backward countries, to take advantage of cheap unskilled labour, and government subsidies on capital cost. The market there is sizeable now, and the production process no longer needs close supervision from headquar-ters. Thus we have a 'product cycle', in which the 'homeland' gets the new products and processes at the beginning of the cycle, and the 'host' gets the older products and processes at the end of it.[11]

This arrangement has some disadvantages from the 'host's' point of view. It might hope to gain managers and men trained in the advanced technology, but it tends not to get them until the technology is no longer advanced. It finds itself exporting low technology products with low value-added per man, and importing high technology products; so its terms of trade and balance of payments suffer. It will thus be still harder for a country, once behind, to catch up if it has not only free trade but also an economy in which many sectors are dominated by foreign firms.[12]

A 'lagging' (low growth, low income) economy is likely under free trade to acquire other structural handicaps:

1   'Native Giants'

While the more successful firms in the 'leading' economy tend to expand abroad, as exporters and multinationals, the stronger firms in the laggard are worse placed to do so. Instead, the easier way to grow is at home, by merger with weaker firms, now under increasing pressure from foreign competition. The result is giant firms, with a large number of plants and products, and diverse management styles. These rather ramshackle giants have a difficult process of corporate digestion to go through before their top managers can turn their energies to real expansion and innovation; and more mergers may come before the digestion is over.[13]

2   Few Small Firms

Small firms play an important part in economic growth, and in particular in many advanced-technology areas where creativity and flexibility are crucial.[14] (Only for small firms can competition work in a Darwinian way to select the best managers.) But a small firm is not at all self-sufficient: it needs to be able to buy in a lot of goods and services from outside, to be close to its market (so as to know what to produce without a market research team and to sell it without a large sales staff) and close to sources of skilled labour and capital. It can be convenient to be near to multinationals' headquarters, for that is where purchasing decisions are taken, and creative scientists, engineers and managers can be poached, or may set up on their own. (It is of little use to be close to multinationals' branch plants.)[15] But above all, being fragile creatures who cannot stand up to economic cold, small firms need a climate of growth.

For all these reasons, small firms do better in Stuttgart or California than in south-east England (but better there than in Glasgow) which helps Stuttgart and California to prosper further and spawn more small firms.[16]

3   Large, Unwieldy State Enterprises

It is commonly believed that nationalisation takes place for political reasons. In fact economic reasons may be at least as important. Where an industrial sector is profitable and expanding it will fight hard against nationalisation and probably win, whatever the government's bias; where it is weak and threatened by foreign competition it may well be nationalised even by a right wing government. Take Sweden, for example. In the twenty-five years of prosperity till 1970 the Swedish Social Democrats nationalised less than the centre-right wing government did in three years from 1976, for these three were years of crisis.[17] Similarly in Britain Rolls-Royce was nationalised by a Conservative government. Thus giant state firms can arise for much the same reasons as giant private ones – failure in international competition. They face similar problems of corporate digestion before they are fit to grow fast.

Polarisation

In this way we can expect free trade and free movement of capital to make for a polarisation of countries, towards two groups: a 'leading' group, with fast growth and high income, and with a structural bias towards small firms, home-based multinationals, and expansion by growth rather than merger; and a 'lagging' group, with slow growth, low income, and a bias towards state enterprise, foreign multinationals, and expansion by merger rather than growth.[18]

The nearest approach to free trade (etc.) has been within Western Europe since 1960, culminating in the enlarged EEC. It is there above all, then, that we should look for such a tendency to polarisation. Certainly the concept of 'leaders and laggards' is extremely useful in comparing Britain and Germany. Germany is now, after Switzerland, the leader *par excellence*: it has high income, and fast growth; a relatively large number of small firms which are strong in some important high-technology areas (like machinery and machine tools);[19] a rapid growth of home-based multinationals since the mid 1960s;[20] a small public sector. Britain is well on its way down to laggard status. It has very slow growth and low income; structurally it shows a paucity of small firms in manufacturing;[21] rapid penetration by European multinationals since the mid-1960s;[22] increasing confinement to low-technology industries and products;[23] and a large and growing public sector.[24]

Effects of Structure

I argued in the last section that the 'laggard' in free trade tended to develop an industrial structure biased towards three types of firm:

(i) giant native firms which have grown by merger rather than by internal expansion;
(ii) foreign multinationals;
(iii) giant state enterprises, formed by takeover of unsuccessful private firms.

Unfortunately for the economy, the wage increases negotiated by all three types of giant will tend to be high, for a number of reasons. The first is related to their origin. The native and state giants have typically been formed out of a number of separate units. To begin with these units will go on bargaining separately, but such a system is increasingly inflationary. As I argued in Chapter 2, Section 1, the pressures on the lower managers involved are such that their strike costs are higher, their concession costs lower, than their superiors'. In particular, they have no reason to take into account the pressure elsewhere in the firm to match any increases they give. This intra-firm emulation is strong nowadays, as Chapter 3, Section 3 showed, and grows stronger as the different components of a new native giant or state firm lose their separate identities. What is more, it is likely to become *reformative*: for the lower-paid plants it is no longer enough to get the same percentage or even absolute increases as others – the cry goes up for *parity*, equal pay for equal work, whether the plant is in the Midlands or Scotland, Longbridge or Bathgate.

So top managers who began by trying simply to keep earnings increases in step in the different plants, have to decide whether to force the lower-paid plants to resist the increasing reformative pressure. The need for central interference grows, and sooner or later a move to a more centralised wage system becomes inevitable; but the move to centralisation can scarcely be made without high average wage increases, in the process of 'evening up' wages to remove disparities between plants. (Any 'evening down' would be fiercely resisted, particularly where there were strong shop stewards to represent the workers who would suffer.)

Once the firm's payments system is more or less centralised, sheer size starts to play its inflationary role. Size makes for strong union organisation, as I have shown, and high wages.[25] That encourages emulation by other firms, and this will combine with the 'evening up' process to disrupt old patterns of relativities. Thus the formation of the British Steel Corporation linked the high wage strip mills of South Wales to the lower-wage special steels works of South Yorkshire; as the Yorkshire steelmen narrowed the gap, they pulled ahead of other workers in their traditionally low-wage area, and these in turn raised *their* aspirations.[26] The general increase in 'linkage' also reduces concession costs (see Chapter 1, Section 3) and thus encourages further wage increases. Finally, greater size usually means greater market concentration, and this too is inflationary, as we saw in Chapter 2, Section 3.

There are other inflationary forces which are specific to one type of giant. The *foreign multinational* has to make comparisons with its high-wage homeland; it would be embarrassing to get the reputation of exploiting cheap local labour. Why should it try, anyway? – its cost structure is unusually capital-intensive, first because it is large, second because it has adapted to high wages at home, third because the processes which it moves to its 'branch plants' are the established, highly mechanised ones. In *state enterprises*, top management's strike and concession costs reflect the pressures put on it by its masters in government and civil service. If they leave it alone, it will almost certainly take a soft bargaining stance, for a quiet life. But if they wish to make it the spearhead of some form of wage restraint policy, they will have to reckon with the likely consequences: a public confrontation with strong unions. And so the laggard's industrial structure has a marked inflationary bias.

The leader is luckier. Its numerous small firms of course tend to have weak unions and a tendency to low wages. The public sector in general is relatively small, and in particular it will contain few of the 'state giants' I have been describing, cobbled together out of weak private firms; for its private sector is more successful. Its large private firms change their shape more gradually as they grow, and have less need to reform their payments systems drastically or suddenly. Foreign multinationals are less important, and tend not to pay high wages, since their wages at home are relatively low.

The leader's home-based multinationals are perhaps the best-placed of all large firms to hold their wages down. First, their home plants are close to headquarters, and can be kept under tight top management control. Second, the operations they prefer to keep at home will tend to be those at the beginning of the 'product cycle', involving a lot of skilled labour and white-collar workers, and small-scale production with relatively little capital equipment. This will make for union moderation and increase management's bargaining power. Management's third and perhaps greatest advantage is that they can continually remind their workers that wages in their plants abroad are lower; if the gap widens too far they will move marginal operations abroad. This threat will be the more convincing because they will be regularly doing just that, as products reach the stage in the product cycle where they can be easily made (and marketed) in the low-wage countries.

Effects of Performance

With its 'disinflationary' structure, and fast-rising productivity, the leader will find its unit costs of production falling relative to other countries. So long as exchange rates do not change, that will make its goods increasingly competitive, widening profit margins and the scope for price rises, thus cutting management's concession costs, and pushing wage inflation back up towards, even above, levels abroad. But how long can the exchange rate be kept fixed? Since the leader is not only cost-competitive, but superior in the quality and design of its new high-technology products, it will earn ever larger balance of payments surpluses. Sooner or later these surpluses will force it to revalue its currency – and to go on revaluing it until the steady gain from new high-technology industry is balanced by falling sales of old low-technology products; and that will happen when the revaluation has gone far enough to turn its cost advantage into a cost disadvantage.

Such a revaluation can be called a *real* revaluation, that is a revaluation which does more than just compensate for slower cost increases. Any real revaluation is bound to change the balance of bargaining power. In the 'old' products the leader now has high costs which make it increasingly uncompetitive, and raise the concession costs of management, who find it harder to pass on wage increases as price increases to the customer; workers' indirect resistance costs also rise, for they fear that a wage increase may lose them their jobs; thus the balance of bargaining power shifts in management's favour. In the new products, on the other hand, the leader faces competition only from other leaders, if at all, so that in them the balance of bargaining power might be expected to favour the union, even after revaluation. But most of these products are made either by small firms, or by new small plants of multinationals; in most small plants collective bargaining is not firmly established, so that the firm pays the 'market rate' for labour, and no more. Heads, management wins; tails it does not lose.

While the revaluation reduces wage inflation, it reduces price inflation further, for imports become cheaper, and foreign competition keeps down the price of home-produced goods; fast-rising productivity helps too.

For the laggard, the argument is reversed. It moves into balance of payments deficit which forces it into real *de*valuation, until its poor performance in new high-technology industries is offset by increased cost-competitiveness in old ones. This increased competitiveness mainly affects 'old' firms and plants where the workers are organised well enough to take advantage of it;[27] the failure to compete on new technology, however, does not strengthen management's bargaining position in new firms and plants, so much as ensure that few of them come into existence.

The laggard's devaluation increases the rate of price inflation, since it makes imports dearer, and allows the price of home-produced goods to rise. The slow growth of productivity means that a given rate of wage increases leads to higher price inflation than it otherwise would – and that in turn will worsen wage inflation. So all aspects of its performance combine to make the laggard's struggle against wage inflation more difficult.

The Escalator

The leader's living standards will obviously rise faster than the laggard's. It will also have a stronger escalator effect, for several reasons.

First, at high levels of GNP there is a relatively high proportion of 'middle class' jobs; the leader's fast growth means a rapid move in this direction, thus more chance for upward mobility and satisfied aspirations. Second, the 'division of labour' between leader and laggard gives the former an even larger share of skilled and middle class jobs. Where a multinational, for example, has its home base in the leader and branch plants in the laggard, a disproportionate share of the skilled and managerial jobs will be in the leader. Similarly, the high technology industries, which are strong in the leader, have more skilled and white collar jobs than the low technology, mass production work which is left to the laggard. Finally, the leader will be more likely, as we shall see in the next section, to keep up a rate of economic expansion which will make room for immigrants on the lower rungs of the job ladder, letting the natives move up. In these ways the leader will have more success than the laggard in satisfying workers' aspirations, and this should encourage union moderation; except, as I pointed out in Chapter 3, Section 3, for the long-term problem that the appetite grows with eating.

Conclusion

I have come now to the end of my theoretical analysis. It began in Chapter 1, Section 2 with bargaining theory, my cornerstone: wage inflation was explained in terms of the concession and resistance costs of management and union, which determined their stances. Chapter 1, Section 3 showed how these costs, in each firm or industry, were affected by the situation in the rest of the economy. Thus a large 'union sector' was a wage-inflationary factor because it tightened the *linkage* between the wages of different firms. A rise in prices also increased wage inflation, although it was unlikely that the effect would be one-for-one; that *could* be said, however, of the ultimate effect on prices of a rise in wages.

The focus then narrowed to the factors at work within each firm and industry: in Chapter 2 I showed how firms' objectives, size, market structure and technology affected their stance, and thus inflation. (Satisficing, large size, high concentration, non-price competition,and high non-wage costs were, other things equal, inflationary.) In Chapter 3 I explained variations in union density and structure (largely by the size and structure of firms, and the strength and nature of the 'escalator') and showed how high density and union decentralisation made for higher wage inflation. These two factors worked largely by toughening the union's stance, i.e. by increasing its militancy; the same effect was produced by emulation of some groups' wages by others (*linkage* again), frustration of material aspirations, and low strike costs.

In Chapter 4 I dealt with the most important 'remedies' tried by governments for inflation. I conceded in Chapter 4, Section 1 that *incomes policies* (voluntary if unions cooperated, statutory otherwise) could work well almost anywhere, for a while – and where unions and employers were centralised, for several years. But they tended to make unions more decentralised, and to encourage emulation, both of which contributed to their ultimate collapse, and increased inflation afterwards. In Chapter 4, Section 2 deflation turned out to be rather similar: though in Chapter 2 I had shown that it had little direct effect on prices, I agreed now that it reduced *wage* inflation, in the short run. But the unemployment it created tended in the long run to increase unionisation and militancy, and (paradoxically) to worsen the supply of labour, and so in the end deflation was inflationary. Finally, in Chapter 4, Section 3 I discussed restriction of the money supply. It was little else than another form of deflation, and not the least damaging.

Now in this Section I have, so to speak, explained the explanation – at least in part: I have shown how, under free trade, success or failure in international competition affects firms' objectives, size, market structure and technology, and on the workers' side, affects the strength and nature of the escalator, and union decentralisation. Chapter 5, Section 1 thus takes the analysis one step further back: we can now not only say what factors are inflationary – we can also explain and predict, to some extent, where and when they will occur. At the price of sticking my neck out further than ever, this extension of the analysis thus makes it possible to see rising inflation not as a more-or-less accidental problem, but as part of a wider economic crisis – and even to get some understanding of that crisis.

There is my analysis, then. As I built it up I related each part of it to the facts – always to those of my trio (Britain, the USA and West Germany) and sometimes to those of the full seven (adding France, Italy, Sweden and the Netherlands). Now it is time to apply the theory as a whole, to explain the facts of inflation – rather briefly, first, in all seven, then more thoroughly, in the trio. After twelve sections, then, explaining my theoretical model, I shall now show that it works.

5.2 THE LULL AND THE STORM: 25 YEARS OF INFLATION IN SEVEN COUNTRIES

This brief sketch of a great subject will be useless and frustrating unless its limits are clear from the start. There will be no attempt here at a rigorous econometric test of the theory, nor at detailed analysis, or even description, of inflation in each country. What is to be explained, for the period from 1952 to 1977, are figures for rates of inflation in each country, averaged over periods of at least five years. I shall reduce the task further by concentrating on wage inflation. I shall be seeking to explain:

(i) the 'league tables' of relative inflation rates for each period;
(ii) countries' movements up or down in the league tables;
(iii) changes in the 'league average' from one period to the next.

For simplicity the various 'explanatory factors' will all be put into one of two groups: 'economic factors' which have their main direct effect through the strike and concession costs of management; 'organisational factors' which work mainly through the strength, structure and objectives of the organisations on either side. The 'economic factors' were explained in Chapters 2 and 4: they include the level of capacity utilisation, profitability and demand for labour, and the degree of industrial concentration, protection and competitiveness in international trade. I shall explain briefly how they moved in each country, for I have not done so before. The 'organisational factors', on the other hand, were discussed quite thoroughly in Chapter 3, and it would be repetitive to do more than sum them up in a few words at each new stage of the argument.

Situations and Strategies in the 1950s

The Second World War and its aftermath explain a great deal about the mild inflation of the 1950s. Two of our countries, the USA and Sweden, can be described, economically, as winners of the war: they began it with high national incomes and advanced industrial sectors, went on developing while the fighting raged elsewhere, and were well equipped to take advantage of the international investment boom afterwards.[28] Both could therefore keep their currencies at a high valuation which put many of their industries at a disadvantage once other countries had recovered enough to compete; competitive pressure was all the stronger in Sweden because its trading policy was liberal.[29] At the same time there was no need to overstretch human or capital resources; Sweden nonetheless kept demand fairly high throughout the decade, but in the US, during the late 1950s, capacity utilisation was distinctly low.[30] In both the 'winners', then, 'economic factors' made for a rather tough management stance.

Three more of our seven – Britain, France and the Netherlands – emerged from the war on the winning side, but in various ways so bruised by the experience that they can best be described as 'apparent winners'. The British were the most inclined to believe they really had won, and having a large amount of old industrial capacity still intact were just able to keep up the pretence.[31] As a result their position both on trade and demand pressure was about midway between Sweden and the US, though their currency valuation was rather lower;[32] thus economic factors in Britain were only slightly less 'toughening' for management's stance than in the 'real winners'.

France and the Netherlands were readier to face facts – indeed they had less choice, for before the war their industrial sectors had been small.[33] Each chose a strategy of rapid expansion, tailored to its own special needs and advantages. The Dutch had little hope of self-sufficiency, but initially an ample labour supply, and therefore chose to undervalue their currency in order to encourage export-oriented investment.[34] France, on the other hand, had little surplus labour, and scant resources to spare to increase investment; its strategy was protectionist, exploiting its larger internal and colonial market. But both succeeded in maintaining high pressure of demand throughout the decade.[35] That, together with French protection and Dutch under-valuation, meant that economic factors made for a decidedly soft management stance.

The last two, West Germany and Italy, had lost the war, and knew it. They could only win the peace by rapid expansion. In Germany that came quickly, which was necessary because of the enormous refugee problem, and possible because of the advanced industrial position Germany still held; so demand (except for labour) was high from the beginning of the decade. Italy, on the other hand, was even less industrialised than France and the Netherlands,[36] and its expansion was slow to get under way: capacity and skilled labour were not over-stretched until the second half of the decade, unskilled labour not even then.[37] Both countries, at all events, were forced to undervalue their currencies. Thus if we take the 1952–60 period as a whole, economic factors in Germany were about as 'softening' as in France and the Netherlands, in Italy less so, though more than in the 'winners'.

Industrial Relations and Inflation Rates, 1952–60

Figure 5.1 shows France at the head of the 'league table' of wage inflation. This is scarcely surprising: not only were economic factors inflationary, but France easily headed the price inflation list too, and wages ran ahead of prices by only enough to give a modest rate of real wage increases (Figures 5.2 and 5.3), so that 'organisational factors' made for some degree of militancy.[38]

Dutch inflation is not far behind the French. Dutch unions, as I explained in Chapter 3, were at this time not only rather weak but extremely moderate, and fast-rising real wages helped to keep them so (Figure 5.3); thus organisational factors made incomes policy at times quite effective (see Chapter 4, Section 1) and did something to offset the strongly inflationary effect of economic factors. From the last sub-section we would expect Germany to be up with the leaders, and when

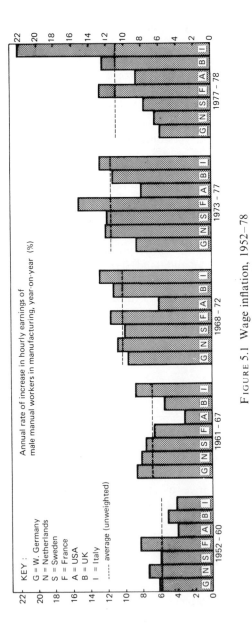

FIGURE 5.1 Wage inflation, 1952–78

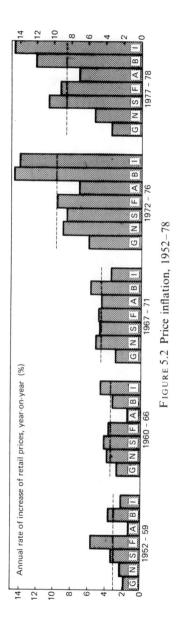

FIGURE 5.2 Price inflation, 1952–78

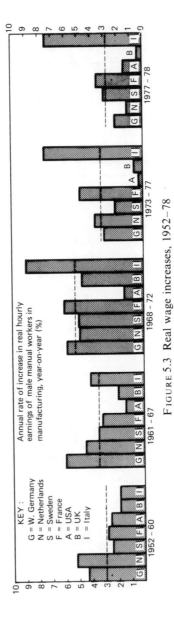

FIGURE 5.3 Real wage increases, 1952–78

we bear in mind that their unions were stronger in numbers than the Dutch (and in the early 1950s quite militant) while their real wages rose less fast, their lower wage inflation rate may seem hard to explain. But the bargaining table has two sides, and the employer stance is not entirely determined by economic factors. I showed in Chapter 2, Section 1 that the formidable cohesion and combativeness of German employers was at its height in the 1950s, while they were reasserting their power. It was unmatched in France or the Netherlands, and explains the difference. It *was* matched, more or less, by the Swedish employers' associations, and their stance was toughened further, as I have shown, by economic factors; on the other hand, the Swedish employers were facing unions of exceptional strength, which had to reckon with high price inflation and lower real wage increases. The two differences between Sweden and Germany roughly cancelled out.

Britain is third from bottom in the table. At this time the unions were not so strong, decentralised or militant as they have since become, nor was price inflation particularly high; and (as explained) economic factors were mildly toughening. Still, in both respects Britain was outdone by the US, and it is no surprise to find that country at the bottom of the table. Italy stands with it – though 'economic factors' were slightly more inflationary – because of the extreme weakness (and disunity) of its unions at this time.[39]

The Last of the Lull: the 1960s until 1968

In all seven countries, the rate of increase of real wages during the 1950s was, by past standards, rapid, and helps to account for the low 'league average' of wage inflation during this period. The same is true for 1961–7, except for the US. But this was the period – from the late 1950s – in which European governments began to divert an increasing proportion of private affluence for their own use, so we have now to take account of rises in income tax. That rose by 2.9 percentage points in Britain between 1953–8 and 1962–4, probably enough to make the increase in affluence less satisfying than in the 1950s. So in Britain as well as the US one could expect real wage frustration to lead to some increase in militancy in the 1960s. In Britain it seems to have done so; in the US, it was outweighed for the time being by the other forces still working to weaken the unions (see Chapter 3). In Sweden the tax increase was extremely sharp, but it is doubtful whether Swedes felt the pinch, by comparison with the 1950s, for real wage increases were a percentage point per year faster than before, and there was an enormous increase in female employment.

In the other four countries the increase in real income, even after tax, was still rapid enough to avoid any real wage frustration, except perhaps in France (which I shall look at in a moment). The only snag lay in the way it was achieved. In the 1950s much of the increase in income had been due to a big improvement in the terms of trade (that is, imported raw materials grew cheaper relative to exported raw materials); in the 1960s the terms of trade only stayed steady (Fig. 5.4). Instead, growth now owed most to a rapid increase in capital per man in industry – investment rates in Germany, France, Italy, and the Netherlands as well as Sweden, were decidedly higher during 1957–66 than in 1948–58.[40] But this made for higher capital intensity and thus for a softer management stance; and the new capital generally required larger plants, which as I showed in Chapter 3 affected industrial relations.[41]

On the 'economic' side the 1960s bring a new and important distinction, between members and non-members of the EEC. The non-members, the US, the UK and Sweden, continued to move towards free trade, but at a rate which probably did no more than balance the increase in industrial concentration nationally and internationally. Germany, Italy, France and the Netherlands, on the other hand, saw a sharp increase in the intensity of competition in the first half of the 1960s, as trade barriers within the EEC were dismantled.[42] The effect of this was greatest on France, because that country had been much the most protected, and because its industry was biased towards products for which there were both rich markets and strong competitors elsewhere in the EEC; firms which had grown used to a protective cocoon now saw that they could not win new markets or even keep their old ones unless they could keep their costs down: so management concession costs rose sharply. Massive southern immigration (and the return of the 'pieds noirs' from Algeria) helped to keep the unions weak and to avoid labour shortages; and now the right-wing governments of the Fifth Republic allowed the minimum wage to lag far behind the average, so that employers could enjoy cheap unskilled labour while keeping their key skilled workers contented (see Chapter 3). So increasing competition outweighed increasing capital intensity, unions stayed weak in spite of increasing plant size, and as a result wage inflation in 1961–7 was lower than that in 1952–60.

In the other EEC countries wage inflation increased, in spite of the increased exposure to international competition. In Italy the rise was much the greatest, and can be explained by both organisational and economic factors. By 1960 the 'Italian miracle' of rapid expansion was in

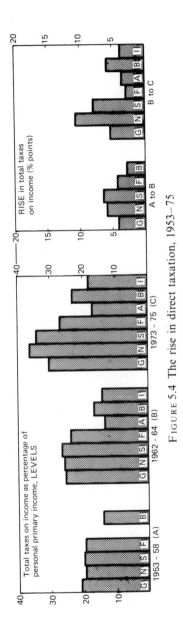

FIGURE 5.4 The rise in direct taxation, 1953–75

full swing, and continued for the first half of the decade. The surplus of unskilled labour dried up, so that labour market conditions gave employers less room to exploit union weakness; at the same time they had less incentive to do so, because of the immense international success of the consumer durables industry, which brought high profitability and capacity utilisation; so economic factors made for a soft management stance in this sector in spite of the increased exposure to international competition.[43] Workers in other sectors then emulated the big increases in consumer durables. At the same time it seems that by 1965 the unions, and workplace organisations, were growing decidedly stronger (see Chapter 3).

In Germany and the Netherlands, as in Italy, the coming of free trade within the EEC did not lead to any toughening of management stance. German and Dutch tariffs had been quite low to start with, and their manufacturing industry began in a strong competitive position: so with high profitability and rising capital intensity,[44] economic factors were still more inflationary than before. In the Netherlands organisational factors seem to have changed little between the two periods; the outcome was a small increase in wage inflation. In Germany the unions appeared to grow weaker, partly through the changing pattern of immigration (see Chapter 3), but this was more than offset, so far as wages were concerned, by a definite loosening of cohesion, a new mood of relaxation, among employers – which is easily explained by the completeness of their economic and political success during the previous decade (see next Section). As a result, wage inflation quickened by more than 2 per cent points, and the rise would have been greater if the average had not been held down by low figures for unskilled workers in the sectors to which most immigrants came.[45]

For the other three countries the intensity of international competition did not increase, but for two of them, the US and the UK, their position in what competition there was, grew weaker, for their currencies became more and more clearly overvalued (see next section). In the US, demand conditions during 1960–7 were roughly similar to those in 1952–60; thus on balance economic factors were even less inflationary than in the previous period. So, as I have already said, were organisational factors; and US wage inflation duly fell even further. In Britain too, demand pressure was no higher than it had been, so economic factors increased the pressure for a tough management stance. But this was more than offset by organisational factors; not only was there increasing union militancy, but the rise of the ramshackle conglomerates described in Chapter 2, Section 1 was eroding what remained of management cohesion. Wage inflation would have increased by more than the 0.3 percentage point shown in Figure 5.1, had it not been for the use of statutory incomes policy in 1966–7. In Sweden it seems that the main changes, on both 'economic' and 'organisational' sides, were the inflationary side-effects of the higher investment rate; these can account for the 1.0 percentage point increase in wage inflation which took place.

The Storm: Inflation since 1968

The middle years of the 1960s were the end of an economic era. Western Europe was finishing a long investment boom with which it made up for the disruption and destruction of the 1940s and pulled back the long technological lead opened by North America during that decade; the boom was given a final impetus by the new unity of its own market. No longer, after the mid-1960s, could Western European expansion be relied upon to keep up demand elsewhere. Now, if they wanted to keep up investment and employment, governments would have to rely on deliberate reflation which pushed up demand to the point where plant capacity and skilled labour were overstretched. The task of getting full employment without high inflation would soon be made all the harder by a new trend towards worse terms of trade: during the 1950s, raw materials had grown cheaper relative to exported manufactures; during the 1960s there was little change; in the 1970s they grew sharply dearer (see Fig. 5.6).

The change in the economic climate coincided with the beginning of the crisis in industrial relations described in Chapter 3, a crisis mainly due to changes in economic structure.

These tendencies were general. Some other developments affected countries most unevenly. Since within Europe there was now a large measure of free trade, its inevitable consequence soon followed: the process of polarisation described in the last section. Britain and Italy were natural 'laggards': one with much the lowest growth, the other with the lowest income in Western Europe, both found themselves by the end of the 1960s at the 'thin end' of the new international division of labour, condemned to export mostly low-technology and import mostly high-technology manufactures. Three fast-growing, high income countries – Germany, Sweden and the Netherlands[46] – took their place opposite, as 'leaders'. France stood between, and the US somewhat aside – the US was less exposed to free trade than any European country. The process of polarisation explains many of the variations either side of the new inflationary trend.

At the beginning, however, the differences in the pace of the inflationary upsurge had most to do with the effects of the Common Market. As the investment boom which celebrated the new freedom of trade petered out, the EEC countries slid into what for most of them was easily the worst recession since their postwar recoveries began. Chapter 3 showed how this recession helped to brew the industrial relations crisis which broke in the next boom. It also speeded up the process of concentration with which industry reacted to the widening of markets,[47] and the result was that firms' concession costs, raised in the early 1960s by fiercer competition, now fell back. Together, economic and organisational factors produced a sharp acceleration of inflation in the EEC after 1968. Between 1961–7 and 1968–72 the average of wage inflation in West Germany, Italy, France and the Netherlands, went up from 7.9 to 11.2 per cent. The size of the increase in each country can be explained by three main factors: the timing of the industrial crisis, its severity, and the effect of polarisation on the exchange rate.

In France the crisis broke earliest, in Italy it was most severe, and neither had a revaluation to toughen management's stance. As a result, both had big rises in wage inflation, of 4.9 and 4.8 percentage points respectively. In the Netherlands the (relatively mild) crisis broke quite late, during 1970, and before long there was a modest real revaluation; the increase was 2.8 percentage points. Finally in Germany the crisis was also less acute than in France or Italy, and although it broke as early as September 1969, there was almost simultaneously a sharp real revaluation which was bound to stiffen management resistance; so the increase was only 0.9 percentage points (see Figure 5.1).

By the next period, 1973–7, it was the *outcome* of the industrial relations crisis which was most important. In Germany the unions were now stronger and more militant, particularly at the workplace, than they had been before 1968, but on the other side the employers had rediscovered much of the spirit of the 1950s (see next section) and the revaluation after 1969, typical of the 'leader', continued to provide the economic incentive for a tougher stance at all levels of bargaining. So their wage inflation fell back one percentage point to 8.6 per cent, just below the 1961–7 rate. In the Netherlands the revaluation and the other 'economic factors' were similar, but the outcome of the industrial relations crisis was quite different. The employers had been protected too long by the 'pillars' to learn German methods or attitudes overnight, but on the other hand Dutch unions became as strong and militant as the German ones; and the Netherlands was steadily raising its new minimum wage. Up went the wage inflation rate in consequence, by a further 1.2 per cent points, to 12.1 per cent, in 1973–7.

On the face of it the industrial relations crisis in France was resolved in the employers' favour, without any apparent increase in the numbers or strength of the unions. But (as I showed) calm was only restored and kept by important concessions, of which the most inflationary was the repeated raising of the minimum wage, relative to the average. The nearer the minimum came to the average the more influence it had on wages, and so although the rises were no greater after 1973 their inflationary effect was greater. Nor did France have the leaders' real revaluation. As a result the rise in wage inflation between the two periods was even greater than in the Netherlands – 3.7 percentage points, to 15.3 per cent.

In Italy alone the industrial relations crisis can hardly be said to have had an outcome, for it remained as acute as ever. I showed in Chapter 3 how it led to a great increase in the strength and militancy of workplace organisation (which after Chapter 5, Section 1 can be partly explained by its becoming a laggard). Employers, who failed to find any effective organisational answer,[48] lacked a strong economic incentive for toughness, as the exchange rate depreciated in true laggard style. This dangerous combination produced an appalling escalation in wage inflation, which nearly doubled, to 24.0 per cent.

In the three 'outsiders', too, industrial relations 'crises' broke at some point between 1968 and 1970. The 'crisis' in the US (between about 1968 and 72) looks in retrospect like little more than an episode of resistance to employer control at the workplace. While it lasted it was inflationary, but it left scarcely a trace on US industrial relations, and the unions in the 1973–7 period were by any standard weaker than at any time since the war. The economic climate, on the other hand, changed in their favour, for the long overvaluation of the dollar came abruptly to an end after 1971 – between 1970 and 1976 its real devaluation was 25.5 per cent. This helped to underpin the long upturn which began in 1975, and upturn and devaluation together sharply reduced management concession costs. Thus 'organisational factors' explain the rise of 2.9 per cent points between 1958–67 and 1968–72; 'economic factors' are responsible for the further rise of 1.9 per cent points (to 8.1 per cent) in 1973–7.

In Sweden too the employers put up spirited resistance to the increase in union militancy which became clear about 1970. But they were facing a union movement of far greater industrial and political strength. Not only did they have to give ground, like the Americans, in the short run – wage inflation rose from 7.3 to 10.0 per cent between 1958–67 and 1968–72 – but they could not prevent a strengthening of the (already existing) workplace organisation, and the militancy by no means died away. Although between 1970 and 1976 Sweden revalued as befitted a leader – by 6.8 per cent – 'organisational' changes outweighed 'economic', and in 1973–7 the inflation rate rose yet again, to 12.0 per cent.

There remains the sick man of northern Europe, Britain. I have shown how there, as in Italy, the unions grew rapidly stronger and more militant after the mid-1960s, particularly at the workplace, and the employers found no way of keeping the balance – nor did governments, in spite of successive experiments in incomes policy. The organisational changes can now be partly explained by a 'laggard's progress' much like Italy's, towards weaker structure and poorer performance; the laggard's currency depreciation helped to reduce the employers' incentive to toughen their stance. As in Italy, too, the economic and industrial relations crises did not erupt, then subside, but went on unfolding, and with them the trend of wage inflation went on rising – from 5.6 per cent in 1958–67 to 11.3 per cent in 1968–72, to 16.7 per cent in 1973–7.[49]

Conclusion

I will end with a short survey of the whole post-war period, taking all seven countries together. It divides quite neatly into two parts, 1952–67, and 1968–77: the Lull, and the Storm. What distinguishes the Lull not only from the Storm, but from almost all previous periods as well, is the placid state of its industrial relations. When we compare wage inflation rates, however, we find the Lull very much in the middle – higher than most previous periods, lower than the Storm. This suggests that in the Lull stances were relatively soft on both sides. The employers had never before been so ready to make peace; the unions would never be so ready again. The employers' behaviour can be explained by generally high capacity utilisation and profitability; the unions' by a fast escalator and satisfying rises in real disposable income. Softness against softness, as I said in Chapter 1, Section 2, makes for peace and moderate inflation.

Splitting the Lull into two, there was a small (1 percentage point) rise in the 'league average' of wage inflation between 1952–60 and 1961–7. The inflationary changes between these periods were a jump in the investment ratio (which made for higher capital intensity and went with larger plant size) and, in some countries, a slackening in the 'march towards affluence'. These were not quite balanced by the disinflationary effects of competition inside the new EEC, and more rapid immigration.

Now we come to the Storm. Between 1961–7 and 1968–72 the wage inflation average leaps from 6.9 to 10.3 per cent – unprecedented for any five-year period in peace-time – and the industrial calm is shattered by a great international wave of (largely unofficial) strikes. An industrial relations crisis has broken (as I explained in Chapter 3) in which the union side suddenly takes a tougher stance. At the same time there is some softening of the employers' stance, as competition, particularly within the EEC, becomes rather less intense.

In the second phase of the Storm, 1973–7, the wage inflation average leaps again to 13.8 per cent. The union stance is in general tougher than ever: the crisis in most countries has led to an increase in union density, and in some to a decentralisation of union power. (Both changes make for a tougher stance.) And lean times have returned: slower escalators, more unemployment, slower rises in living standards, all make for militancy. But there is little else that can be said generally, for the other great change in this most recent period is the much wider dispersion of wage inflation rates. In 1968–72 the lowest had been in the US, 6.1 per cent, the highest in Italy, 12.9 per cent, and the six European countries had been bunched within 3.3 per cent points of one another. In 1973–7 the US was still the lowest, Italy still the highest, but the figures were now 8.0 and 24.0; and even the European countries were spread out now over 15.4 per cent points.

The field, as they say about runners, is suddenly spreadeagled, and for two main reasons: the polarisation process, and the very different outcomes of the industrial relations crises. The first gives a range from the clearest leader, West Germany, through the Netherlands and Sweden, to Italy and Britain (with the US), the clearest laggards. In industrial relations, the range is from the US, where the employers come out clearly on top, through West Germany (where they regrouped very effectively) to Britain and Italy, where they were forced to recognise, and negotiate with, union power within their walls. West Germany, at or near the top on both counts, emerges with relatively low inflation; Britain and Italy, at the bottom on both, have the highest. So in some countries the storm abates, in others it grows worse. There is no hope that the gap will close; the differences underlying it are growing ever wider.

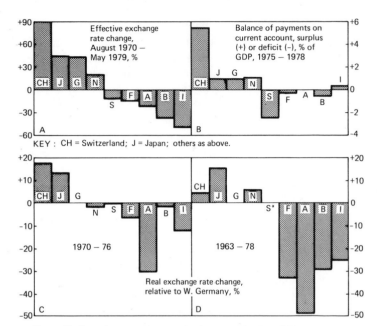

KEY : CH = Switzerland; J = Japan; others as above.

Note: *effective* exchange rate changes measure de- or revaluations of the currency relative to the Western (weighted) average. *Real* changes also take price and wage changes into account (in the case of D, only wage changes). Thus the UK devalued in "effective" terms more than the US, but in "real" terms less, because of its faster inflation.

FIGURE 5.5 The process of polarisation, 1963–78

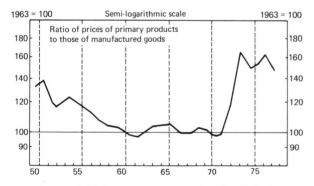

FIGURE 5.6 The western terms of trade, 1950–78

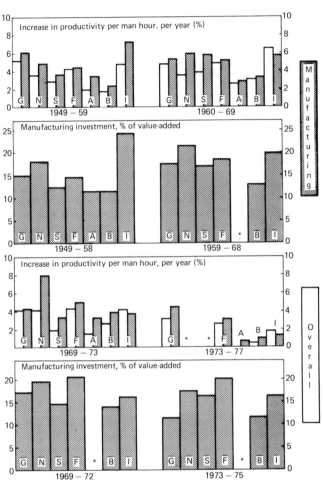

* Figures not available.

KEY : G = West Germany, N = Netherlands, S = Sweden,
F = France, A = USA, B = UK, I = Italy.

FIGURE 5.7 Investment and growth, 1949–77

5.3   WHY BRITAIN FAILED, GERMANY DID NOT SUCCEED, AND THE US MIGHT HAVE MANAGED, WITH MORE OIL

It is time now for more detail, and more rigour. In the last section I showed how the theory could be applied, but not how it could be tested. But I have tested it for one country: Britain. The method and results of the tests are reported mathematically in the Appendix; here I shall describe them briefly, in plain English.

I set out to explain changes in the rate of increase of wages between 1959 and 1975, of male manual workers in manufacturing industry (this is a large group, much emulated, for which accurate figures are available every six months). First I looked for factors which would affect the union side of the bargaining process. Clearly the rate of price inflation is one. Wages elsewhere are another – and the group which will be most visible and important to our manufacturing workers are manual workers in the public sector, who in Britain are numerous and highly-unionised. So I assumed that the militancy of manufacturing workers would increase with any fall in their own earnings relative to those in the public sector;[50] our second explanatory variable, then, is 'relative wages in the public sector'. Two more variables with less certain effects are the rate of increase of real wages after tax (if that is high, militancy should decrease) and unemployment (if that is high, militancy should, on balance, increase). Finally, while a statutory incomes policy is in force, this is bound to restrain the unions to some extent.

On the management side, the level of capacity utilisation will affect strike and concession costs: if it is low, management's stance will toughen. I took the standard measure of capacity utilisation (actual production relative to potential) and also the rate of overtime working, which gives some idea of *human* capacity utilisation. With less confidence, we can look again at unemployment – perhaps high unemployment may toughen the management stance. Since I argued in Chapter 4, Section 3 that a credit squeeze would soften management's stance, I took a measure of the cash and credit available to firms ('liquidity'). Finally, following Chapter 5, Section 1, we can use a measure of 'trade competitiveness', on the assumption that an overvalued currency, giving poor price competitiveness in international trade, forces employers to toughen their stance, while undervaluation encourages them to soften it.

It worked. Taken together, these factors turned out to explain about 90 per cent of the variations in manufacturing wage inflation. For six of them – price inflation, relative wages, unemployment, incomes policy, overtime working, and trade competitiveness – the regression results confirmed, as far as statistics can, that they had an effect. In Fig. 5.8 I show how these factors moved. It is clear that some of them help particularly to explain the rising *trends* in wage inflation, for at least since the late 1960s, price inflation, unemployment and trade competitiveness have been on a rising trend too.[51] Others help explain *fluctuations* over shorter periods; thus the fall in wage inflation in 1966–7 followed the imposition of incomes policy, a decline in competitiveness, and a fall in overtime working. The dramatic rise during 1974–5 followed big rises in trade competitiveness, overtime and price inflation, and it was kept going into 1975, in spite of falling overtime and competitiveness, by a further rise in price inflation and a big rise in the relative wages of the public sector. Since the end of the 'testing period' the pattern has continued – during 1976 a new incomes policy, falling price inflation, and low overtime, helped to bring the wage inflation rate down. By early 1977 a rise in trade competitiveness and overtime was tending to push it up, but was offset by low public sector wages; these fell further during the next year, and competitiveness fell back, balancing the weakening of incomes policy. At the end of 1978, incomes policy collapsed; the private sector workers who had already evaded it were now emulated by the public sector workers. With the public sector catching up, and prices responding to the surge in wages, the stage was set for a rapid acceleration of wage inflation in manufacturing. This was held back, during 1979–80, by falling overtime and trade competitiveness, but both of these were bound to be reversed before long.

Could we use a similar econometric explanation for Germany and the United States? Germany resembles Britain in some important ways – in the size of its union sector, for example, and the importance of international trade – but there is a crucial difference, which makes *any* econometric explanation difficult: the character of the employers. For Britain I was able to predict the employers' stance from the economic pressures upon them – capacity utilisation, trade competitiveness, and so on. The predictions were accurate, because British employers make their decisions on wages, as on everything else, individually and rather short-sightedly – in response to the immediate pressures upon them. German employers, on the other hand, are capable of acting collectively, and for long-term objectives, and as a result their actions cannot be predicted or explained mechanically from the immediate pressures upon them.

Let me show how the German employers responded to broader considerations. I have already described, in Chapter 2, Section 1, the great effort they made in the early 50s to reassert their power in industry,

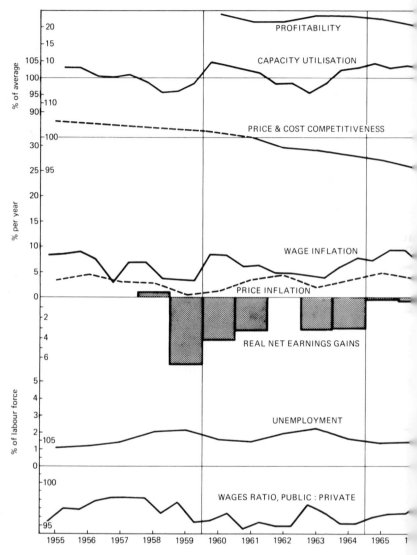

FIGURE 5.8 British wage inflation and some of its causes

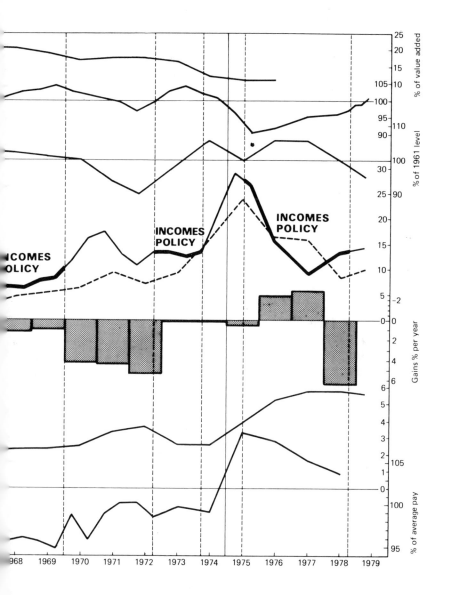

INCOMES POLICY

INCOMES POLICY

INCOMES POLICY

society and State. The unions had to be tamed, and that required a tougher stance than might have been expected from the economic situation. In the sixties, finding themselves remarkably successful, they eased up. In the deep recession of 1966–7 the steep fall in wage inflation was achieved without any need for fifties-style toughness – the unions amicably agreed, in the 'concerted action' discussions, to restraint of negotiated wages, and all the employers had to do was to hold down their (non-negotiated) wage 'supplements', individually.

After more than a decade of peace, then, the German employers were deeply shocked by the upsurge of workplace militancy in and after 1969 – the more so because it coincided with a political recovery by the Left. Their great achievements of the fifties seemed suddenly at risk. The immediate response was to concede to union leaders large increases in wage rates; this ensured that their 'social partners' regained their prestige among workers, that the accepted structure of relativities was restored, and that those groups of workers which had not taken part in the September strikes did not learn too well the lesson that militancy paid. This tactic of retreat was of course made more or less painless by the very high levels of capacity utilisation and competitiveness in 1969–70 (see Fig. 5.9); but it demonstrated nonetheless a shift in the industrial – and social – balance of power away from the employer. It would have been quite out of character for German employers to see such a shift without making a great effort to get back to the *status quo ante*. They could do little in Parliament, where their allies were much weaker than in the early 1950s, so they concentrated on strengthening their industrial front.

The new mood and strategy of the German employers was symbolised by one man, Dr Hanns-Martin Schleyer. Schleyer had made a name for himself in 1963 as the pioneer of the lock-out in post-war collective bargaining; his background[52] and personality made him the natural leader of the hard-liners. As such, when the hard line was adopted in the 1970s, Schleyer rose rapidly to the top: in 1973 he became President of the BDA, in 1977 also of the BDI – the first man to lead both the 'peak organisations' of German industry. The new 'Schleyer' policy was of course partly a response to new economic pressures – the revaluation after 1969 was raising concession costs – but it reflected also the particular attitudes and objectives of the German *Unternehmer*. Schleyer would have looked as out of place among the ineffectual gentlemen of the British CBI as a wolf among poodles – and they could never have asked from their members the discipline he demanded, and got, from his.[53]

Although German employers are ready to look beyond economic pressures, that does not mean that they ignore them. Capacity utilisation, profitability and trade competitiveness can all be expected to influence the broad negotiating policy worked out at national and industrial level, and they will definitely affect the firm's individual decisions on wage supplements.[54] So the movements of these variables can go some way to explain changes in employer stance. On the union side, too, some of the variables relevant in Britain are relevant in Germany – unemployment and price inflation, for example. Incomes policy is relevant too; a statutory policy has never been applied, but on the other hand voluntary restraint is meaningful, because the unions are centralised. (I would describe the first 'concerted action' period, from early 1967 to the September Strikes of 1969, as the only voluntary incomes policy so far.) I ignore relative wages in the public sector, because this sector in Germany is smaller, and its wages tend to keep rather closely in line with the rest of the economy. On the other hand, union strength and militancy has been considerably affected by immigration, and the escalator it helps to fuel, so I shall take as additional variables, the proportion of foreign workers in the labour force, and changes in that proportion.

All these factors are shown in Fig. 5.9. We can see that in some respects wage inflation in Germany follows the same rules as in Britain. It seems to respond to the pressure of demand, to price inflation, to trade competitiveness, in much the same way. The big rise in unemployment during the 1966–7 recession, and the sharp reduction in foreign workers, could have been expected, in Britain, to be followed a year or so later by an increase in union militancy. That did in fact happen in Germany, and helps (along with capacity utilisation and trade competitiveness) to explain the sharp rise in wage inflation during 1969/70. High wage inflation continued until 1974 (in spite of falling competitiveness) largely because capacity utilisation stayed high and people got used to relatively fast price inflation. The fall after 1974 can be explained fairly well by falling price inflation and plummeting capacity utilisation.

What is harder to explain, from the charts, is the *continuing* low rate of wage inflation since then. With the 'immigration stop' since 1973, a high rate of unemployment, and slowly rising living standards, there should have been an upsurge in militancy. It is in fact generally agreed that there was. Then where is the consequent upsurge in wage inflation in 1977–8? Employer resistance prevented it; but why was this resistance so strong? Profits were lower than in previous cycles, but the fall was much less than in Britain. Capacity utilisation was quite high again, and

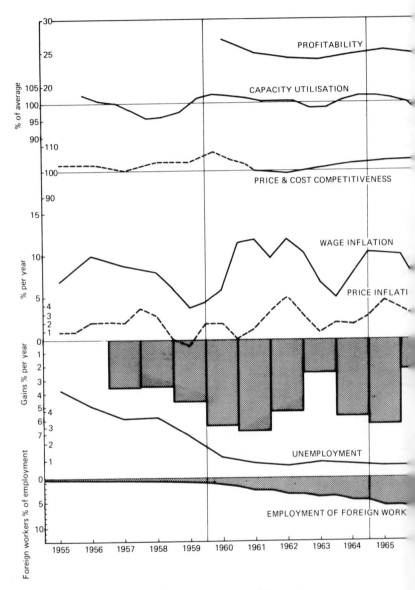

FIGURE 5.9 German wage inflation and some of its causes

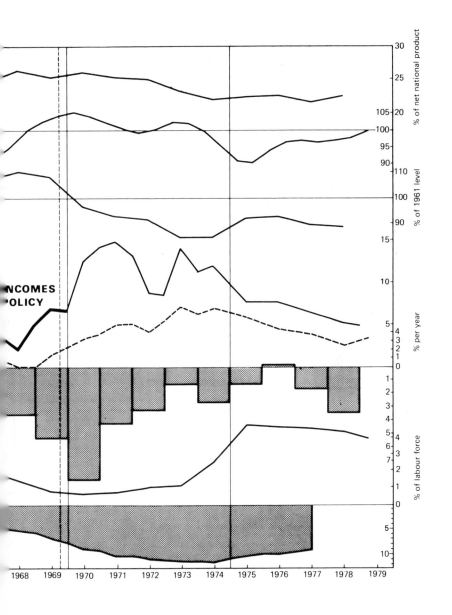

% of net national product

30

25

105 20

100

95

90

% of 1961 level

110

100

90

15

10

% per year

5
4
3
2
1
0

1

2

3

4

5
6
7

% of labour force

4

3

2

1

0

5

10

1968   1969   1970   1971   1972   1973   1974   1975   1976   1977   1978   1979

trade competitiveness was higher than in 1973–4, and high enough to produce a huge trade surplus.

We have here to remember the 'Schleyer' policy, the renewed hard line; to show its importance we can contrast the 1977/8 situation with the German past, and the British present. In the early 1960s the 'economic factors' taken together, were not much more 'softening' than in 1977/8, and the unions, for good reason, were much more moderate; yet the inflation rate was considerably higher. Compare Britain: in 1977/8, the pound was held up by North Sea oil, and British manufacturers lost much of the competitiveness gained through devaluation, by giving wage increases above incomes policy limits. By the autumn of 1978 it must have been clear that the incomes policy was on the verge of collapse, and that another disastrous upsurge in inflation could only be avoided by the strictest discipline on the part of employers. Collectively, they now had the strongest incentive to stand firm, and the government was using every power it had, to make them do so. CBI leaders did not stump the country, like Schleyer and his successors, organising employer resistance to wage demands.[55] On the contrary – they demanded that the government stop punishing firms for breaking the incomes policy (in Germany such punishment would have been administered by the employers' organisations themselves). The incomes policy duly collapsed, and inflation accelerated – hardly the goal of employers' policy, if they had had a policy. Meanwhile, across the water, in an economic climate no more 'toughening' than Britain's, German employers were stubbornly resisting long strikes, resorting readily to lockouts, and were succeeding in holding wage inflation down to around 6 per cent.[56]

It is hopeless, then, to try to explain or predict the stance of German management using purely economic indicators; but as long as one bears this in mind, and takes due account of changes in employer strategy, it is possible to explain trends and fluctuations in German inflation in much the same way as I used for Britain. That cannot be said of the US. To begin with, the union sector is too small. In Britain and Germany, such employers as can fix their wages without bargaining have to follow the union sector rather closely–or be swallowed up in it. In the US, non-union employers have much more freedom to respond to the labour market, and the boot is partly on the other foot – the union sector, as I argued in Chapter 1, Section 3, has to take a great deal of notice of non-union wages. This, and the toughness of employers generally, has helped to frame different rules for bargaining in what there is of the union sector. Unofficial strikes are usually ineffective, and in the US, unlike the

UK and Germany, there is usually little or no increase in wage inflation in the early upturn, when conditions are most favourable for unofficial action. The cyclical high point usually comes, in fact, well after the peak of the boom (see Fig. 5.10). Conditions for unofficial strikes by then are no longer particularly favourable; nor would they be for official ones, if it was not for the peculiar character of US wage bargaining. As almost all their wage contracts last two or three years,[57] US employers can prepare for the possibility of strike action for many months in advance; they (and their customers) normally pile up large stocks to safeguard supplies. During the boom this is most difficult: not only is there, of course, little production to spare for stockbuilding, but the rate of interest which has to be paid on money borrowed for the purpose is usually highest in the boom. It is at this point, too, that labour market pressures are most inflationary – shortages of skilled workers in the non-union sector are most acute at about the peak of the boom, so at this time wages rise fastest there, and the union sector follows behind. Thus it is for wage negotiations towards the end of the boom that employers are worst prepared.

No more in its trends than in its fluctuations, does US wage inflation follow European rules. Otherwise we should have expected the rise both in concentration and in unemployment in US industry between 1965 and 1975 to have led to a definite increase in union strength and militancy. They did not. In fact, as I argued in Chapter 2, Section 3, it has been management which gained by increased concentration, for as firms grew larger they could better exploit the close economic integration, and deep social division, of the North American continent. Nor have the unions been able, so far, to benefit from the rise in unemployment – they have been prevented from doing so by the racial and sexual divisions of the labour force. Meanwhile the unions have been steadily weakened by Mexican immigration, and the shift of economic activity into the 'non-union' Sunbelt.

There was one force at work, however, which was bound, even in the US, to encourage militancy. During the 1940s and 1950s real wages, after tax, had risen steadily. In the sixties the rises slowed; in the seventies they virtually stopped. The real disposable income of manual workers in industry, in 1978, was no higher than it had been in 1966.[58] In a society organised to raise consumer aspirations, they must have *felt* poorer. Yet during the 1976–8 boom, wage inflation was running no more than one or two percentage points ahead of price inflation – not enough, after tax, to give any noticeable increase in living standards. Of course, this low rate could have been achieved *in spite of* union militancy – by statutory

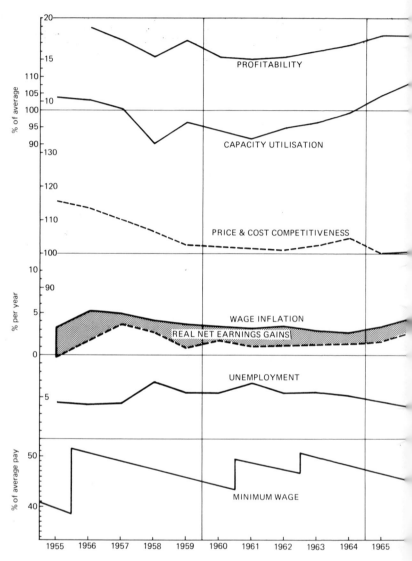

FIGURE 5.10 US wage inflation and some of its causes

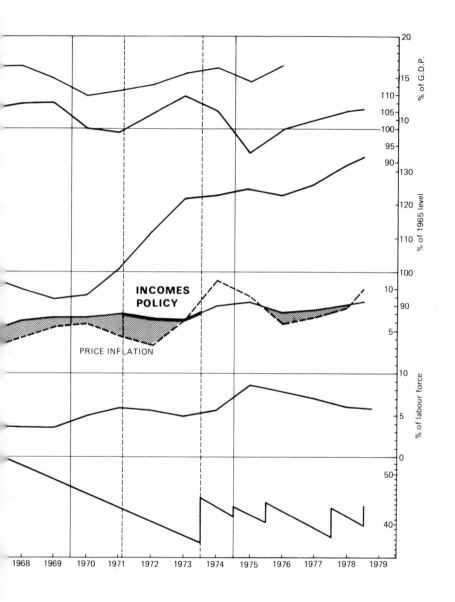

INCOMES POLICY

PRICE INFLATION

% of G.D.P.

% of 1965 level

% of labour force

1968 1969 1970 1971 1972 1973 1974 1975 1976 1977 1978 1979

incomes policy, as in Britain; by stubborn employer resistance, as in Germany. But there was no statutory incomes policy, and there is no more sign in the strike statistics than in union membership figures that US employers have been struggling against a rising tide of union pressure.

Still, inflation has risen: at the time of writing (early 1979) wages were rising at about 10 per cent per year, an extraordinary rate for the US, even for the end of a boom. Inflationary changes must have taken place, if not on the union side, then on the other. It is not hard to see what they were. The massive real devaluation of the dollar since 1971 – about 30 per cent – has drastically reduced wage costs in the US relative to its main competitors. Once, before the opening of US and foreign markets to international competition, that might not have been of great significance; now, it is bound to reduce management concession costs greatly (it is also largely to blame for the stagnation of living standards). This does not simply explain the rise in inflation which has taken place in the last decade – it over-explains it. Imagine the effects of so large a real devaluation on Britain, where a much smaller one had, as my econometrics showed, devastating effects. Imagine the effects on Germany, where *re*valuation played a vital part in bringing inflation down. Without the weakening of the US unions it would be hard to explain how the rate of inflation had stayed so low.

Conclusions

The United States stands out from the comparison as a country where *organisational factors* – the attitudes of workers and managers, the strength (or rather weakness) of unions, the degree of discipline within management, the extent of collective bargaining – are now, by current international standards, highly disinflationary. They have been moving in that direction ever since the Korean War, except for the late 1960s. The *economic* factors which directly influence management and unions – trade competitiveness, capacity utilisation, purchasing power, availability of labour – have (taken together) shown a strongly inflationary trend over the last decade which has outweighed the organisational changes.

As the key economic change has been the devaluation of the dollar it is worth looking for a moment at the reasons for it. At first it could be seen as a corrective to a long overvaluation, needed to win back the competitive edge and expansionary confidence of US industry. The huge rise in world energy prices after 1972 made the necessary correction larger, for US firms found themselves at a disadvantage in the new era, with a range of products designed for lavish energy use. It was clear, nonetheless, by 1977 that US firms were reasonably competitive again. The trade deficit remained, the dollar went on falling, but that was now due, more and more, to the rise in imports of oil. If the energy deficit had been eliminated – as it would have been at European levels of energy use – the devaluation could have been halted, at least for a time.[59]

Compare Britain. 'Organisational factors' there were inflationary throughout, and became sharply more so after the mid-1960s. If after that time economic factors also became, on balance, more inflationary, that was mainly because the pound too was falling (though in real terms, much less far than the dollar). This, as I have shown, was due above all to Britain's miserable status as 'laggard' in the process of international polarisation. For that reason, the same devaluation was not enough to prevent a steady worsening of the balance of trade in manufactures, and Britain would have been forced to devalue much further but for some remarkable geological luck – the existence of large gas and oil reserves under the North Sea which by the end of the seventies brought the UK back to rough self-sufficiency in energy and thus did much to rescue the balance of payments. But the resulting *re*valuation was so calamitous for British manufacturing that by 1981 it would surely have to resort again to real devaluation. That would have frightening consequences. Even with the pound buoyed up by the North Sea, the situation by 1979 was already desperate. For the short-term benefits of deflation and incomes policy, the country was now paying the long-term price, in an upsurge of inflation which none knew how to control save by stiffer doses of those same drugs.

Is it not refreshing to turn to Germany? True, some organisational factors were much less favourable than in the US – unions were stronger and more militant, collective bargaining was more widespread – but this was partly offset by the remarkable strength and discipline of the employers. And on the 'economic' side, Germany's place as a 'leader' had led to a substantial real revaluation which had had distinctly disinflationary effects. The proof of the pudding, anyway, was in the eating – inflation in Germany in 1978 was much lower than in the US, let alone Britain, and tending to fall. If Germans seemed worried by it, the Anglo-Saxon observer was inclined to put that down to the fussy perfectionism of the politically insecure.

In fact, for the long term, Germans still had very good reason for concern. If the rate of investment in new jobs was not sharply increased, the escalator in Germany would stay virtually at a standstill, and this would increase union strength and militancy. But the only way to overcome business reluctance to invest was to push up demand until existing capacity was over-stretched, and profits high. This would be particularly dangerous, because the present balance of bargaining power was precarious: if lower managers in large firms again began conceding big increases in wage supplements, the employers' bargainers at industry level would be outflanked and forced by 'conservative emulation' to retreat from their tough stance. Wage supplements were under control at the moment because managers at all levels were under pressure to hold down wage costs; but once return to excess demand like that of the early 1960s or 1969–70, and the temptation to 'buy' maximum output by whatever concessions were necessary, would be too strong.

There is an old German word used in chess to describe a situation where you would be safe if you did not move; but you *must* move. Germany is in *zugzwang*. If German policy has not succeeded, Britain's has certainly failed: it is facing 'economic' and 'organisational' problems which combine to make its inflation almost uncontrollable. It is in check, so to speak, and would be facing mate but for the North Sea. Finally, the United States is so well placed 'organisationally' that with an economy as strong as Germany's it would have no inflation at all. Its immediate economic problems are, for the most part, not fundamental. The US would have managed as well as most, if it had had a better energy policy, or more oil.

6 Prospects and Remedies

6.1 THE OUTLOOK FOR WESTERN INFLATION

In this Section I shall try to predict what will happen to the present inflation, if no important changes are made in the economic policies of Western governments – or rather, if the important changes which they will be forced to make, take place through the usual process of drift, through a jumble of disconnected responses to political pressure. I hope the grim prospect I offer in this Section will concentrate the mind sharply on the remedies I prescribe in the next.

It will be clear by now that it is hopeless to try to forecast inflation without first forecasting (a) the growth of demand and employment, (b) how economic relationships between countries will evolve. I shall have to look at these matters together, because each affects the other so much.

The West has been wallowing since 1974 in what deserves to be called the Second Great Slump, though those who prefer less dramatic phrases would describe it as a protracted period of low demand and high unemployment. All elected governments no doubt dislike this . . . slump as much as their electors do; they could end it, if all or most of them reflated, and all, or most of them, know this. Yet they do not reflate. What holds them back is a problem I have already explained, in Chapter 2, Section 3: for each state individually, under free trade, the results of reflation are, on balance, unpleasant, because it gains less in higher growth and unemployment than it loses in currency devaluation and higher inflation. That is a little oversimplified, perhaps, because the consequences depend on the country's balance of payments position to start with. Countries in deficit are, as Francis Cripps puts it, *constrained*:[1] any serious attempt to reflate would be likely to lead to a drastic fall in the currency and a dangerous quickening in the inflation rate. Countries with a large surplus on current account, on the other hand, are *unconstrained*: they could reflate quite a lot without driving their currencies down far, if at all. Obviously it is much harder to explain reluctance to reflate in an unconstrained country. No Western country is *currently* unconstrained, but four – Germany, Japan, Switzerland and the Netherlands – have been recently, and probably will soon be again. Why have they been reluctant to reflate? They have at least two reasons in common: their governments are afraid that higher demand will increase inflationary pressures at home, and their most influential lobbyists on economic policy are exporting or multinational firms which look above all to foreign markets and have rather little to gain, perhaps something to lose, from reflation at home.

We can apply much the same distinction to the countries of the Eastern bloc and the Third World. Almost all Third World and Eastern bloc countries are constrained, many of them severely, by an embarrassingly large foreign debt; again, there are only three or four countries which are really unconstrained, and these are the oil producers with large revenues and small populations: Saudi Arabia, Kuwait, the United Arab Emirates and Libya. These countries are in fact also 'constrained', by the difficulty of finding any more exports they could usefully buy; unfortunately the accidents of geology and history have given these few countries enormous oil revenues, and thus surpluses on a still larger scale than the Western 'leaders'. Like the Western leaders, by exporting more than they import they reduce demand elsewhere.

It is difficult to see what, short of a big fall in the real price of oil, could solve the problem of the oil surpluses. The surpluses of the Western 'leaders' seem easier to deal with. Increasing freedom of capital movement allows market pressures to force up their currencies, and large real revaluations should in due course get rid of, or much reduce, their current account surpluses. But there is only faint reason for optimism in that. First, the leaders' real *re*valuations are the laggards' real *de*valuations, and devaluations of course have extremely serious consequences for inflation; so the laggards may restrict demand to keep their devaluations to a minimum. Second, most of the deficit countries (in the Third World and the Eastern bloc as well as the West) have been in serious deficit for some years now, and have run up large debts; they really need several years in healthy surplus before they can escape from constraint. Third, the oil surpluses are likely to persist or get even larger (see below). So most countries will for the foreseeable future be extremely nervous of expanding demand on their own.

What few dare to do on their own, all should be able to manage collectively. The Western surplus countries could be browbeaten into reflation if the others made common cause and threatened to discriminate against their exports. Unfortunately the political process *between* states is a great deal less effective at promoting the common good than is the political process within them (which is saying something). Negotiators often do not have power to implement the promises (or the threats) that they make (this is a particular problem in federal states with a separation of powers, like the USA and West Germany) and even when they do, they may choose to backslide once the heat is off them from abroad, and on them from lobbyists and voters at home. So a succession of summits has produced many fine phrases but few jobs. Still, these are early days yet in international economic politics, and as their desperation increases the statesmen of the world may learn to give their threats more conviction and their commitments more respect. If they do, we may look forward to a modest recovery from the Slump.

An international upswing, however, may not get very far before it runs into another obstacle. Between 1975 and 1978 the real price of oil was progressively reduced, essentially because Saudi Arabia thought lower prices politically desirable and was able to supply enough oil at critical periods to keep demand satisfied at those prices. This price fall, while it lasted, did a good deal to keep payments imbalances within bounds. But it was made possible only by a margin of excess capacity: as soon as the Iranian revolution (and a mild upswing) got rid of that margin, the OPEC 'hawks' had their way, and the price recovered. Any upswing in world demand for goods in general would cause a greater upswing in demand for oil which would ensure that the 'Iranian shortage' continued, or recurred, and high prices were maintained.[2] The direct impact of higher oil prices, outside the oil exporters, is bound to be deflationary, and the increase in oil surpluses makes reflation more difficult.

So the persistence of the slump will be due to the nature of international economic, and political, relations; at the same time, those relations will be powerfully affected by the persistence of the slump. The key to the situation is the position of the laggards. Even in a world boom they would not be very comfortably placed – pushed gradually off the 'high ground' by competition from the leaders, while their markets for traditional 'low technology' goods were invaded by 'advanced developing' countries like South Korea and Brazil. In a boom, however, all that would happen is what Britain suffered for twenty years from the mid-1950s (and for fifty years until the first slump) – *relative* decline; a steady fall in shares of world markets, but growth in absolute income nonetheless. But in a near-stagnant world market, relative decline may mean absolute decline. In summer even the weak survive; come winter, the weakest go to the wall.

As they lose the free-trade game, the governments of the laggards find it harder and harder to resist the pressure to change the rules. This pressure takes two forms. There is a general form, the dislike of voters for the policies forced on them (under existing rules) to cope with failure: deflation and devaluation to prop up the balance of payments, deflation and incomes policy to hold down the inflation which the devaluation and previous deflation have aggravated. (In a politically-stable laggard like Britain it merely becomes rather difficult for governments to win elections; in an unstable one like Italy the whole structure of state and society is threatened.) There is also specific pressure, from workers, managers and owners in industries which are suffering severely from foreign competition.

This increasing pressure to move away from free trade, to (re)impose tariffs and import controls and subsidies of various kinds, has been outweighed until recently by counter-pressure from those with a stake in the existing system: at home, exporters and multinationals; abroad, governments and bankers; everywhere, neoclassical economists. The foreign pressure becomes more and more effective as the laggard becomes dependent on foreign loans to avert a collapse of the currency; the domestic pressure too, as what remains of private manufacturing industry is increasingly dominated by exporters and multinationals.

Happily, the politicians find a way to face in both directions at once (that is, after all, their profession). They reassure bankers, other governments, and the world in general that there is no question of departing from the sacred principle of free trade; and no doubt they mean every word; then they make some temporary, exceptional . . . *adjustment* . . . to the rules of free trade in order to cope with the (temporary and exceptional) problems of the steel industry, the shipbuilding industry, the textile industry, the clothing industry[3]. . . . You see, these (declining) industries are in a particularly bad state, and need help to tide them over the *transitional* period until their surplus workers can get jobs in the new growth industries and their surplus capacity is taken up by . . . the world recovery . . . and besides, someone else broke the rules first. And we have to give subsidies and preferential contracts to our new growth industries, just to get them started, and keep them going until the world recovery comes. . . .

Nothing lasts like the temporary; the world recovery will do almost as well as the Greek Kalends as a future date to start being virtuous again. And nothing is so much copied as the exceptional. Other industries copy: protection is harder to refuse to Industry B once it has been granted to Industry A. Other countries are also likely to copy, whether in retaliation, or because they will now be less exposed to criticism. (Or because of the real effects of the action on them: other importers face a larger inflow once one importer closes his doors, while the exporter may need to make up for the loss of a foreign market by cutting imports into his own.) And so, step by step, looking always to the front, the retreat from free trade begins.[4]

This retreat could offer great advantages. Import controls, as I shall argue in the next Section, could do much to help escape from the slump; but they would have to be applied systematically. In particular, they would have to be used *selectively*, against goods from the surplus countries, so that the deficit countries could escape from their constraints. But it is very difficult to do systematically what you are pretending, even to yourself, not to be doing at all. Instead, the interference with free trade at each stage will follow – is already following – the line of least political resistance and greatest short-term political gain.[5]

Unfortunately the line of least resistance turns out to be the one which does least good and most damage. It consists of finding ways of breaking the free trade rules which can be either hidden or excused. The easiest to hide are preferential contracts and subsidies to home producers – but these discriminate equally against all foreign competitors. The easiest to excuse are restrictions on imports which compete with a home industry in deep crisis – but these are usually low-technology products (standard textiles, for example) in which the leaders have little interest anyway. The best excuse for import restrictions is that the seller is pricing below cost – but that can rarely be said against the leaders, who tend to get their competitive edge by superior quality, not low price. So those who suffer most are not the leaders, but Third World and Communist countries; but these are some of the most constrained – a dollar off their exports very quickly means a dollar off their imports, and the West as a whole merely loses a market as well as a source of cheap goods. Worse, the Western industries protected are declining already, and the effect is merely to slow the decline: so they still invest very little, but the West's capital goods industries lose a market in some Eastern or Southern country which cannot now expand so fast. Worst of all, the pretence and deceit which surrounds the whole business takes away from the increase in protection what ought to be its greatest advantage – that it provides businessmen with the stability, the confidence in future sales which they need in order to invest.

The result is that the retreat from free trade may hinder, rather than help, the process of world economic recovery; but the longer that is delayed, the further the retreat will go.

At the same time the continuing slump is speeding up another process which tends to reduce competition: the rapid increase in national and international concentration. I have argued before that the main reasons for mergers are the wishes of firms in general to reduce uncertainty caused by competition, and the urge of strong ones to go on growing when the scope for 'internal' growth is limited. The conditions I have been describing are clearly ideal for mergers, and also for the destruction of smaller and weaker firms – which further reduces competition. We are thus moving rapidly nearer to the domination of the world economy, and above all world trade, by a few hundred multinationals.[6] These large multinationals have the extra advantage that they are well placed to lobby against trade restrictions which hurt them; they can usually argue that their *imports* should be left alone, since they are *exporters* too.

Continuing Trends

Some trends which I have shown at work in the past, can be expected to go on grinding forward in future in much the same way, regardless (more or less) of the level of demand or the fate of free trade. We can expect the 'Adam Smith effect' – the increase in the complexity and interdependence of production, described in Chapter 2, Section 2 – to continue gradually, tending to soften management's stance. At the same time workers are encouraged to take a tough stance by the changing pattern of consumer expenditure described in Chapter 3, Section 3 – the shift from 'consumption' to 'investment', and from private renting to home ownership. The slump has slowed this trend down, but has not stopped it; nor has it stopped the trend to the two-income family, as more wives go out to work (even three-income, as the husband takes a 'moonlight' job to help evade taxes). Both trends reduce workers' strike costs.

Probably the most important effect of married women working, however, is on their attitudes, and those of male workers. As I showed in Chapter 3, Section 1, so long as the fact of women working runs ahead of the attitudes to it, it divides the labour force and weakens the unions; as attitudes begin to catch up, the division fades and the unions tend to grow stronger. Every Western country appears by now to be in the second, catching-up phase, with women insisting ever more strongly on equal rights and men coming to terms with the consequences – including reduced promotion for themselves. There are, then, a number of inflationary trends in the background, moving slowly, but moving.

Conclusion: the Outlook for Inflation

What we can expect, then, over (say) the next five years, is the persistence of the old inflationary trends just described, and the development of new ones arising essentially from the slump: increasing trade union strength and militancy, due mainly to the stopping of the escalator; slower productivity growth; reduced pressure of competition, particularly price competition, on management, because of increasing concentration and protection. These new trends will go furthest in the *laggards*, where growth is slowest and the retreat from free trade fastest. But they will affect the *leaders* too – even other countries' import controls reduce management concession cost, because they take away the incentive to hold down wage costs in order to win or keep that market. Still, the laggards will be most affected. What will create the greatest difference between leaders and laggards is the process of devaluation and revaluation, which still has a great deal further to go (indeed in Germany it has scarcely started, and in Britain it has been temporarily reversed).

The position of the laggards, then – Italy, Britain after the North Sea bubble has burst, and perhaps, in time, France and Belgium – is likely to become desperate. The further they retreat from free trade, the less they will be forced to devalue and deflate, but the stronger will be the inflationary effects of reduced competition. They will certainly be forced to use fairly strict forms of incomes policy, and as these increasingly fail, the yet more desperate remedies discussed in the next Section. If its wastefulness of energy forces the United States to go on devaluing, like a laggard, it will probably have to resort again to incomes policy, like a laggard. In other 'intermediate' countries inflation will tend to get worse, but how much worse must depend on their industrial relations and economic performance, as well as international developments, and would need more detailed analysis than I can offer here. Finally, for the leaders, like Germany, their situation gives them hope, so long as it lasts. Revaluation will keep the employer stance tough; modest growth may be enough to moderate the unions. But if other countries retreat very far from free trade, the leaders' growth and revaluation will be at risk, and so in turn their relative stability.

6.2 DESPERATE REMEDIES

I expect this section to annoy almost everyone who reads it. It certainly annoys the writer. It puts forward no easy solutions, for I know of none.

It mentions cures which I think worse than the disease, and refuses to call them impractical merely because they are hateful. (I can only say that these policies will be put forward anyway, and that a cool understanding of them will, in the long run, help their opponents.) As for my positive proposals, they leave many questions and objections unanswered, for lack of space. I ask the reader to judge them for what they are: not a detailed blueprint for immediate action, but a brief sketch of the principles on which future policy should be based. Meanwhile, I hope this Section serves to mark the rocks, and bell the cat.

I will begin with what many will find the most painful implication of my analysis: that union strength contributes to inflation; ergo, if the unions were weaker (other things being equal) there would be less inflation. That suggests a number of policy measures, some of which will be quite alarming (I hope). Before examining them, it is worth recalling another implication: that unions are *counter-organisations*, which arise among workers in response to their needs in the organisations in which they spend their working lives. As a result, the more naive attempts to weaken or restrict unions are ineffective; others, less naive, may still be undesirable. In the first category come most policies aimed at directly weakening the unions.

Policies aimed at Direct Weakening of Unions

This category would include, for example, the banning or limitation of strikes of various kinds, and the banning of closed shops or encouragement of non-recognition by the employer. Such policies may be effective in sectors and places (like the American South) where there are other factors at work making for union weakness anyway. Where they are applied to a union movement already well entrenched – as they were by the British Conservative government in 1972–4 – they are quite as likely to result in a backlash of militancy and public sympathy for militancy which may be more inflationary than the previous situation, particularly because the activity which is hardest to repress is the most decentralised kind. Often, legal limitations on union actions will seem effective when they express, and somewhat reinforce, social attitudes which the workers share. This could be said of the German restrictions on plant bargaining and prohibition of unofficial strikes – in the 1950s and early 1960s; when workers' attitudes changed, the law against unofficial strikes was neither respected nor enforced, and the main effect of the restrictions on bargaining was to encourage the 'dual' bargaining system which I have argued has serious inflationary effects.

Policies aimed at Direct Weakening of Union Bargaining Power

By trying to increase workers' strike costs, these policies are open to similar criticism. It *may* be possible to drive people back to work sooner, or discourage them from coming out in the first place, by refusing them social security benefits; but as I have shown, very few strikers apply for such benefits even when they can get them, and the effect on public sympathy for a strike may be counter-productive. Much the same could be said against other steps to make strikes more expensive. It has to be remembered that nowadays strikes normally involve only a small proportion of the workers in any community. If their own savings, etc., are not enough to tide the strikers over, they can certainly manage with help from relatives and friends. If the law or government policy, by seeming unfair, makes it easier for them to get moral and financial support within their community – which if feelings run high enough means half the country – it will be self-defeating. As Edward Heath was reminded in the British miners' strikes, this is not 1926 – you cannot starve half of South Wales into submission, and you had better not seem to be trying to.

Policies aimed at Indirect Weakening of the Unions

These are more subtle, and more likely to be effective. To get the most nauseating of these quickly out of the way, it seems clear (from Chapter 3, Section 1) that anything which tended to increase racialism, and so set workers against one another, would weaken the unions, and tend to reduce inflation. (So the National Front in Britain, the NDP in Germany, the Ku Klux Klan in the United States, can proudly call themselves anti-inflationary organisations, the consumer's friends.) I daresay one pogrom would do more for price stability than a dozen Price Commissions. Shall I drop the subject now?

Another policy, which will seem morally more acceptable, is to stress as much as possible the selfishness of unions and strikes, and their damaging effects both on the national economy and the interests of the workers themselves. This is a matter more for the mass media than for governments directly; papers like the *Sun*, the *Daily Mail* and *Bild Zeitung* seem to take their responsibilities here particularly seriously. Probably this sort of campaign has more effect on what might be called wider solidarity – blacking, and financial or moral support for strikers – than the workers' willingness to join a union or come out on strike themselves; where they have personal knowledge of an issue they will be inclined to make up their own minds. The mass media can also help to discredit militant union leaders, particularly at higher levels in the union, where they are not known to their members personally; but the media can do little to prevent moderate leaders discrediting themselves, in their members' eyes, if they accept restraint. Sooner or later this will cause a swing to militancy at the grass roots, and possibly also at the centre.

In principle it is likely to be most effective to strike at the root causes of union strength: the remoteness of authority, etc., and the economic self-interest of the workers. But it is no use tinkering with the problem. Easy institutional solutions to remoteness, such as works councils, may perhaps *forestall* unions, but cannot supplant them once they are established, for it is easy for the union to prevent the works council operating effectively. Similarly, profit-sharing schemes designed to make the workers feel an economic bond between them and the firm, would have to go much further than most managements would be prepared to take them before workers began to see collective barganing as an irrelevance. Short of really drastic changes, like the wholesale break-up of giant firms into smaller units or their transformation into workers' cooperatives, it hard to see such institutional reforms as important, though there is a lot to be said – on grounds of efficiency as much as anything – for much tighter control of mergers and for the encouragement of worker participation. (I return to the question of mergers later.) Another way of weakening the unions would be to give workers more scope to look after their interests *individually*. But that would require a fast escalator – and so long as the slump lasts we will be lucky to have any escalator at all.

Governments are likely, then, to prefer the most direct and certain way of weakening union power – interfering at the very point where it is exercised, the wage negotiation:

Statutory Incomes Policy

I have shown that incomes policy can only be expected to work for long in a bargaining system where both unions and employers are strongly centralised, and workers are unable or unwilling to organise strongly at the grass roots. These conditions do not now exist in any of our seven countries, and as a result all incomes policies will break down in a few years at most, and leave a situation which is more inflationary than when they started. Unfortunately that is not reason enough to dismiss them. If governments avoid the remedies I have been criticising, as I hope, and, as I fear, balk at those I shall be proposing, then they *will* resort to incomes policy.

The beginning of wisdom in framing an incomes policy for a decentralised bargaining system with strong unions, is to recognise from the start that it is going to break down fairly soon, and that there will then have to be an interval of more-or-less free collective bargaining before the government interferes again (or finds a better solution). During that interval inflation is certainly going to accelerate; very well, while the policy is *on* you have to make sure that it decelerates at least as much as it accelerates when the policy is *off*. While restraint is in force, inflation must be slowed down as far and as fast as possible. Actual wage reductions are of course politically out of the question – but a complete freeze is quite another matter. It is rigid, of course, but so what? Any incomes policy must be, to work; and it creates less distortion of relativities than for example a flat-rate £x per week increase. The brutal equity of a complete wage freeze is a definite advantage, politically; the main political disadvantage is that if prices continue to rise there will be a sharp reduction in real wages. The main economic case against a freeze is that when inflation does fall sharply (as it will), this will cause economic distortions wherever continuing fast inflation has been assumed: for example, in medium and long term interest rates, and in long-term contracts. Because the real rate of interest rises sharply businesses (and State) may find their debt burden uncomfortably high.

Fortunately the government can guard against both these effects. It can encourage indexation of loans so that the *real* interest rate is fixed (it would have a marvellous effect on firms' willingness to invest if it were brought home to them by indexation just how low real interest rates have fallen) and indexation of contracts so that real prices are fixed. And then before implementing a wage freeze it must prepare means of bringing price inflation down more or less to zero within a matter of weeks. This could be done by a three-pronged policy:

1. Use price controls to make sure that prices stop rising where costs have stopped rising.
2. Use the exchange rate to check rising import costs as quickly as possible. This should not be difficult: by now, foreign exchange markets have learnt that exchange rates must sooner or later reflect inflation rates, and if the freeze is announced convincingly enough they will go along with a central bank move to revalue the currency accordingly.

3. Use temporary subsidies to balance whatever price rises are still in the pipeline from home or abroad. (Since the wage costs of central and local government would suddenly be lower than tax rates had allowed for, there would be a short-term windfall to distribute without any need for increased borrowing.)

If price inflation *were* rapidly reduced the public delight would strengthen union moderation and the incomes policy would erode more slowly.

Still, the policy *would* erode in time: rigidity would have to be softened, and when it was the loopholes would be exploited, as I have explained before . . . Government and civil servants would have to bring themselves to let go in good time. It is a hard thing for a bureaucrat to give up a new toy, but a point comes with an incomes policy where the distortions the restrictions are causing are storing up more trouble for the future than the policy is worth in lower inflation now. In particular the temptation is to go on restricting pay in the public sector when private sector workers are already laughing behind their hands; but it is absolutely essential not to leave powerful groups of workers with a grievance which makes them militant opponents of the next rigid incomes policy. Before the rigid phase comes round again, the 'free collective bargaining' period must be used to clear the decks by setting distorted relativities right; but if many severe distortions have been unnecessarily introduced during the twilight of the last incomes policy, inflation will quicken very rapidly and the free-for-all will have to be brought to an end too soon, before all the distortions have been removed. In short, if governments insist on using incomes policy, they must accept that it is temporary, make the best of it while it lasts, and drop it in good time.

Nonetheless, what I have just put forward is no more than the least bad form of a bad policy. Each time the on – off cycle is repeated the shop stewards who can evade the policy are stronger, and so is the emulation it encourages. At the same time, it would be harder to operate after the changes I predicted in the last Section: unions stronger and more militant; managers less inclined to resist them as their firms grow larger and authority more remote, while the pressure of competition declines. In the end, politicians and public may be prepared to consider a remedy which goes to the root of the problem. There is one.

A Modest Proposal

We have to find some way of reversing the process which has taken place: we have to make the unions, if not weaker, then more moderate:

to soften their stance. We have to make management, if not stronger, then more determined: to toughen their stance.

Take the unions first. Some of the causes of greater union strength and militancy are inherent in the nature of what we call progress, but others are self-inflicted, through unnecessary increases in organisational size, and economic stagnation. Small firms are beautiful:[7] they are not only much more efficient than they are thought to be, they are also much less inflationary than big ones. They must be encouraged – through changes in the financial system, by sweeping changes in monopoly and merger policy, and through confidence in a stable and expanding market. The last condition, it must now be clear, cannot be squared with free trade. To provide conditions where small firms can flourish, and to get the escalator restarted, there must be some retreat from free trade. But that retreat must not be the ragged, futile one at present under way, but one carefully planned and limited, which will reduce payments imbalances and restore continuing high demand.

I leave the detailed case for import controls to the New Cambridge economists round Godley and Cripps, who have by now shown beyond any reasonable doubt that a British recovery is impossible without them.[8] Let me just sketch briefly how controls would work. They would be imposed mainly by the laggards, to protect not only sectors like steel (and in Britain cars) which are threatened with bankruptcy or slow extinction, but also those like electronics, where the losers are being gradually pushed off the 'high ground' by competition from the leaders. By reducing payments deficits they would make reflation possible, and industries now 'sick' would be encouraged by a secure market and high demand to carry out the massive long-term programmes required to bring them back to competitive health; with unemployment falling, workers' resistance to rationalisation would fall too.

There are three important objections to import controls which I must not leave unanswered. The first is that Britain and Italy and most of the other countries which might wish to use import controls are members of an Economic Community that would be threatened by such measures, which are quite against its rules. True, in principle; but a greater threat to the EEC, as a community of democratic nations, would be the economic decline and social demoralisation of any of its members. It is my case that this is just what we can expect if the present system of trade is not radically changed. The Community must either leave its members to protect themselves, or it must do the job itself. Nothing that I am proposing for the individual state could not be done as well or better at a European level, as I shall argue later.

The second objection is that the industrial weakness of the laggards (of the Italian public sector, and British industry as a whole) cannot be blamed on the recent vicious circle of decline, because it goes back well before it. If British industry invested little, and mismanaged that, in the palmy days of the 1950s when profits and demand were high and funds plentiful, why should it do better if protection and high demand returned? Secure from foreign competition, would managers not be as sleepy as they were then? Perhaps; but there are ways of waking them. One, long overdue, is for the financial institutions of the City of London to take their duty to control industrial management as seriously as the German banks traditionally have done (control in the Italian public sector could be similarly tightened up).[9]

The third objection is akin to the second. If management's stance is too soft already, it would be softer still behind import controls, as I argued in the last section. If small firms grew stronger, that would provide increased competition domestically, which would help; but any radical change in industrial structure would take a long time. One remedy is much the same as to the second problem. Tighter control of management, by outsiders concerned with long term profitability, could force it to take a tougher stance; that appears to happen in Germany, in Sweden, in the United States – wherever the professional manager is firmly controlled by owners and financiers.

But that would not be enough. It would be absolutely necessary to come to grips with the problem of market power, increased by import controls, for it is that above all which reduces concession costs. There is only one way to do that effectively: price control. The argument for price control is simple. If firms operated in competitive markets they would be *price-takers*, having to accept whatever price the market set and do their best to make a profit at that price – which would normally imply taking a tough stance in wage bargaining. But most large firms today operate in oligopolistic or monopolistic markets, where they are to a large extent *price-makers* – which lets them take a soft stance, confident that the wages and prices of their close rivals (if any) will rise more or less in line with their own. Well, we must make them price-takers again.

Price control as normally practised does not in fact achieve this. The general rule is to set a limit to profit margins, either at some 'fair' level or according to what the firm was earning before. This method (I shall call it Type 1) is quite suitable if the controls are being used as a political prop for incomes policy (which is usual): if wages are held down, then workers can be assured that prices will be held down too. But in the present context – as a way of toughening the bargaining stance – a Type

1 policy is useless, or even worse than useless. For the firm now knows that any rise in costs entitles it to a rise in price, while if it holds down costs (perhaps by holding down wages) only the consumer will benefit. This reduces not only concession costs, the incentive to hold down wages, but also the incentive to hold down costs in general, by increasing efficiency.

Instead, the price controls must *mimic the market*. A competitive market would let prices rise to pass on rises in the price of raw materials, or components, and so forth, because these rises would raise the marginal costs of all or most of the competing firms. So the price ceiling must be adjusted too, whenever such unavoidable changes in costs take place. The competitive price would rise, for the same reason, to reflect any *general* increase in wages; so must the price ceiling, to reflect the rate of wage increase that is thought reasonable (what that rate will be, I discuss below). The competitive price would fall, to the extent that there was a general increase in productivity; the price ceiling too must take account of the increase in productivity that can reasonably be expected (what *that* increase should be, see below).

Mimic the market: set the price ceiling so that the firm can make a *reasonable* profit if it gives a *reasonable* wage increase and makes *reasonable* gains in productivity. If it can do better, either on productivity or wage restraint, then it gets its reward in extra profit; if it does worse, it will suffer – and ought to. So the price ceiling on firm *A* for product *X* would be set, and adjusted, as follows: First decide whether its profits are 'reasonable' to begin with; if they are, then its present price should be taken as the initial ceiling level. If profits seem too high, or too low, then the ceiling should be respectively lower, or higher, than the present level. Change the ceiling without fuss whenever *external* costs (raw materials, components, interest charges, etc.) change, for these are beyond the firm's control. The other, *internal* costs are largely within the firm's control, and the ceiling should reflect not what they *are*, but what they *should be*.

This requires, first, a view of what wage increase is 'reasonable'; when in doubt, set that at the 'norm' fixed for the whole economy. This would probably have to be on the low side since there would be fury if any group's 'reasonable' increase was set at less than the norm; above-norm increases would be allowed for, grudgingly, if wages were judged to be too low on grounds of fairness or need to attract labour. These decisions should be taken by some representative body with a large proportion of trade union members, to which interested parties could come and plead their case; the 'Pay Council's' natural generosity would be curbed by giving it a 'fund' of so many per cent of the national wage bill to dish out every year in above-norm 'allowances'.

We also need a view of what productivity increase is reasonable. The ideal would be to do case-by-case studies of firms' operations, and comparisons with 'best-practice' technology abroad, and work out from that, what improvement could reasonably be expected. That would take time, and a lot of skilled – and incorruptible – manpower. Meanwhile, an adequate rule of thumb would be to take the average rate of productivity increase in the relevant sector over the previous few years. Any injustice would amount to no more than a few per cent of the price; competitive market forces are no more precise.

With the price ceiling set, one could sit back and leave the pay bargainers to it, to share out whatever cake had been allotted – and by productivity bargaining, to increase it. For they would now be subject to the harsh market discipline which monetarists falsely claim to result from following a monetary 'rule'.[10] Managements would be free to make fake productivity deals of the sort used to evade flexible incomes policies – but if they did so they would be only cutting their own throats. Unions would be free to be irresponsible, to ask for the moon and strike if they did not get it; but management would be able to tell them, truthfully and convincingly now, that they would be risking their jobs if they got what they were asking for, since the bill could not be passed to the consumer. Forget the cartoon images – union bargainers are realists, and so are the vast majority of their members.

Probably the greatest effect of this 'Type 2' system of price control would not be on inflation at all, but on productivity. Market discipline restored, market incentive restored. The manager in a large firm who can always make the consumer pay the cost of his inefficiency, as long as he markets his product well, and merges or colludes with any dangerous rival – that manager would now be face to face with the problem he should have been concentrating on all along: getting a fair day's work for a fair day's pay, and getting his production methods up to date. In Britain at least most top managers of large firms pay most attention – in the time they have left from day-to-day administration of their overgrown empires – to marketing, finance, mergers; and labour re-lations when a major strike threatens. Production itself, as Alastair Mant has shown,[11] they neglect – and production managers, the backbone of the firm, are paid worst and promoted least. But once forced to hold their costs down below a price ceiling, their lordships would have to take a serious look at the shambles on their shop floors –

the out-of-date methods and equipment, the men and machines idle much of the time for lack of proper coordination.[12] They might even find, if they got the process of production back under control, that their labour relations improved – for production and labour relations go together like horse and cart, and the greatest bond between management and men is the interest they share (if management shares it!) in making their product.[13]

For the time being, however, the people who best understand the process of production are sitting at the other side of the bargaining table. Shop stewards know what is going on on the shop floor; they could make an enormous contribution to improving efficiency – if it was worth their members' while. At the moment they are inclined to think that – supposing management made good use of their cooperation – it would be shareholders and consumers who would gain rather than the work force. But if they saw it as the only way to get a wage increase above the norm. . . .

So much for the effects of a 'Type 2' system of price controls – if it worked. But by now I shall probably have lost all credibility with readers who know the complexity of the modern economy. Price (and import) controls, even of the rough-and-ready kind we had in the 1940s, were an administrative nightmare then; would they not be worse, thirty years on, for there are now hundreds of thousands of prices, each for a product with an ever-increasing number of input costs, shared between it and other products of the same firm? *Would* top managers be getting to grips with production problems? Wouldn't they rather be spending their time pleading with some ignorant bureaucrat – or working out how to switch their output away from products with tight ceilings to those with looser ones? *Would* they toughen their stance – or simply go on as before on the assumption that the whole crazy scheme would collapse soon anyway?

But the saving grace of this scheme would be its very limited extent. It would not cover the public sector – wages there would be controlled by some form of incomes policy, although a successful Type 2 scheme could be extended to nationalised industries once their managers were properly disciplined by profit objectives. It would not apply to the service industries, or any small firms, or any markets strongly affected by price competition from imports; it could in fact be restricted to those products of large firms sold on markets which were either highly concentrated or protected by import controls. And that would be enough, for although the controls would only affect between ten and twenty per cent of the labour force, it is precisely these workers who (together with the public sector, which would be controlled more directly) provide most of the wage leadership. Not surprisingly (because it is their firms which are least subject to the discipline of competition), these workers tend to be better paid, and to get higher wage increases, than the rest.[14] Once hold *them* in check, and you take the pressure of emulation off the rest of the economy, where, outside the public sector, unionisation is low and employers rarely feel obliged to do more than keep in step with wage rises elsewhere.

We are still talking about a large and complex part of the economy. Fortunately it is the giant manufacturing firms which are most suitable for price control, for their own structure of administration provides Head Office with most of the information the control agency would need, and for their own administrative purposes they avoid changing prices often. It would still be a tremendous task to work out price ceilings for all their products; a good way of limiting the task would be to impose ceilings only on *representative* products or product specifications, while carefully monitoring other products and the average price for the range. Then if output was switched away from the controlled product, and/or prices of uncontrolled ones were raised more, the ceilings could be switched accordingly, to defeat the evasion. In this the control agency would have the big advantage that it could expect many buyers to help, by 'blowing the whistle' on evasion (complaints could be confidential, to avoid damaging relations with the supplier); this is not an advantage that a *pay* control agency generally has, as I argued in Chapter 4, Section 1.

The greatest difficulty in price control is probably quite different. There have been many public bodies set up, particularly in the United States, to regulate or supervise some part of the operations of big business, and it has been found that the agency deputed to ride the tiger almost invariably ends up inside it.[15] No doubt with the best intentions, the controller soon looks more like a spokesman. Clearly the price control agency I am proposing would be under enormous pressure from industry to go the same way. Whether it resisted successfully would depend above all on how much counter-pressure there was from politicians, public opinion and small business customers of controlled firms. Regulatory agencies are generally brought into being when some abuse has become a scandal; they mutate after public interest in the matter has waned. It is unlikely that there will be much waning of interest in *this* agency's raison d'etre!

Nonetheless, such a scheme would not work without import controls, if it was only applied on a *national* basis. A *national* price control scheme could not be applied to exports or imports, so that firms which exported much of their output might not feel much constrained by it, and multinationals would be able to evade it to a large extent by arranging their operations so as to export most of what they made within the country and import most of what they sold there; yet major exporters and multinationals tend to be wage leaders. Import controls, however, could be used to prevent multinational evasion; and they would have a less direct but still important effect on exporters. For, as I have shown, one of the strongest inflationary pressures on a laggard is that devaluation (in real terms) makes most of its exporters, and many import-competing firms, highly competitive on price, and this weakens management's bargaining stance. The aim and effect of an import control strategy would be, by improving the balance of payments, to halt or even reverse the devaluation; so, as their sales became less profitable, exporters would toughen their stance. (The same would happen in import-competing industries, except for those which were now protected; and the latter would certainly be under price controls.) Of course, re-valuation would soon depress exports, at least for a time, but there would be ample room to switch into protected home markets, and this would make price control all the easier. Thus the import control strategy, which would make price controls absolutely essential, would at the same time help to make them effective.

And so goodbye to European unity? It need not come to that; as I said earlier, nothing I am proposing for London or Rome could not be as well or better administered, or at all events coordinated, from Brussels by a European Commission under proper parliamentary control.[16] Price controls on multinationals would clearly be more effective on a continental scale. The go-it-alone import control strategy could be replaced by an equally effective, and less disruptive, European strategy:

1. Controls where necessary on imports from outside the Community (there is the Common External Tariff already).
2. General reflation, leaders (i.e. Germany and the Netherlands) first.
3. Some form of protection for weaker industries in the losers (and perhaps elsewhere). This could take the form, in each case, of output controls, investment controls (suitable for very large projects) or import controls agreed between states or decided in Brussels. (The Davignon Plans for steel and textiles have already taken us a long way in this direction.)[17]

However, I doubt if the time is yet ripe for such a European solution. We still lack an effective supranational authority, and without one such a scheme would not work: it is too complex and delicate to be negotiated, let alone administered, by sovereign governments. The best we can realistically hope for is that national schemes of import (and price) control are adopted only after consultation and within a European framework of agreed rules, designed to limit the disruption of trade as far as possible; that would not be bad, for a second best solution.

The vacuum of power at the centre in Europe points to a more general problem which lies at the heart of our double crisis of inflation and depression. Our economic organisations, firms, now operate world-wide, and their movement of goods and capital across frontiers sets the context in which our political organisations, states, operate. Yet these political organisations are much more limited in their geographical scope. Governments' writ does not run outside the frontiers of the nation-state, and so they find themselves trying to deal with the effects of economic forces whose causes are partly outside their territory and thus outside their control.

This situation is not wholly new. The last great era of (relatively) free trade and movement of capital, after the First World War, ended in a depression from which the West began to escape only after a retreat into protection. The switch to protection was disorderly and initially, then as now, made the depression worse. But it placed the responsibility for reflation in each country firmly with that country's government, and at the same time gave governments back their freedom to act. We must learn in the 1980s what should have been clear since the 1930s: that a government which does not control the flow of goods and capital across its frontiers cannot freely choose its economic policy.[18] In the 1930s there was only one solution: control at the boundaries of the nation-state. Now, we have alternatives: either (as then) the market must shrink; or the State must grow.

6.3 CONCLUSION

This book has dealt with two closely related crises, one of theory, one of policy. Both have the problem of inflation at their heart, but both extend far beyond it, indeed far beyond economics.

The crisis of theory arises from the failure of the dominant intellectual current in economics, the Neoclassical School, to provide convincing answers to the most pressing questions of the day; and it is made acute by the fact that these questions are posed by the crisis of policy: the failure to solve the twin problems of inflation and unemployment. The theorists are asked, what should be done; their proposals are put into practice; and they are seen not to work.

The policies fail because the theory is bad; and the theory is bad because it starts from assumptions which, though once half true, are now blatantly false. Today it is absurd to imagine that workers are selling their labour, firms their products, in competitive markets, and with nothing but individual profit in mind. We must assume instead that most wages are *negotiated* between managers and unions (or keep in step with negotiated wages); that most firms are *oligopolists*, with few rivals in each market; and that unions and firms behave unlike individuals and with much more than profit in mind. To make anything of these assumptions, we then have to face the fact that all of them lead us well outside economics, into sociology, psychology, and various kinds of history, and still further afield. These other disciplines are particularly useful in exploring the concepts of concession cost and resistance cost, which explain bargaining power, and thus in approaching what I think is the heart of the matter, the question of wages.

I have argued in four steps: that wage inflation speeds up or slows down in response to shifts in the balance of bargaining power between unions and management; that this balance depends on the *stances* of the two sides; that their stances depend in turn on their concession and resistance costs; and that these costs change and vary according to the economic structure and situation, the industrial relations structure, and the motives of those who have power within the structures. So we must look deeper and wider than a few superficial, economic variables like the rate of unemployment or the supply of money. When we do, we begin to find answers to the most important and mysterious questions about inflation.

– Why has the *trend* of inflation, in most countries, been rising? Because there have been inflationary changes everywhere in *economic structure*: larger firms, higher concentration; and (in most countries) in *industrial relations*: more decentralised and stronger unions, more emphasis on wage comparisons. The bargaining stance of firms has also been softened by changes in cost structures and forms of competition; the unions' has been toughened by changes in the pattern of consumer expenditure.
– What can account for *fluctuations* in inflation in each country?

Changes in capacity utilisation (at home and abroad), in cost-competitiveness in international trade and in voluntary or statutory restraint of wages.
– What can best explain *recent variations* in inflation between Western countries? Differences in industrial relations, economic structure, and social attitudes. What in turn, can explain these differences? First, economic, social and political history; second, each country's experience of the current process of *international polarisation* between 'leaders' and 'laggards'.

It is much more complex, then, this world I have been describing, than the world of neoclassicism and its monetarist offspring. Is it not also much more real? In this real world there are no simple (if harsh) solutions. The causes of fluctuations, I have argued, can only fluctuate: it is either futile or even counter-productive to seek a permanent change in any of them which would reduce inflation. The causes of variations between countries are embedded deep in the history or at best the economic performance of each, and are very hard to alter, impossible to alter quickly. Our best hope is to work upon the causes of the rising trend. To do so most effectively, and least destructively, we have to isolate what is most nearly the root cause, the prime mover, of the change; and that is the change in economic structure.

To roll back this change in structure completely – by breaking up large firms, fragmenting concentrated industries, etc. – is out of the question (though that is not to rule out any move in this direction). We have rather to find some way to offset the change, to counterbalance it. I have put forward such a way, but I have to recognise that it leads, via a harsh paradox, to a cruel dilemma. The discipline of the market upon the wages of large firms can only be restored by the greatest interference with the market activities of those large firms ever seen in peacetime. That is the paradox. Yet the state, which must interfere, extends less far than they do, much less far than their markets. That brings us to the dilemma. If wage discipline is to be restored it can only be by increasing the extent of the state, or reducing the extent of the market. (And one or other of these measures will be necessary to allow the expansion which is the only way to reduce union militancy.) Those are the horns of the dilemma: the market must shrink, or the State must grow.

It is a most unattractive solution. You could say of it, much as Churchill said of democracy, that it is the worst – except for all the others. For I have argued that ultimately no other solution will work – within the limits of our political and social system. We could try to weaken the unions by legal restrictions on their activities, or by increasing unemployment; or we could use compulsory pay restraint to obstruct them directly. But each theory which predicts that one or other of these methods will work, neglects central features of the economic and social structure of our society. They will all fail; in failing they will be economically and socially destructive; and their worst danger is that those who commit themselves intellectually, politically, morally, to their success may be tempted to take desperate measures to *make* them succeed. Desperate measures, as we have seen in South America, may work; may make a desert which some can call peace. Better, though, to face that harsh paradox, and infuriate the loudest defenders (most timid practitioners) of the market economy. And better to face that dilemma, to sacrifice a large part either of national sovereignty, or of free trade. The horns are uncomfortably sharp, but if we do not choose one, we shall fall between, and at the end of that long fall we shall have to bury our democracy.

Appendix

Symbols

$\dot{w}$	percentage change negotiated in average hourly earnings
T	toughness of negotiating stance
m, u	subscripts for management, union
C	concession cost: the cost (broadly defined, i.e. disutility, throughout) resulting from an increase (for m) or a decrease (for u) of 1 per cent point in $\dot{w}$
R	the cost resulting from or required for a decrease (for m) or an increase (for u) in $\dot{w}$
$R \equiv$	R direct $+ R$ indirect $= Rd + J$
$Rd \equiv$	$S.P$
S	strike cost per day
P	the mean of the probability distribution of increases in strike duration required for a 1 per cent point decrease (for m) or increase (for u) in $\dot{w}$
J_m	value of productivity, recruitment, etc., lost due to 1 percentage point fall in $\dot{w}$
J_u	value of job prospects, etc lost due to 1 per cent point rise in $\dot{w}$
em, eu, e	superscripts for *value expected by management, union, both sides*.

We assume:

$$\dot{w} = f(T_u, -T_m) \tag{1}$$

$$T_u = f(C_u^{eu}, -S_u^{eu} \cdot P_u^{eu}, -J_u^{eu}); \quad T_m = f(C_m^{em}, -S_m^{em} \cdot P_m^{em}, -J_m^{em}) \tag{2}$$

$$P_u^{eu} = f(C_m^{eu}, -S_m^{eu}, -J_m^{eu}, \ldots); \quad P_m^{em} = f(C_u^{em}, -S_u^{em}, -J_u^{em}, \ldots) \tag{3}$$

[Equation (2) can be deduced from a number of simpler and obviously plausible assumptions: that the aim in choosing T is to minimise the integral of $C + R$ for the actual value of $\dot{w}$; that R^e is a decreasing (for m) or increasing (for u) function of $\dot{w}$, and C^e an increasing (decreasing)

192

function of it. Thus T will be set to give $R^e = C^e$, and the point at which this will be true will be a function of C^e and the components of R^e, as in equation (2). The missing determinants which appear from equation (3) onwards arise from the circular complexities of decisions by m being based on m's expectations about u's expectations. . . . These can be shown to reinforce rather than weaken the effect of the 'underlying' factors set out.]

We deduce:

$$T_u = f(C_u^{eu}, -C_m^{eu}, S_m^{eu}, -S_u^{eu}, J_m^{eu}, -J_u^{eu}, \ldots); \tag{4}$$

$$T_m = f(C_m^{em}, -C_u^{em}, S_u^{em}, -S_m^{em}, J_u^{em}, -J_m^{em}, \ldots)$$

and from equations (1) and (4)

$$\dot{w} = f(C_u^e, -C_m^e, S_m^e, -S_u^e, J_m^e, -J_u^e, \ldots). \tag{5}$$

In the econometrics described below I made no attempt to estimate expected values as such, but took them to correspond to actual values in so far as I could measure these. However, I chose determinants which I thought the relevant party could hope to gauge with reasonable accuracy.

RELATIVE WAGE INFLATION, BETWEEN INDUSTRIES
(see Tylecote, 1975).

The first phase was to try to identify variations in determinants of $\dot{w}$ between industries, over a given period, and use them to explain variations in $\dot{w}$: cross-section regression analysis. To summarise: The dependent variable $\dot{w}$ was the percentage rate of change of average hourly earnings (AHE) of adult male manual workers in 58 manufacturing industries in the UK, 1954–70. The main independent variables were proxies for C_m and S_m:

Cr, a measure of absolute firm concentration; it was expected that high Cr made for low C_m, and thus high $\dot{w}$.

L, a measure of the ratio of total selling price to the manual wage cost component. High $L \to$ low $C_m \to$ high $\dot{w}$.

Sc, a measure of the ratio of non-wage value-added to the manual wage bill. [L and Sc are distinct and not very highly correlated ($r = 0.6$) since one relates to gross, the other to net output.] Since the former was normally a loss to the firm during a strike, while the latter was saved, high $Sc \rightarrow$ high $S_m \rightarrow$ high $\dot{w}$.

It was found, indeed, that these three variables, above all Cr and L, explained about 50 per cent of variations in $\dot{w}$ among the 58 industries. However, it seemed likely that these factors would explain more in industries which were strongly organised and thus conformed closely to our bargaining model's assumptions, than in the weakly organised ones where J_m would presumably play the major role. What was required was a proxy for strength of union organisation, by which industries could be *weighted* so that the regression results would be more affected by the more strongly organised ones. Union density figures were not available; instead I used Es, the average number of adult male manual workers per establishment (for rationale see Chapter 3, Section 1). Weighting by Es pushed $\overline{R}^2$ above 0·8 (see Table A1, 'Core Model'). Slight further improvements in fit were gained by introducing as additional independent variables Es, and W (the initial level of AHE): Es should serve as proxy for S_m, and P_m: high $Es \rightarrow$ high S_m, $P_m \rightarrow$ high $\dot{w}$. High wages should make workers relatively content. So high $W \rightarrow$ low $C_u \rightarrow$ low $\dot{w}$. (Also, arguably, high $W \rightarrow$ low J_m, high $J_u \rightarrow$ low $\dot{w}$.)

All the variables were indeed highly significant and correctly signed in the weighted regressions ('Full Model'), except for W, which was marginally significant. I then introduced three more variables favoured by others.

$\dot{P}$, the average annual rate of increase of labour productivity over the period;

Pr, the proportion of the relevant workers *paid by results*;

$\dot{E}$, the rate of change of employment in the industry over the period.

$\dot{P}$ is seen in some bargaining models (perhaps with Japan in mind) as, in effect, a determinant of C_m – high $\dot{P} \rightarrow$ low C_m – though the arguments seem to me unconvincing. Pr is seen by e.g. Lydall (H. F. Lydall (1958), 'Inflation and the Earnings gap', *BOUIES*, vol. 20, pp. 283–304) as a factor pushing up W steadily and not fully compensated for in bargains; again unconvincing. $\dot{E}$ should proxy the pressure of demand for labour fairly well (the alternative view that it rather reflects labour supply implies absurd over-estimates of labour supply variations, and of supply constraints or employer sensitivity to those variations as expressed in differential W). All three performed poorly in the weighted regressions. (Table A1 only shows E; the other two were weaker still). This tended to confirm my view of P and Pr and to suggest that for well-organised

TABLE A.1

The figure given for each independent variable is its coefficient, with (in brackets) its t statistic for significance. The proportionate effect of a change in the independent variable on the dependent variable, w (the rate of change of hourly earnings) can be calculated by multiplying its mean by its coefficient.

Independent variable	Mean (weighted)	Core model	Full model	Agnostic model
Constant		2·94 (65·26)	3·31 (13·44)	3·39 (12·35)
Cr	77·91	0·00356 (3·86)	0·00261 (2·35)	0·00266 2·36)
L	10·93	0·0226 (10·14)	0·0216 (9·88)	0·025 (5·90)
Sc	1·97	0·0567 (2·98)	0·0458 (2·42)	0·0312 (1·15)
Es	342·70		0·00000177 (2·05)	0·00000180 (1·65)
$\dot{E}$	53·01		−0·00789 (1·78)	−0·00926 (1·93)
R	−19·78			0·000236 (0·63)
Degrees of Freedom		54	52	51
F statistic		98·96	65·55	52·40
Corrected R^2		0·84	0·85	0·85

workers the effect of $\dot{E}$ on $\dot{w}$ through J_m and J_u $\left(\text{high } \dot{E} \rightarrow \dfrac{\text{high } J_m}{\text{low } J_u} \right.$ $\left. \rightarrow \text{high } \dot{w} \right)$ was cancelled out in the long run by the escalator/mobility effects (see Chapter 3, Section 1 and Chapter 4, Section 2); roughly, high $\dot{E} \rightarrow$ low $C_u \rightarrow$ low $\dot{w}$. However when the weighting was reversed to $1/Es$, to emphasise weakly organised industries, $\dot{E}$ was significant and correctly signed: there, predictably, the effect through J is dominant.

My more recent unpublished work, for the later, 1959–75 period, has generally confirmed the above results, and added a further significant group of determinants: 'foreign trade exposure' variables. The argument is that as UK industry grows more exposed to foreign competition, Cr is less adequate as an index of *effective* concentration. Measures of export ratios and import penetration, and changes in them, were used to supplement Cr as proxies for C_m. The import variables were correctly signed and significant; the export variables were insignificant (presumably because they also proxy *success*, which has opposite effect on $\dot{w}$).

WAGE INFLATION OVER TIME (see Tylecote, 1976)

This required the use of the econometric technique most popular with economists and most notorious with statisticians: time-series regression analysis. This suffers from two faults which are both much less acute in cross-section work: (1) the existence of many variables correlated with the dependent variables, for most of which the relationship is more-or-less accidental; (2) where there *is* a causal relationship between variables, it is more complex than is shown by the simple Indep. → Dep. link assumed by ordinary least squares (OLS) regression. (For further criticism of time series analysis, see Wiener (1964), *God and Golem, Inc.: A comment on certain points where cybernetics impinges on religion* (Cambridge, Mass: MIT Press), quoted in Robinson (1977)).

These problems cannot be remedied simply by greater sophistication of technique. The use of two-stage least squares, for example, may merely replace one over-simplified causal assumption with another, slightly less over-simplified, and does not touch the first problem. I preferred to use the simplest technique, OLS, with two precautions: first, making sure that the lags employed on independent variables were sufficient to exclude reverse causation – e.g. 1973(i) price inflation may be affected by 1973(i) wage inflation, but scarcely by 1974(i) wage inflation, to which a 1-year lag connects it; second, checking that the value of the Durbin–Watson statistic for autocorrelation of residuals was not such as to suggest mis-specification of the equation. A third precaution, most useful of all, was to build a model in which I had full confidence *a priori*, by reasoning (in the language of Chapter 1, Section 1) downwards and sideways as well as upwards. (It turns out that I have been something of a Bayesian without knowing it. See L. D. Phillips (1973) *Bayesian Methods for Social Scientists* (London: Nelson) and A. Zellner (1971) *Bayesian Methods in Econometrics* (New York: Wiley)).

$\dot{w}$ was again, percentage change in average hourly earnings, for male manual workers in UK manufacturing industry; this time the period was 1959–75, the observations were 6-monthly, and there was adjustment for the effect of overtime.

The main independent variables used were $\dot{P}$, the rate of retail price inflation, with a distributed lag of $1-2\frac{1}{2}$ years; w/w, the level of average weekly earnings of private-sector manual workers, relative to those in the public sector, with a simple lag of 1 year (other lags are 6 months unless specified, except for the dummies, which are unlagged); Ot: the rate of overtime working; Hu: the level of capacity utilisation (standard measure); U: the percentage of manufacturing labour force registered as unemployed (lagged 1 year); Tc: the ratio of weighted average export prices of manufactures for major competitors to those for the UK; π: profitability in manufacturing (pre-tax gross trading profits, percentage of total corporate value-added); Fu: the weighted average level of capacity utilisation in industry in other industrial countries; Li: liquidity (current assets/current liabilities in large manufacturing firms); Id: incomes policy dummy, value 1 during statutory incomes policy (1966(ii)–1970(i), 1972(ii)–1974(ii)), otherwise 0; Sd: seasonal dummy, value 1 in the winter 6 months, 0 in the summer.

In later regressions $\dot{P}$ was replaced by $\dot{P}s$, which is $\dot{P}$ with a distributed lag which becomes slightly shorter over the period (reflecting assumed quicker responses to price inflation), and Id was replaced by Idw, which is Id weighted by a factor based on the values of Tc, W/w and Ot. (The assumption is that incomes policy ceilings make most difference when $\dot{w}$ would otherwise have been high, which depends on the values of other variables, of which Tc, W/w and Ot seemed 'stronger' – $\dot{P}$ was ignored because it was assumed that ceilings made some allowance for prevailing rates of price inflation.) Fits were already good with $\dot{P}$ and Id but still better with $\dot{P}s$ and Idw. The argument is, then, that:

$$C_m = f(Tc, \pi, Fu, Li, Idw); \quad S_m = f(Ot, Hu, Li, Sd); \quad J_m = f(U, Ot);$$
$$c_u = f(\dot{P}s, U, Idw, W/w); \quad S_u = f(Ot, Sd); \quad J_u = f(U, Sd)$$

such that all variables except Id, W/w and Idw are positively signed (note that the predictions of negative sign on Li and positive sign on U are 'perverse' in orthodox terms).

The preferred equation leaves out Hu as too highly correlated (0·77) with Ot (and not significant when 'alongside' it) and the result is (in brackets, t values; beta coefficients):

$$\dot{w} = -82\cdot09 + 0\cdot03\,Ot\,(1\cdot88;\,0\cdot38) + 0\cdot14\pi(0\cdot71;\,0\cdot10) + 1\cdot75\,U$$
$$(3\cdot54;\,0\cdot35) + 1\cdot62\,Fu\,(3\cdot49;\,0\cdot38) + 0\cdot39\,Tc\,(5\cdot73;\,0\cdot48)$$
$$+ 0\cdot75\,\dot{P}s\,(2\cdot10;\,0\cdot44) + 0\cdot02\,Li\,(0\cdot32;\,0\cdot11) - 0\cdot52\,W/w$$
$$(3\cdot62;\,-0\cdot35) - 0\cdot73\,Idw\,(6\cdot17;\,-0\cdot46) - 1\cdot07\,Sd\,(2\cdot86;\,-0\cdot17)$$

$\overline{R}^2$ 0·91; D.W. statistic 1·90; F stat. 33·66; degrees of freedom 22; correlation determinant 0·00015.

Thus all but Li (which is thoroughly insignificant) have the predicted sign. $U, Fu, Tc, \dot{P}s, W/w, Idw$ and Sd are significant at the 95 per cent level, and Ot very nearly so. The following points are of interest.

The coefficient on prices is, plausibly, below 1 but not very far. U is 'perversely' signed and supports my case on unemployment. The high beta coefficients on W/w and Tc indicate the importance of emulation and the disastrous effect of devaluation, respectively. The coefficient on Idw is misleading because of the weighting factor: it in fact implies that statutory incomes policy, while 'on', reduces $\dot{w}$ on average by between 5 and 6 per cent points, a large but plausible figure. The fit is extremely good and the D.W. statistic indicates no autocorrelation of residuals.

Notes

NOTES TO CHAPTER 1

1. Alfred Marshall, of Cambridge, was the foremost of the British neoclassical economists; Walras, of those on the Continent of Europe. See E. Roll (1973), *A History of Economic Thought*, 4th ed. (London: Faber & Faber) ch. VIII, for an uncontentious account of their doctrines; Joan Robinson (1972), for a highly critical one.
2. See A. Marshall [1890] (1916), Books V and VI – or almost any modern introductory textbook.
3. Ibid., Book V on prices, Book VI (chs III–IV) on wages.
4. Cf. Joan Robinson (1972), Introduction.
5. The main exception was Sweden, where economists building on the tradition of Wicksell anticipated much of Keynes' work. (The spur was similar – socio-political normality, and high unemployment.) See B. Gustafsson (1973), 'A Perennial of Doctrinal History: Keynes and "the Stockholm School" ', *Economy and History*.
6. See, for example, Pollard (1969), chs 3 and 4.
7. A. C. Pigou (1931), 'Limiting Factors in Wage Rates', pp. 20–34 in Pigou and Robertson (1931).
8. See D. E. Moggridge (1976), *Keynes* (London: Fontana), for landmarks along this road.
9. J. M. Keynes (1936), particularly ch. 19.
10. See J. Robinson (1972); L. L. Pasinetti (1974), *Growth and Income Distribution: Essays in Economic Theory* (Cambridge: CUP); R. F. Kahn (1973), *Selected Essays on Employment and Growth* (Cambridge: CUP); and A. S. Eichner (ed.) (1979), *A Guide to Post-Keynesian Economics* (London: Macmillan).
11. See A. Leijonhufvud (1969), *Keynes and the Classics* (London: IEA) p. 20 citing Samuelson, 'A Brief Survey of Post-Keynesian Developments', in R. Lekachman (ed.) (1969), *Keynes' General Theory; Reports of Three Decades* (New York: Macmillan), p. 332.
12. See A. M. Ross (1948), and J. T. Dunlop (1944). For the hostility see ch. 3 below.
13. See ch. 3 below.
14. See J. C. R. Dow (1964), *The Management of the British Economy 1945–60* (Cambridge: NIESR) Part I.
15. In the first group was Barbara Wootton (1955), *Social Foundations of Wage Policy* (London: Allen & Unwin).
16. In A. W. Phillips (1958).

17. See Pigou (1931).
18. On the role of expectations in modern inflation theory, see H. Frisch (1977), 'Inflation Theory 1963–1975: A "Second-Generation" Survey', *JEL*, pp. 1289–317, section IV.
19. For a definition of the 'natural rate' of unemployment see Friedman (1968), p. 8; for criticism of the concept see F. H. Hahn (1971), 'Professor Friedman's Views on Money', *Eca.*, February, pp. 61–80, and H. Otruba (1974), 'The Optimum Quantity of Money: A Delayed Criticism', *Zeitschrift der Nationalökonomie*, pp. 125–36; for further discussion see ch. 4, sect. 2 and ch. 4, sect. 3 below.
20. See Friedman (1968) and Phelps (1967).
21. See M. Kalecki (1939), *Essays in the Theory of Economic Fluctuations* (London: Allen & Unwin) for his contribution, or the discussion in Joan Robinson (1977).
22. Simon and March (1958), p. 141.
23. On bilateral monopoly see e.g. J. Johnston (1972), 'A Model of Wage Determination under Bilateral Monopoly', *EJ*, September, pp. 832–52.
24. 'A theory cannot be tested by comparing its "assumptions" directly with "reality" '; rather, 'a hypothesis can be tested only by the conformity of its implications or predictions with observable phenomena'; it is futile to have as 'objective . . . a set of assumptions that are "more" realistic.' M. Friedman, 'The Methodology of Positive Economics', in Friedman (1953), pp. 32, 40 and 41.
25. See Appendix.
26. See for example Alfred Marshall (1916), p. 316, discussed in Joan Robinson (1977). For a denunciation of theorising from unrealistic assumptions, by one of the most distinguished of modern economists, see W. W. Leontief (1973), 'Theoretical Assumptions and Nonobserved Facts', *AER*, vol. 61, pp. 1–7.
27. See Kuhn (1970).
28. For their procedure see Kuhn (1970).
29. E. H. Phelps Brown (1972), 'The Underdevelopment of Economics', *EJ*, March, pp. 1–10; address given 8 July 1971.
30. Ibid., p. 9.
31. The difference between this approach and the methodology of positive economics is similar to that between Bayesian and conventional, 'classical' statistics. (Friedman is a distinguished 'classical' statistician.) On Bayesian statistics see references in Appendix.
32. See Appendix for a brief mathematical summary of the bargaining theory which is described in this section.
33. I take 'union' to mean any association of workers, however loose or informal, which is prepared to exert pressure upon the employer.
34. An equivalent schema for the non-union employer's wage policy is (with a causal chain from left to right): [see facing page]
35. This is not to say that BF cannot increase its prices a little, at first – that depends on its competitive position – but the fact of increasing its wages doesn't give it any *more* scope to do so.

Wages and unionisation elsewhere	Employer's costs		Wage increase
HIGH ⟶	**LOW** Concession **HIGH** Indirect resistance		HIGH
LOW ⟶	**LOW** Indirect resistance **HIGH** Concession		LOW

36. If it is a satisficer this toughening will only take place after it falls below its 'satisfactory' level of profits.
37. Thus the balance of bargaining power in different firms, as expressed in the rate of wage increases, *tends to equality*; the nearer they are, in terms of competition and wage comparisons, the faster the convergence.
38. See ch. 3 and ch. 5, sect. 3.
39. But if there was to be a return to the old system of fixed exchange rates – inside the proposed European Monetary System – the effect would be slower; in fact if the rates were really fixed, come what may, there would be virtually no effect on import costs at all. This would obstruct the wage-price spiral just as a large non-union sector may obstruct the wage-wage effect. For stable import costs help to keep retail prices down, and home producers find themselves a sort of international British Fordsler, forced by competition to hold down first their prices, then, as a result, their wages. But the cost of not budging, or reduced competitiveness, is higher unemployment and lower profits first, then lower investment and higher unemployment. In the past this has always, in the end, forced governments to let the exchange rate adjust; this removed the blockage, and the wage-price spiral went ahead all the faster as the prices and wages which had been held back, caught up with the rest. For Britain, North Sea oil has delayed this effect; it has not abolished it.
40. I have made one omission: those prices, or parts of prices, charged by the self-employed – doctors, perhaps, or electricians. It is easiest to treat these as wages; if the group concerned are well organised, then they are like the wages of a strong union, which will (at worst) keep closely in line with the rest; if the group is badly organised, like perhaps peasant farmers in a poor country, then, like non-union workers, they may be at the mercy of market forces. They belong in the union or non-union sector accordingly.
41. A recent study of US wage inflation (Flanagan (1978)) found that once wage-wage effects were taken into account there was a sharp reduction in the estimated effect of prices on wages. Gordon (1977), pp. 253 ff found that US wage-inflation was better explained by product prices (which affect firms' concession costs) than by consumer prices. He could explain it very well by adding just one more variable, the change in the margin of spare capacity – which itself affects the scope for passing on wage increases in prices.

NOTES TO CHAPTER TWO

In most of this section the argument is essentially the same as that in a discussion paper (Tylecote (1977), 'Managers, Owners and Bankers in British and German Industry: Causes of the German Industrial Superiority') which is already copiously documented, and will be developed in a forthcoming article. For that part I shall therefore save space by giving no references here.

1. C. H. Wilson, quoted in Shonfield (1965), p. 261.
2. Quoted in Taylor (1961).
3. Winschuh, quoted in Hartmann (1959), p. 242.
4. Stein (ed.) (1954), pp. 10–11.
5. K. Pritzkoleit (1963), *Die Neue Herren* (Munich: Desch), p. 164.
6. See ch. 3 below.
7. See ch. 3 below.
8. Cf. Ward and George (1975), pp. 25–6.
9. See Adams and Rosenbaum (1962), pp. 162–4.
10. British Institute of Management (1976), *Front-line Management* (London).
11. See A. Nicholson (1976), 'The British Production Cinderella: 1, Causes', *Management Today*, June, and K. Lockyer (1976), 'The British Production Cinderella: 2, Effects', *Management Today*, June.
12. See Lockyer (1976) op. cit., and 'Decline and Fall in Salary Trends'. *Engineering Today*, 9 May 1977.
13. J. Levy (1976), *The Education of Graduate Mechanical Engineers* (London: City University).
14. Child *et al.* (1978); Granick (1975).
15. Partridge (1979).
16. Fores *et al.* (1978), 'Germany's Front-line Force', *Management Today*, March, pp. 86–9; Agartz (1973), ch. 3; and Hartmann (1959), pp. 175–85.
17. Hartmann (1959), p. 157.
18. See ch. 3 below.
19. See W. Patman (1963), *Chain Banking: Stockholder and Loan Links of 200 Largest Member Banks* (Washington).
20. See E. J. Epstein (1975), 'The Rockefellers', *Sunday Times Magazine*, 12 December, and C. L. Schwartz (1975), *International Socialist Review*, January, pp. 12–37.
21. See article by Kramer (1974), *Wall Street Journal*, 21 October, p. 8.
22. See Schwartz (1975); and G. C. Zilg (1974), *Dupont: Behind the Nylon Curtain* (New York: Prentice-Hall).
23. See Patman (1963); Schwartz (1975); and *FT*, 20 January 1978.
24. Patman (1963); Pahl and Winkler, in P. Stanworth and A. Giddens (eds) (1974), *Elites and Power in British Society* (London), p. 108.
25. Except in the most competitive sectors. See Flanagan (1976), pp. 667–9.
26. See e.g. Mitchell (1978), p. 575 on the rubber industry.
27. See ch. 3, sect. 2 below.
28. See e.g. report, *FT*, 20 February 1979, p. 30.
29. See ch. 3, sect. 2.
30. On the growing competition with the Big 3 see 'Survey of German Banking', *FT*, 27 March 1979, particularly p. 22. On the increasing political challenge to the industrial power of the banks see e.g. G. Hawtin (1979), 'Call to cut industrial stake alarms German banks', *FT*, 9 April, p. 32.

31. See Hannah (1976), chs 1 and 2.
32. Ibid., on the evolution of markets between the late 19th century and the present day.
33. On modern oligopoly see e.g. F. M. Scherer (1970), *Industrial Market Structure and Economic Performances* (Chicago: Rand McNally).
34. In consumer markets, the 'differentiation' is produced mostly by advertising, so that customers will probably switch to rivals straight away; that will be even worse, for once their 'brand loyalty' is broken they will be hard to win back.
35. Through the organisation of Japanese firms in *Zaibatsu* and their successors: groups of enterprises in different fields with a degree of central coordination and a commitment to buy from one another whenever possible; see M. Y. Yoshino (1968), *Japan's Managerial System* (Cambridge, Mass.: MIT Press) ch. 5.
36. See e.g. A. B. Laffer (1969), 'Vertical Integration by Corporations, 1929–65', *RES*, February, pp. 91–3 on the USA.
37. See Ward and George (1975).
38. Adam Smith [1776] (1950), *Wealth of Nations* (London: Cannon ed.) vol. I, p. 75. If the reader is wearying of quotations from *The Wealth of Nations*, I apologise; that was the last. I hope they have served incidentally to suggest how far from a neoclassical economist Adam Smith was.
39. See e.g. Clegg, Fox and Thompson (1964).
40. It appears from the modest response of sales to large changes in exchange rates (see ch. 5 below) that international oligopolists either cooperate effectively or have no need to – perhaps because of the product differentiation discussed below.
41. There can be world-wide oligopoly without world-wide free trade, if multinationals straddle trade barriers – as they do. This makes cooperation particularly easy.
42. See C. Wilcox (1966), *Public Policies towards Business* (Irwin) especially pp. 472–3.
43. See e.g. Blair (1972), ch. 13.
44. See ch. 3. The alternative, paying 'well' – relative to other firms and occupations – is by definition only possible for some employers.
45. Even within the US, union density varies between over 35 per cent in some Northern states, to under 10 per cent in the Carolinas (US Department of Labour, 1978).
46. The lowest density in any country of Western Europe is over 20 per cent, in France. (See next section.)
47. R. J. Hall and C. J. Hitch (1939), 'Price Theory and Business Behaviour', *OEP*, May; A. D. H. Kaplan, J. B. Dirlam and R. F. Lanzilotti (1955), *Pricing in Big Business* (New York: Brookings Institution), esp. pp. 130 ff.
48. Kaplan *et al.* (1955), and J. Blair (1972), pp. 475–97.
49. See the argument of Rothschild, 'Price Theory and Oligopoly', in G. Stigler and K. Boulding (eds) (1952), *Readings in Price Theory* (New York: Irwin), pp. 455–61.
50. See the arguments in ch. 1, sect. 3 and ch. 3, sect. 3.
51. See P. W. S. Andrews (1949), *Manufacturing Business* (London: Macmillan) ch. 5.
52. See Blair (1972), pp. 475–97.

53. See National Economic Development Office (1977).
54. See T. Hultgren (1965), *Costs, Prices and Profits: Their Cyclical Relations* (New York: NBER) esp. Tables 21, 24 and 26.
55. See Blair (1972) pp. 419–37.
56. See *FT* reports, 9 June 1978, 5 July 1978, 8 August 1978 and 25 September 1978.
57. For an argument predicting such structural responses, see A. Phillips, 'Structure, conduct and performance – and performance, conduct and structure?', in J. W. Markham and G. F. Papanek (eds) (1970), *Industrial Organisation and Economic Development* (New York: Houghton Mifflin).
58. Export prices are more sensitive to the cycle than domestic ones (OECD, June 1977, p. 62).
59. For evidence for counter-cyclical pricing in concentrated industries see Blair (1972).
60. W. Godley and W. D. Nordhaus (1972), 'Pricing in the Trade Cycle', *EJ*, September, and K. Coutts, R. Tarling and F. Wilkinson (1976), 'Costs and Prices 1974–76', *EPR*, March.
61. See G. C. Means *et al.* (1975), *The Roots of Inflation: the International Crisis. . . .* (London: Wilton House) Introduction, ch. 1 and Appendix.

NOTES TO CHAPTER 3

The arguments in this section, like those of ch. 2, sect. 1, closely follow those in a discussion paper (Tylecote (1980), 'A New Theory of Union Density', (University of Sheffield Division of Economic Studies DP 80.12) and forthcoming article. As these are copiously documented I shall save space by keeping the notes here very few and brief.

1. They can indeed do any of these things without formal membership of any union, and strictly speaking I use 'union' and 'unionisation' here and elsewhere to mean informal as well as formal organisation of workers.
2. Cf. Nickel (1973), p. 215, and Dahrendorf (1956), p. 63.
3. Cf. Hinton (1974), p. 94.
4. See Nickel (1973), p. 174, and G. K. Ingham (1970), *Size of Industrial Organisation and Worker Behaviour* (Cambridge: CUP).
5. A fast escalator also reduces the number of workers with long personal experience of industrial labour, who show much the highest propensity to unionise (Nickel (1973), p. 120) if only because they have had a longer time to join (ibid., p. 259).
6. Racism can be seen as a rational response to advantage gained from discrimination (D. J. Wellman (1978), *Portraits of White Racism* (London: CUP)).
7. See for example Bain and El Sheikh (1976).
8. There may, however, be a *compositional* effect in the other direction, where non-unionists – marginal workers in marginal firms – are most likely to be fired in a recession, hired in a boom.
9. Unions may *favour* minimum wage laws, for the benefit of the workers concerned or to protect unionised employers and *their* workers from

'undercutting'. Either way, the implication is that they won't be able to unionise the low-paid workers whatever happens. This attitude is typical of US unions, which are not only weak but seem mostly not much interested in organising the more downtrodden groups. British unions have tended to oppose legal minima. (So have Swedish).

10. Union density in the USA is lower in states with 'right-to-work' laws outlawing compulsory union membership (R. L. Miller (1976)).

11. Note that it is when people *believe* about social mobility, etc., that counts. The facts of the situation influence beliefs, but so do other things; there will certainly be a delay before perceptions catch up with changes in actual mobility.

12. See Fig. 3.1.

13. 1930, 21.9 per cent; 1940, 25.4 per cent; 1945, 36.1 per cent; 1947, 27.9 per cent; 1974, 39.4 per cent.

14. In 1940 30 per cent of them were married and living with their husbands; in 1975, 58 per cent.

15. See Fig. 3.1.

16. The most important single change was Kennedy's Executive Order 10988 in January 1962 on union representation of federal employees.

17. Which is one reason for the surge in unionisation everywhere just after each world war (Fig. 3.1).

18. A 'median estimate' of illegal aliens in the USA was 8 million, of which 5.2 million were guessed as Mexicans (Briggs *et al.* (1977)).

19. The Mexicans went mainly to the south-west (ibid.).

20. 'Right-to-work' laws exist in a majority of Sunbelt states, a minority elsewhere (Miller (1976)).

21. Mexicans' earnings, though very low for the US, are far higher than in Mexico; the difference between the two countries in income per head is enormous (Briggs *et al.* (1977)).

22. These effects are *direct*, where blacks are treated better than Mexicans, in return (implicitly) for separate organisation, or none; *indirect*, where firms in a 'Mexican area' like S. Texas pay less than rivals in a 'black area' like Detroit.

23. See Fig. 3.1.

24. Married women made up only 18.0 per cent of the *female* labour force in 1950

25. Ludendorff and Hitler, unlike British governments, had preferred to keep married women out of the wartime labour force. By 1975 they made up 57.2 per cent of the female labour force.

26. By the late 1960s density among immigrants was similar to that among natives (Bergmann and Müller-Jentsch, in S. Barkin (ed.) (1975)).

27. FDP leaders (see *Frankfurter Rundschau*, 28 March 1978).

28. For a comparison of the legal situation of commonwealth immigrants to Britain, and non-EEC immigrants to Germany, see Castles & Kosack (1973), pp. 98–107.

29. Promotion from the shop floor used to be unusually easy in Britain (Granick (1975)); in making it difficult, Britain has only fallen back into line. What is unusual now – and disastrous for industrial relations – is the technical ignorance of the new graduate managers (see A. Mant (1977)),

The Rise and Fall of the British Manager (London: Macmillan), and ch. 2, sect. 1).

30. M. Massenet (1970), 'Les travailleurs étrangers en France . . .', *Hommes et Migrations, Documents*, no. 793, 1 September, estimated that foreigners made up 20 per cent of manual workers in manufacturing.
31. The Workers' Statute of 20 May 1970 marked the turning point in state policy towards unions in Italy.
32. See Peper, in Barkin (ed.) (1975), ch. 4; and Kruijt and Goddijn, in A. J. den Hollander (ed.) (1962), *Drift en Koers* (Assen: van Gorzum).
33. Catholics tended initially to be near the bottom, coming mainly from the more backward South and East.
34. Figure 3.3 shows the relatively good position of agricultural workers in the Netherlands.
35. See ch. 5, sect. 2.
36. The state's friendship is not unconditional, however. It has not, for example, interfered with the rather pro-managerial judgments of the Labour Court, and has at times put heavy pressure on the unions for discipline and moderation (Korpi (1978)).
37. For how members and stewards see the stewards' function in the UK, see McCarthy and Parker (1968).
38. Beynon (1973). CIR Study 2 (1973) Table 15, shows a high correlation between shop steward activity and size of establishment; higher than that shown in Table 14 (ibid.) between *unionisation* and size.
39. In a 1971 survey in the UK, 94 per cent of the workers who were in plants with unions recognised by management, had stewards recognised by them too (CIR Study 2 (1973) Tables 13 and 14). A substantial minority of these stewards were not even recognised as such by their unions! Seventy-four per cent of managers in a 1972 survey *preferred* stewards to local union officials as negotiating partners on workplace issues (von Beyme (1977), p. 70).
40. See H. Braverman (1974), *Labour and Monopoly Capital* (New York: Monthly Review Press), and D. Wray (1949), 'Marginal Men of Industry: the Foreman', *American Journal of Sociology*, pp. 298–310.
41. J. G. Rayback (1965), *A History of American Labor*, 2nd ed. (New York: Macmillan) pp. 396–400, and P. L. Taft (1964), *Organised Labor in American History* (New York: Harper & Row) p. 588.
42. See e.g. Beynon (1973), pp. 66 and 309–16 on Ford's attempts in Britain to copy their methods in the US.
43. See Child *et al.* (1978).
44. In a large 1973 sample, 46 per cent of foremen, as against 59 per cent of employees, were union members (Parker (1975), Table 1).
45. Beynon (1973), p. 156.
46. See Hinton (1973), pp. 56–102.
47. For the effects of the war on industry and labour, see Pribicevic (1959), pp. 32–7, and Hinton (1973), ch. 1.
48. See Hinton (1973), pp. 48–55.
49. See Pribicevic (1959), p. 35, and Hinton (1973), pp. 73–6.
50. See Hinton (1973), Part II, and pp. 332–4.
51. Ibid., ch. 9.

52. Ibid., pp. 270–1, Pribicevic (1959), p. 103.
53. Ibid., pp. 37–8.
54. Ibid., pp. 38–40 and 53–64.
55. See A. Bullock (1967), *The Life and Times of Ernest Bevin* (London: Heinemann) vol. II.
56. H M. Pelling (1976), *History of British Trade Unionism* (London) ch. 11.
57. My judgement; see ch. 2, sect. 1.
58. G. Goodman (1969), *Brother Frank: the Man and the Union* (London: Panther).
59. For an example of T&G support for their stewards, see Beynon (1973), chs 3 and 10.
60. Out of 22½ million employees in civilian employment in 1971, there was a total of about 350,000 'workplace representatives' of which about 60,000 were non-union. The growth since the early 1960s had been 'substantial'. (CIR Study 2 (1973), pp. 3–4.)
61. McCarthy *et al.* (1971), *The Reform of Collective Bargaining at Plant and Company Level* (London: HMSO) D.E. Manpower Papers no. 5.
62. Wilders and Parker (1975), and Daniel (1976), ch. III.
63. Pryor (1972).
64. On the difference of attitude to unions between foreign-born and native Americans, see Rosenblum (1973), ch. 6, *passim.*
65. See ch. 2, sect. 1 above.
66. Galenson and Smith, in Dunlop and Smith (eds.) (1978), ch. 1.
67. Ibid.
68. See J. Steiber (1968), 'Unauthorised Strikes in the American and British Industrial Relations Systems', *BJIR*, July, and H. A. Turner (1969), *Is Britain Really Strike Prone?* (London: CUP).
69. This is also the conclusion of Rosen, in Barkin (ed.) (1975), ch. 10.
70. On the nature of Swedish unions and their workplace organisation, see van Otter, in Barkin (ed.) (1975), and Korpi (1978).
71. On the prevalence of PBR see e.g. Korpi (1978), p. 359.
72. For the background of Swedish industry and industrialists, see L. Jörberg, in S. Koblik (ed. 1975), *Sweden's Development from Poverty to Affluence, 1750–1970* (Minneapolis: University of Minnesota Press) ch. 4, pp. 92 ff, Heckscher (1954), pp. 250–1, and Myers, in Harbison and Myers (eds) (1959), ch. 15.
73. See Korpi (1978), p. 356.
74. 'The employer is entitled to direct and distribute the work, to hire and dismiss workers at will, and to employ workers whether they are organised or not . . .' – clause which SAF rules insist – with the support of the Labour Courts – be included in all collective agreements (van Otter, in Barkin (ed.) 1975), p. 202. On strike compensation and on illegality of unofficial strikes, see Korpi (1978), pp. 361–3.
75. Korpi (1978), pp. 356–7.
76. Ibid., conclusion, p. 366.
77. Skandinaviska Enskilda Banken (1975/6), *Some Data about Sweden*, p. 16.
78. See van Otter, in Barkin (ed.) (1975), pp. 213–16.
79. For the opposition of *French* employers, see H. Lesire-Ogrel (1967), *Le Syndicat dans L'Entreprise* (Paris: Edns. du Seuil).

80. The Comité d'Entreprise as such was set up in February 1945 by an Ordonnance in order to contain the committees spontaneously set up by the workers themselves (CIR Study 4 (1974), pp. 45–8). An Act of December 1968 gave unions the right to establish *union sections* for representative purposes (ibid., pp. 480–9). On employers' neglect of the first in the 1960s and the second in the 1970s, see ibid., pp. 51–3.

81. M. Seeman (1972), 'The Signals of 68: Alienation in Pre-Crisis France', *American Sociological Review*, 57, pp. 387–402.

82. See Brandini, in Barkin (ed.) (1975), p. 86 and CIR Study 4 (1974), pp. 99–101. The Italian term is *commissione interna*, internal commission.

83. See CIR Study 4 (1974), pp. 100–5, and Regalia *et al.*, 'Labour Conflicts and Industrial Relations in Italy', in Crouch and Pizzorno (eds) (1978).

84. Ibid.

85. Ibid., on changes in the bargaining structure; also Brandini, pp. 96–117.

86. See Peper, in Barkin (ed.) (1975), pp. 129–32.

87. CIR Study 4 (1974), p. 60.

88. Ibid., pp. 129–40.

89. Ibid., pp. 66–76.

90. Ibid., pp. 62 and 73; Peper, in Barkin (ed.) (1975), p. 140.

91. CIR Study 4 (1974), p. 67.

92. Ibid.

93. Akkermans *et al.*, 'From Corporatism to Polarisation . . .', in Crouch and Pizzorno (eds) (1978), ch. 5.

94. Peper, in Barkin (ed.) (1975), p. 146.

95. On the history of workplace organisation in Germany see e.g. Nickel (1973), pp. 209 ff; on the employers' response, see Erdmann (1966), pp. 40 ff.

96. Kolb (1962).

97. Ibid., for history of Weimar works councils.

98. On the new works council structure, see Bergmann and Müller-Jentsch, in Barkin (ed.) (1975), pp. 248–51.

99. On the supervisory and management board provisions, see CIR Study 4 (1974), pp. 16–23, and Agartz (1973), pp. 126–9.

100. Ibid.

101. On changes in firm structure see Hartmann (1959), pp. 175–85, and Ward and George (1975), pp. 25 ff.

102. E.g. 24 per cent more in the metal industry, 20 per cent more in chemicals, in 1970. (Müller-Jentsch and Sperling (1978)).

103. On the rapid wage drift at this time, and its causes, see Bergmann and Müller-Jentsch, in Barkin (ed.) (1975), and Teschner (1977), ch. II.1.

104. Teschner (1977), ch. II.2.

105. Ibid., ch. V.3.

106. See CIR Study 4 (1974) pp. 25 ff.

107. Ibid., on the special efforts of the engineering and chemical unions.

108. Ibid., p. 33.

109. Teschner (1977), ch. V.1.

110. See Teschner (1977), ch. V.

111. Müller-Jentsch and Sperling (1978).

112. Ibid.

113. One index of continuing strength is the steady rise in numbers of Vertrauensleute, stewards. See M. Weiss (1978), *Gewerkschaftliche Vertrauensleute* (Cologne) pp. 94–7.
114. Durand and Dubois, in Dubois *et al.* (1978).
115. On the causes of wage emulation see Patchen (1961), Hyman and Brough (1976), Hyman and Singer (1968), and Brown and Sisson (1975).
116. Adams and Rosenbaum (1962).
117. For a typology of emulation see Hyman and Brough (1976), pp. 10 ff.
118. On Ford militancy, causes and effects, see Beynon (1973), ch. 11, and J. Mathews (1972), *Ford Strike: The Workers' Story* (London).
119. On the miners' militancy, see J. Hughes and R. Moore (1972), *A Special Case?* Harmondsworth: Penguin.
120. Patchen (1961), and Brown and Sisson (1975).
121. On reasons accepted for differentials see Hyman and Brough (1976), ch. 3, and D.T.B. North and G.C. Buckingham (1969), *Productivity Agreements and Wage Systems* (London: Gower).
122. On changes in attitudes see Chafe (1977); on changes in the law, see Eastwood, in Stromberg and Harkness (eds) (1978), ch. 5.
123. Ford workers in Britain now quote relative pay levels in Germany, etc., in their pay claims (Mathews (1972)). Emulation of Ford's German workers by its Belgian workers is already established (W. Kendall (1975), *The Labour Movement in Europe* (London: Allen Lane) ch. 11).
124. On the example of the British Leyland merger as a broadener of comparisons see e.g. Fryer, *Sunday Times*, 20 February 1977; also Hyman and Brough (1976), p. 241.
125. On moves away from sectional deals to plant and firm bargaining, see Brown and Sisson (1975), p. 30.
126. Or within a local labour market; but no present-day union could control that.
127. See Teschner (1977), ch. V on the negotiating role of works councils.
128. Adams and Rosenbaum (1962).
129. S. Rosen (1969), 'Trade Union Power, Threat Effects and the Extent of Organisation', *RES*, April, pp. 185–96.
130. In Germany the 'union sector' is large because most employers belong to EAs and pay bargained wages.
131. Flanagan (1976), pp. 635–73.
132. Flanagan (1976), in *BPEA*, p. 457.
133. For relative levels of the minimum wages, 1951–77, see Perry (1978), p. 283, and ch. 5, sect. 3.
134. Gramlich (1976), pp. 426–30 finds a significant impact on wages and prices, 1965–75; on his own reasoning, the impact must have been higher when the relative level was.
135. Compliance was 43 per cent in 1973 (Gramlich (1976), p. 424).
136. See below, p. 97. German workers thought it was unfair that profits grew much faster than wages in 1968/9 (Müller-Jentsch and Sperling (1978)).
137. For further discussions in this area, see Goldthorpe in Hirsch and Goldthorpe (eds) (1978), and Müller-Jentsch and Sperling (1978).
138. See e.g. Jackson, Turner and Wilkinson (1972), part 3.
139. On the rapid increase in expectations in Germany in the 1960s, see Müller-Jentsch and Sperling (1978).

140. Durcan and McCarthy (1974) and others have shown that strikes in Britain do not cluster at the times of year when they would lead to the largest tax rebates; but strikers have many other considerations to bear in mind.
141. See Daniel (1976), chs. VIII, IX and X.
142. The rate of saving in Britain rose from 1.9 per cent of household disposable income in 1951 to 12.1 per tent in 1974; in Germany, from 8.5 per cent in 1960 to 15.1 per cent in 1974. (CSO Blue Books, and *St. J., passim*).
143. The latest figures (from *FT*, 4 August 1978) on the percentage of owner-occupation (of all households) are 53 per cent in UK, 41 per cent in West Germany, 61 per cent in Belgium.
144. Immigrant workers are an important exception to this, where their right to stay in the country depends on the employer's goodwill. In general most immigrants in Britain have been better placed than most in Germany (see ch. 3, sect. 1) but the latter are catching up as more gain the protection of long residence.
145. See Gennard (1977), ch. 2, and Fisher (1973), Table 26 for comparisons between countries.
146. Except in West Germany and Sweden; see Gennard (1977), and Fisher (1973).
147. See Gennard (1977), pp. 83–5.
148. For an example of such popular support in Sweden see Gennard (1977), pp. 32–3.
149. *Economist, passim.*
150. *Economist, passim.*
151. My own recollection of the atmosphere.
152. On the Teamsters, see P.L. Taft (1964), *Organised Labor in American History* (New York: Harper & Row).
153. See above, p. 65.
154. See above, p. 78.
155. On the unusually frustrating and powerless position of white-collar workers in France before 1968, see Burgess, in Harbison and Myers (eds) (1959), and *FT*, 13 June 1978.
156. See *ESE*, 1968.
157. On the power of government over business, and business over government, see Macrae (1968), in 'Survey of France', *Economist*, 18 April; on the revolutionary tradition of the French working class see e.g. CIR Study 4 (1944) pp. 40–1.
158. On the demands made, see Dubois *et al.* (1978).
159. Ibid., for the story of the events of May.
160. On the increase in minimum wage, see CIR Study 4 (1974) pp. 39–40.
161. This is the extreme case of the situation often found and already cited above, where dissatisfaction over other matters is channelled into wage claims.
162. On the revolutionary tradition in Italy, see Regalia *et al.* (1978).
163. See Brandini, in Barkin (ed.) (1975).
164. On the upsurge of militancy and the employers' response, see Regalia *et al.*, 'Labour Conflicts and Industrial Relations in Italy', in Crouch and Pizzorno (eds) (1978), ch. 4.
165. On the unions' justification for moderation from 1973 onwards, and the growth of shop floor independence, see Regalia *et al.* (1978).

NOTES TO CHAPTER 4

1. On Dutch incomes policies see Kervyn (1965), and Akkermans *et al.* (1978); on Swedish, see T. L. Johnston (ed. and trans.) (1963), *Economic Expansion and Structural Change* (London).
2. On British incomes policies see National Board for Prices and Incomes (1970), L. C. Hunter (1975), 'British Incomes Policy, 1972–74', *Industrial and Labour Relations Review*, and W. W. Daniel and D. McIntosh (1973), *Incomes Policy and Collective Bargaining at the Workplace* (London: PEP).
3. On US incomes policies see Weber and Mitchell (1978).
4. National Board for Prices and Incomes (1970).
5. On the provisions of the 1970s legislation, see *British Journal of Industrial Relations*, Chronicle, *passim*.
6. For TUC, in Germany read DGB, in US read AFL/CIO, in Sweden read LO. . . .
7. See Kervyn (1965), and Akkermans *et al.* (1978).
8. See J. Duesenberry (1952), *Income, Saving and the Theory of Consumer Behaviour* (Harvard).
9. Richard Cowper (1978), 'How Britain Wastes Skilled Workers' and 'Allocating Blame for Skilled Worker Shortage', *FT*, 26 and 27 September. The *FT* findings were confirmed by official reports summarised in *Guardian*, 15 August 1978, p. 15.
10. See W. Brown (1977), 'Incomes Policy and Pay Differentials', *BOUIES*, pp. 27 ff.
11. See ch. 3, sect. 1 above.
12. For Britain, see Hill (1977) and Department of Employment (April 1976); for Germany, see A. Wacker (1976), *Arbeitslosigkeit; Sociale und Psychische Voraussetzungen und Folgen* (Frankfurt), and M. Jahoda *et al.* (1975), *Die Arbeitslosen von Marienthal, ein Soziographisches Versuch* (Frankfurt).
13. See Department of Employment (1975), 'Unemployment among Racial Minority Groups', *DEG*, September, and idem (1976) 'Racial Disadvantage: A PEP Report', *DEG*, March, and A. Sinfield, 'Unemployment and the Social Structure', in Worswick (ed.) (1977).
14. Thus there were shortages even of semi- and unskilled labour in West Central Scotland, a notorious unemployment blackspot, in the mid 1970s – though there were plenty of 'bodies' available (Hunter (1978), pp. 39 ff). The skilled labour shortage was of course worse.
15. See Doeringer and Piore (1971), *Internal Labour Markets and Manpower Analysis* (New York: Heath), and Hunter (1978), ch. 4.
16. See ch. 1, sect. 3 and ch. 3, sect. 3 above.
17. Hunter (1978), ch. 4, found that increasing pay had become one of the least common responses to shortage.
18. See K. Kügel (1973), *Die Lohnentwicklung in der BRD, 1951–71* (Basle) on W. Germany, and N. S. Barrett *et al.* (1973), *Prices and Wages in U.S. Manufacturing* (New York: Heath) on the US.
19. See for example the efforts of Parkin, Sumner and Ward, in K. Brunner and A. H. Meltzer (eds) (1977), 'The Economics of Price and Wage Controls', supplement to *Journal of Monetary Economics*, 2, pp. 193–221.

20. See e.g. M. T. Sumner, 'Wage Determination', in Parkin and Sumner (eds) (1978).
21. See Sumner in Parkin and Sumner (eds) (1978), and D. Maki and Z. A. Spindler (1975), 'The effect of unemployment compensation on the rate of unemployment in G.B.', *OEP*, pp. 440–55.
22. Sumner in Parkin and Sumner (eds) (1978), Table 4.
23. Sumner refers to a 'serious problem of social choice . . . the stark choice' which is, in context, clearly that between raising unemployment and cutting benefits.
24. J. Hill (1977).The comparison was with the findings of P. Eisenburg *et al.* (1938), 'The Psychological Effects of Unemployment', *Psychology Bulletin*.
25. Of these, just over three-quarters were female, mostly married (A. R. Thatcher, 'Statistics of Unemployment in the UK', in Worswick (ed.) (1977), ch. 4, p. 88.
26. Department of Employment (1976), 'The Changed Relationship between Unemployment and Vacancies', *DEG*, October. In particular, no one who leaves a job *voluntarily* in Britain is entitled to unemployment benefits or (for a period) to social security benefits. So welfare payments cannot encourage people to *become* unemployed; at best they make it less miserable to *stay* unemployed.
27. Jim Taylor, quoted by Cairncross (1979), *Guardian*, 26 April, p. 18.
28. For the US,it is more difficult to say. There, as I have shown at various points, (1) high unemployment does not shut off the supply of cheap and willing immigrant labour; (2) the non-union sector is large and less affected by the other; (3) employers are more inclined to use unemployment as a weapon against the unions. So there are stronger arguments for a US Phillips Curve than for any other, and it is possible that over a five, even ten year period, deflation does, on balance, disinflate – particularly when the effects on the exchange rate and commodity prices are taken into account (see ch. 2, sect. 3). But in the very long run the inflationary effects of a stopped escalator (see ch. 3, sect. 1) and slower growth (see ch. 5, sect. 1) are likely to be overwhelming. The last, at least, is now coming home to roost. (On the econometric debate, see Perry (1978), Gordon (1977), Flanagan (1976), and Mitchell (1978).)
29. For statements of monetarist views, see e.g. Friedman (1975, 1974, 1969); Laidler and Parkin (1975), Parkin and Zis (1976). For a sympathetic examination of monetarism, see Congdon (1978).
30. For more-or-less Keynesian counter-attacks, see Tobin (1970, 1974), J. R. Hicks (1975), M. Miller and D. Williams (1976).
31. See Congdon (1978), pp. 53–4, and von Hayek (1978).
32. Friedman (1975), Addendum; (1974), p. 46.
33. von Hayek (1978).
34. On the effect of a higher 'dole', see above, ch. 4, sect. 2. On the effect of prices and incomes policy, see Friedman (1975).
35. Unless we take into account effects through fluctuations in wages and the exchange rate.
36. The new monetarist emphasis on *expectations* has confused the picture further. Suppose an increase in the money supply leads, in some way, to a big increase in price expectations; then firms may hold or cut output in spite

of rising prices *now* because they regard them, relative to future prices, as too low. Or the trade unions, seeing the money supply rising, may raise *their* 'price' even before demand for labour has increased, and firms may cut back their output because the price of their main input, labour, is too high.

37. M. Friedman, 'The supply of money and changes in prices and output', in Friedman (ed.) (1958).
38. William Rees-Mogg (1976), in *The Times*, 13 July.
39. See the amusing correspondence in 'Letters to the Editor', *The Times*, 4 and 6 April 1977.
40. See Friedman (1973) *Money and Economic Development* (New York: Praeger).
41. For example, when UK M_1 and M_3 diverged in the mid 1970s, one leading authority (M. Parkin (1975), 'Where is Britain's Inflation Going?', *LBR*, 117, July, pp. 1–13) took M_3 as 'the indicator of monetary policy'; over the same period his distinguished colleague D. E. W. Laidler (1974), 'A Brief Note on Fiscal Policy . . .', reprinted in *Public Expenditure, Inflation and the Balance of Payments*, HC 328, took M_1.
42. For example, (1) average hourly earnings, (2) ditto adjusted for overtime, (3) retail prices, (4) wholesale prices. . . .
43. The increase in money supply may even come first. Firms' demand for money increases when they are merely *planning* an increase in output, before they have actually carried it out; and when the government wishes to stimulate the economy it is likely to increase the supply of money even if the main stimulus comes from other measures implemented at about the same time. This is consistent with the most common view of the lag between money and output – six to nine months (see Friedman (1974), and A. A. Walters (1974), *Money and Inflation* (London: Aims of Industry) p. 3).
44. But where they *have* made their predictions precise in the course of econometric studies, the main exponents of monetarism have been guilty of grave inconsistencies which offend against even *their* methodology. See Tobin (1970), on Friedman's work, and Miller and Williams (1976) on Laidler and Parkin's.
45. In Ayer (1967). See e.g. the Introduction, pp. 5–16.
46. This has been conceded now by Ayer himself (Ayer (1967), pp. 20–2).
47. Of course, if you accept *my* criteria for judging theories, monetarism is theory as well as ideology, for its propositions can be assessed by the realism of the assumptions behind them; but by that yardstick it is a poor theory. It is either a poor theory or no theory at all.
48. von Hayek (1978). The other Nobel prizewinner, Prof. Friedman, has implied as much: 'The brute fact is that a rational economic programme for a free enterprise system . . . must have flexibility of prices (including wages) as one of its cornerstones.' ((1952), *AEA*, p. 380).
49. A. C. Harberger (1954), 'The Welfare Loss from Monopoly', *AER*, Papers and Proceedings.
50. F. von Hayek, interviewed in *Diario de Noticias*, 2° Caderno, 19 December 1977.
51. For a detailed, and empirically based, argument quite similar to what follows, see Miller (1978).
52. See E. W. Davies and K. W. Yeomans (1974), *Company Finance and the*

Capital Market: a study of the effects of firm size (Cambridge: CUP).
53. For this argument put with rigour and in detail, see Tylecote (1975), July.
54. For the intellectual lineage of Chilean economic policy since 1973, see Michael Moffitt (1977), 'Chicago Economics in Chile', *Challenge*, September–October. For accounts of that policy, the repression which was indispensable to it, and its economic and social results, see O. Letelier (1976), *Chile: Economic 'Freedom' and Political Repression* (New York: Transnational Institute), A. G. Frank (1976), *Economic Genocide in Chile* (London: Spokesman), I. Letelier and M. Moffitt (1978), 'Human Rights, Economic Aid and Private Banks', *Institute for Policy Studies Issue Paper*. Hayek's remarks are drawn from the interview with *Diario de Noticias*, quoted above (my translation from the Portuguese). Compare them with those of a Chilean economist: 'To do what we've done here, you have to be a real son-of-a-bitch. If you start looking in the faces of the poor people, you can't get anything done' (*Washington Post*, 25 September 1977). Harberger expressed his enthusiasm in an interview in *El Mercurio*, 14 July 1974, quoted by Frank (1976), p. 7, and opined that Chilean social and medical security was much too developed.
55. Count Czernin, one of the last of their Foreign Ministers, quoted in A. J. P. Taylor (1955), *The Hapsburg Monarchy* (London: Hamilton) p. 232; I have slightly changed the wording of Taylor's translation.

NOTES TO CHAPTER 5

1. See Joan Robinson (1974), citing Samuelson (1948).
2. This explains the apparent 'Leontief paradox' that in the 1940s and 1950s the exports of the US, the country with the highest wages, were relatively *labour*-intensive. See W. W. Leontief (1953), 'Domestic Production and Foreign Trade: The American Capital Position Reexamined', *Proceedings of the American Philosophical Society*, vol. 97, reprinted in Bhagwati (ed.) (1969).
3. Of course, specialisation is well known, and in some forms desirable; but for economy A to specialise mainly in 'high-technology' goods, and economy B to do so mainly in 'low-technology' goods, may seem less desirable, at any rate to the people of B. I shall be arguing below that free trade encourages just such a tendency.
4. These investments may not involve much movement of capital or labour. They are often financed by funds raised within the host country. In the post-war period there has been a net *inflow* of skilled manpower and (arguably) capital into the more developed countries where skills and capital are already abundant.
5. See Hymer (1972). For the advantage of being already 'in occupation' of a high-technology industry, see C. Freeman, 'Technical Innovation and British trade performance', in Blackaby (ed.) (1979), ch. 3.
6. Note that the multinational can operate efficiently within a country without having all its know-how there.
7. On the process of *polarisation* between rich and poor areas and countries see G. Myrdal (1963), *Economic Theory and Underdeveloped Regions* (London:

Duckworth), and Hymer (1972). On the determinants of success in high-technology industries see C. Freeman, in Blackaby (ed.) (1979).

8. On the explosive growth of multinationals since the mid 60s, see Ronald E. Muller, 'Systematic Instability and the Global Corporation at Home', in Jacquemin and de Jong (eds) (1976), pp. 239–63.

9. On the motives for direct investment in manufacturing abroad, see R. E. Caves (1971), 'International corporations: the industrial economics of foreign investment', *Eca.*, vol. 38, pp. 1–27., idem (1973), 'The causes of direct investment . . .', (Harvard Institute of Economic Research DP), J. H. Dunning (1973), 'The determinants of international production', *Oxford Economic Papers*, November, and J. Hurst (1972), 'The industrial composition of US exports and subsidiary sales to the Canadian market', *AER*, March.

10. See D. T. Brash (1966), *American Investment in Australian Industry* (Canberra: Australian National UP), and A. E. Safarian (1966), *Foreign Ownership of Canadian Industry* (McGraw-Hill) pp. 183–6, on the retention of R&D activity near headquarters; see Vernon (1966) on the retention of production in the home country in the early stages of the product cycle.

11. See Vernon (1966).

12. For a corresponding argument from the 'homeland's' point of view, see A. D. Morgan, 'Foreign Investment by UK Firms', in Blackaby (ed.) (1979), ch. 4, pp. 87–91, *passim*.

13. On the motives of British firms, and others, for merger, see de Jong, 'Theory and Evidence concerning Mergers', in Jacquemin and de Jong (eds) (1976), pp. 95–123.

14. On the advantages of small firms in certain types of innovation, see C. Freeman (1974), *The Economics of Industrial Innovation* (Harmondsworth: Penguin) ch. 6, and D. Shimshoni (1970), 'The mobile scientist in the American instrument industry', *Minerva*, vol. 8, no. 1, pp. 59–89. Shimshoni (p. 61) found that their main advantages were in motivation, low costs, lead-time in development work (from speed in decision) and flexibility.

15. Shimshoni (1970) pp. 61 ff stresses the external economies gained by new small firms from technological expertise brought from elsewhere in the R&D system.

16. On the advantages of the US over the UK in spawning new small high-technology firms see C. Freeman (1974), ch. 6.

17. See 17 May 1980., *Economist*.

18. I should stress that it is only a tendency, though a strong one; there are other factors which affect growth and industrial structure, and one cannot expect every country to fit neatly into one or other group, though on the whole we can expect the groupings to become clearer as time goes by.

19. On the W. German machine tool industry see *FT*, 27 November 1978, p. 32, and 20 September 1977, p. 17. On small firms in the W. German economy see G. F. Ray, in Blackaby (ed.) (1979), pp. 73–7.

20. For a comparison of the growth of German, British and other multinationals since the mid 1960s, see Holthus (ed.) (1974), *Die Deutschen Multinationale Unternehmungen* (Frankfurt: Athenäum) pp. 11–14, *passim*.

21. On small firms in the UK see Ray, in Blackaby (ed.) (1979).
22. Franko (1976).
23. See Stout (1977), NEDO, App. B, which shows how UK import/export unit values in engineering are now much inferior to those of Germany; also D. K. Stout, 'Deindustrialisation and Industrial Policy', in Blackaby (ed.) (1979), ch. 8.
24. Although since the late 1950s there has been a high level of merger activity in Germany, compared to their British counterparts German firms stress internal expansion. (Ward and George (1975), ch. 5.) 'Leader' features in Britain, such as the importance of home-based multinationals, and 'laggard' features in Germany – such as the importance of foreign-based ones – can be traced back to the time before European trade was freed.
25. K. D. George *et al.* (1977), 'The Size of the Work Unit and Labour Market Behaviour', *BJIR*, July.
26. This information comes from my own contacts with BSC.
27. The increased cost-competitiveness does *not* stimulate new high technology industry significantly; see Stout (1977), NEDO and M. Posner and A. Steer, 'Price Competitiveness and the Performance of Manufacturing Industry', in Blackaby (ed.) (1979), ch. 7.
28. For Sweden's high GDP per head before the war see Paige *et al.* (1961).
29. Free trade is an old Swedish policy; its main industries have always been export-oriented. (S. Koblik (ed.), 1975).
30. On the level of demand in Sweden see United Nations *Economic Survey of Europe* (ESE) *passim*.
31. On the economic damage to Britain (due largely to the sale of overseas assets to the US) see C. Barnett (1972), *The Collapse of British Power* (London). The French and Dutch suffered not only invasion and occupation but also traumatic loss of empire after the war.
32. See *ESE, passim*.
33. Their GDP per head in 1938 had been 82 and 80 per cent of the British level, respectively (Sweden's 97 per cent), and had then stagnated until 1945 (Paige *et al.* (1961)).
34. On Dutch policy after the war, see Kervyn (1965), and van den Beld, in Blackaby (ed.) (1979), ch. 6.
35. On French policy in this period see *ESE*, 1956. The gross investment ratios of France, the Netherlands and the UK in 1949–59 were respectively 20.6, 25.0, and 16.1 (*ESE* (1961)).
36. Italian GDP per head in 1938 had been only 48 per cent of the UK level (Paige *et al.* (1961)).
37. Regalia *et al.*, in Crouch and Pizzorno (eds) (1978). The German and Italian gross investment rates in 49–59 were 24.2 and 21.9 respectively (*ESE* (1961)).
38. On the factors which kept the unions weak nonetheless, see ch. 3 above.
39. See ch. 3.
40. Where investment had been high during the 1950s it tended to be capital-widening, which increased the number of jobs, in contrast to the capital-deepening of the 1960s. The table below shows the rise in investment ratios:
41. On rising capital intensity in the Netherlands, see van den Beld, in Blackaby (ed.) (1979), pp. 126 and 128.

Investment, percentage of value-added, manufacturing industry
(ESE, passion.)

	France	West Germany	Italy	Neth.	Sweden	UK	USA
1949–53		14.7		18.6	13.5	11.0	
1954–8		15.8		17.6	11.9	11.7	
1957–61	16.7	18.7	24.4	19.2	17.3	13.4	
1962–6	19.2	18.0	20.0	22.1	16.8	12.9	
1967–71	19.6	16.3	15.5	21.3	15.0	13.5	

42. Jacquemin and Phlips, in Jacquemin and de Jong (eds) (1976), p. 71 show that aggregate concentration within the EEC grew very slowly between 1960 and 1965 – far too slowly to counterbalance the freeing of trade.
43. See I. Regalia *et al.*, in Crouch and Pizzorno (eds) (1978), p. 140.
44. On profitability and capital intensity see OECD (1977), *Towards Full Employment and Price Stability* (Paris) pp. 307 and 301.
45. Calculated by the author from WG official sources.
46. And, above all, Switzerland; but that lies outside my scope here.
47. Between 1965 and 1968 aggregate concentration within the EEC rose very sharply (Jacquemin and Phlips, p. 71).
48. By now some of them *have* found an answer, in the increased 'de-centralisation of certain operations, or entire production processes, to small or very small enterprises and outworkers . . . even in the modern manufacturing sectors' (Regalia *et al.*, in Crouch and Pizzorno (eds) (1978), p. 103).
49. The importance of the outcome of the industrial relations crises is underlined by the table below, which shows that in the Netherlands, Britain and Italy the share of profit fell by more than a quarter, while in the other 4 (and by the way in Canada and Japan) it fell, if at all, by less than a tenth.

Gross property income share in corporate value-added

	France	Germany	Italy	Neth.	Sweden	UK	USA
1960–5	29.9	27.4	32.0	42.2	22.8	22.7	27.6
1966–71	31.5	27.8	30.8	36.0	21.4	19.4	26.8
1972–6	32.4	26.5	23.8	31.9	21.5	13.9	24.9

Source: OECD (1977), p. 307.

50. The converse is of course true for public sector workers. So if *their* wages increase faster, manufacturing militancy increases after a while, therefore wages *there* increase faster; which soothes workers in manufacturing at the price of provoking those in the public sector . . . and so the see-saw goes on.
51. Price inflation responded, of course, to the rise in wage inflation. The trend in trade competitiveness has been interrupted since 1976 by the 'North Sea bubble'.

52. He had been a leader of the Reichstudentenwerk (the Nazi student organisation) and a member of the SS. (*The Times* obituary column, 21 October 1977, is the source of this and the other biographical information).
53. On the CBI see Grant and March (1977).
54. Capacity utilisation is a good indicator of skilled labour shortage (see ch. 4, sect. 2) and therefore of the 'labour market' pressures for higher wages – much better than unemployment.
55. From the middle of 1977 the Chairman of *Gesamtmetall* (the engineering employers) went round the various 'bargaining regions' to stiffen his colleagues' resolve. The Solidarity Fund for strike bound firms was fuller than ever before (*Spiegel*, 3 April 1978, p. 26).
56. The incomes policy collapsed in the winter of 1978–9 after, and partly because, Ford had been forced by a long strike to concede increases far above the ceiling. There is no evidence that Ford were offered any financial inducement to stand firm by any employers' organisation. (For the information in this para., see *Economist* and *Spiegel, passim.*)
57. Mitchell (1978), p. 565. 68 per cent of days lost in strikes, 1968–75, were lost at the end of wage contracts (ibid., p. 566.)
58. Calculated from US Department of Labour, *Handbook of Labour Statistics, passim.* In 1972–6 real disposable income per employed person rose 0.3 per cent in the US, 3.0 per cent in the UK, 5.2 per cent in Germany, 6.4 per cent in Italy, and 8.2 per cent in France (OECD (1978), *Economic Survey of USA*, p. 24).
59. In a longer perspective, the US seemed on its way to becoming a 'laggard'. But that process (which would require another book to discuss) was far from complete.

DEFINITIONS AND SOURCES FOR FIGURES 5.8, 5.9 AND 5.10

Profitability: Britain: gross property income share in corporate value added (Source: *TFE*, p. 307). Germany: Share of profits in net national product at market prices, adjusted for changes in employment structure (Source: OECD). USA: Net profits plus net interest, for non-financial corporations, as percentage of gross domestic product (Source: OECD).

Capacity utilisation: Britain: ratio of actual to potential industrial production, relative to trend (own calculations assuming full capacity utilisation in 1960(i), 1965(i), 1969(iii) and 1973(iii)) (Source: *Economic Trends* and CBI *Industrial survey*). Germany: as for Britain (Source: St. B). USA: Wharton index for manufacturing (Source: *ERP*,January 1979).

Competitiveness (On costs): Unit labour costs (trade weighted average) of main competitors, relative to home country, in common currency, 1961 = 100 (for Britain and Germany), 1965 = 100 (for USA) (Sources: OECD, UN, and *ERP*, January 1979). (*On prices*): unit value of exports (trade weighted average) ditto (Sources: OECD and UN). (Note: price competitiveness is shown by a dotted, cost by a continuous, line. Cost seems more relevant, but data are not available earlier than shown.)

Inflation: Britain: percentage increases, year on year, of average hourly earnings of male manual workers in manufacturing, adjusted for overtime;

and of retail prices (Source: *DEG*). Germany: as Britain; (Sources: St. B. and OECD). USA: as Britain but earnings figures are for all private non-agricultural industries. (Source: *ERP*, January 1979). (Continuous line shows wage inflation; dotted line price inflation. Incomes policy periods are bounded by dotted vertical lines and shown by a thicker wage inflation line.)

Real net earnings gains: percentage increase, year on year, of real hourly earnings in manufacturing, after tax (Sources: for Britain, own calculations to 1975, from *DEG* data plus tax information supplied by Caroline Atkinson of the *Economist*; then *ERP*, April 1979. For West Germany (where social welfare benefits are included from 1968), St. B. and OECD).(Figures are not available for USA; the hatched area between wage and price inflation lines shows the rate of *pre-tax* gains in earnings.)

Unemployment: rate of unemployment, as percentage of all employees. National definitions (Source: OECD).

Wages ratio, public/private (for Britain): ratio of male manual workers' weekly earnings in public sector to those in private industry (Source: *NIER*, 1975 (A. J. H. Dean) and 1979).

Employment of foreign workers (for Germany): as percentage of total employment (Sources: St. B. and OECD).

Minimum wage (for USA): as percentage of average hourly earnings of manual workers in manufacturing (Sources: Dunlop and Galenson (1979), p. 79; *ERP*, January 1978, p. 177). (Note: minimum wage coverage was extended in 1961 and much extended in 1967. The sloping lines only show approximate values.)

N.B. 'Own calculations' were largely the work of Ann Anson and David Newlands.

NOTES TO CHAPTER 6

1. In Francis Cripps (1978), 'Causes of growth and recession in world trade', in *EPR*, no. 4 ch. 4. The following argument on the demand outlook is similar to Cripps' there and partly inspired by it.
2. For an explanation of the instability of the oil price, see A. B. Tylecote, 'A Theory of The Price of Exhaustible Resources' (University of Sheffield Division of Economics, DP 77.10).
3. For recent reports on increasing protectionism in these industries, see *FT*, 24 October 1978 and 4 December 1978.
4. For recent reports on the general trend to increased protectionism, see *FT*, 10 November 1977 and 15 April 1978.
5. For a similar argument on the causes and effects of '*ad hoc* creeping protectionism', see Cripps and Godley (1978).
6. See the arguments in ch. 4, sect. 3 and ch. 5, sect. 1; for the trend already to multinational control, see Muller in Jacquemin and de Jong (eds) (1976).
7. The reference is of course to E. F. Schumacher (1973), *Small is Beautiful: A Study of Economics as if People Matter* (London: Blond & Briggs).

8. See Cripps and Godley (1978), for a crisp summary of the arguments presented for years in *EPR*.

9. See ch. 2, sect. 1 and Tylecote (1977).

10. If a monetary rule imposes any discipline it is on firms and unions as a whole – high wage inflation on *average* leads to a credit squeeze on all. Since wage settlements are not made between firms as a whole and unions as a whole – least of all in Britain (see ch. 4, sect. 1) no firm or union can by restraining its own settlements avert the monetary 'punishment'; it will merely seek to adjust to it when it takes place. Such adjustment as I argued in ch. 4, sect. 2 and ch. 4, sect. 3 tends on balance to *increase* inflation.

   Contrast the discipline of a price ceiling. Suppose labour costs are 25 per cent, gross profit margin 10 per cent of sales. Then 5 percentage points extra wage increase, if there were no increase in productivity, would mean $1\frac{1}{4}$ percentage points, or one-eighth, subtracted from the gross profit margin, much more from the *net* margin. Even if half the extra wage increase were balanced by a consequent increase in productivity, the cut in gross margin would still be one-sixteenth, which in net terms will be considerable. (Without a price ceiling, and assuming price leadership, and wage emulation by rivals, as argued in ch. 2, sect. 2 and ch. 2, sect. 3, most of this loss can be avoided by a price increase.) Thus management concession costs would be drastically raised, relative to strike costs.

11. See Mant (1977), and ch. 2, sect. 1.

12. Barry P. Smith (1977),'Managing for Productivity', *Management Today*, October, pp. 66–9, argues that output in UK manufacturing and distribution could be increased by from 20 to 40 per cent with much the same human and plant resources – by improving operational technology, management systems and control, and personnel motivation.

13. Mant (1977).

14. Tylecote (March 1975). Summarised in the Appendix.

15. See Bernstein (1955).

16. A call for a new EEC strategy, based on a diagnosis similar to mine, was made by a group of fifteen Italian, French and British economists in 'Unequal Community development and a need for re-evaluation', *Guardian*, 8 February 1979, p. 18.

17. See *FT*, 24 October 1978 and 4 December 1978.

18. Cf. Keynes in *The General Theory*, ch. 23.

Bibliography

Adams, J. S. and Rosenbaum, W. B. (1962) 'The relationship of worker productivity to cognitive dissonance about wage inequities', *Journal of Applied Psychology*, 46 (1962) 161–4.

AEA (1952) *Readings in Monetary Theory* (London: Allen & Unwin).

Agartz, V. (1973) *Gewerkschaft und Arbeiterklasse*. . . . (Munich: Trikont).

Akkermans, T. *et al.* (1978) 'From Corporatism to Polarisation . . .' Ch. 5 in Crouch and Pizzorno (1978), vol. I.

Ayer, A. J. (1967) *Language, Truth and Logic*, 2nd edn. (London: Gollancz).

Bain, G. S. and El Sheikh, F. (1976) *Union Growth and the Business Cycle* (Oxford: Blackwell).

—— and Price, R. (1976) 'Union Growth Revisited: 1948–74 in Perspective', *BJIR* 14 (November), pp. 339–55.

Barkin, S. (ed., 1975) *Worker Militancy and Its Consequences 1965–75*, (New York: Praeger).

Bernstein, M. H. (1955) *Regulating Business by Independent Commission* (Princeton: Princeton UP).

Beyme, K. von (1977) *Gewerkschaften und Arbeitsbeziehungen in kapitalistischen Ländern* (Munich: Piper).

Beynon, H. (1973) *Working for Ford* (Harmondsworth: Penguin).

Bhagwati, J. (ed., 1969) *International Trade* (Harmondsworth: Penguin).

—— (ed. 1972) *Economics and the World Order from the 1970s to the 1990s* (New York: Collier-Macmillan).

Blackaby, F. (ed., 1979) *Deindustrialisation* (London: NIESR/Heinemann).

Blair, J. (1972), *Economic Concentration* (New York: Harcourt).

Briggs, V., Fogel, W. and Schmidt, F. H. (1977) *The Chicano Worker* (Austin and London: University of Texas).

Brown, W. and Sisson, K. (1975) 'The Use of Comparisons in Workplace Wage Determination', *BJIR* (March), pp. 23–51.

Castles, S. and Kosack, G. (1973) *Immigrant Workers and Class Structure in Western Europe* (London: OUP).

Chafe, W. H. (1977) *Women and Equality: Changing Patterns in American Culture* (New York: OUP).

Child, J., Pearce, S. and King, L. (1978) 'Class Perceptions and Social Identification of Industrial Supervisors', *University of Aston Management Centre W.P. No. 100*, July. Commission on Industrial Relations (1973) *Industrial Relations at Establishment Level: A Statistical Survey*, CIR Study 2 (London: HMSO).

——(1974) *Worker Participation and Collective Bargaining in Europe*, CIR Study 4 (London: HMSO).

Clegg, H. A. (1970) *The System of Industrial Relations in Great Britain* (Oxford: Blackwell).

—— (1976) *Trade Unionism under Collective Bargaining* (Oxford: Blackwell).

——, Fox, A. and Thompson, A. F. (1964) *A History of British Trade Unions Since 1889* (Oxford: OUP).

Commons, J. R. and associates (1918–35) *A History of Labor in the United States* (New York: Macmillan).

Congdon, T. (1978) *Monetarism: An Essay in Definition* (London: Centre for Policy Studies).

Cripps, F. and Godley, W. (1978) 'Control of imports as a means to full employment and the expansion of world trade: the UK's case', *CJE* (September), pp. 327–34.

Crouch, C. and Pizzorno, A. (eds., 1978) *The Resurgence of Class Conflict in Western Europe since 1968*, 2 vols. (London: Macmillan).

Dahrendorf, R. (1956) *Industrie- und Betriebssoziologie* (Berlin).

Daniel, W. W. (1976) *Wage Determination in Industry*, June (London: PEP).

DE (1976) 'The Demoralising Experience of Prolonged Unemployment', *DEG* (April).

Deppe, F. *et al.* (1977) *Geschichte der deutschen Gewerkschaftsbewegung* (Köln).

Dubois, P. *et al.* (1978) 'The Contradictions of French Trade Unionism', ch. 3 in Crouch and Pizzorno (1978), vol. I.

Dunlop, J. T. (1944) *Wage Determination under Trade Unions* (New York: Macmillan).

——and Galenson, W. (eds., 1978) *Labor in the Twentieth Century* (New York: Academic Press).

Durcan, J. W. and McCarthy, W. E. J. (1974) 'The State Subsidy Theory of Strikes . . .', *BJIR*, March.

Erdmann, G. (1966) *Die Deutschen Arbeitgeberverbände . . .*, (Berlin: Duncker and Humblot).

Fisher, M. (1973) *Measurement of Labour Disputes and Their Economic Effects* (Paris: OECD).

Flanagan, R. J. (1976) 'Wage Interdependence in Unionized Labor Markets', *BPEA*, 3, pp. 635–81.

Franko, L. G. (1976) *The European Multinationals* (London: Harper & Row).

Friedman, M. (1953) *Essays in Positive Economics* (Chicago: University of Chicago Press).

—— (1958) *The Relationship of Prices to Economic Stability and Growth* (Washington: US Govt Printing Office).

—— (1968) 'The Role of Monetary Policy', *AER* (March), pp. 1–17.

—— (1969) *The Optimum Quantity of Money and Other Essays* (London: Macmillan).

—— (1974) *The Counter Revolution in Monetary Theory*, IEA Occ. Pap. 33 (London: IEA).

—— (1975) *Unemployment versus Inflation?* (London: IEA).

Fryer, J. (1977) 'Will the Unions Collar IBM?' *Sunday Times Business News*, 20 February.

Gennard, J. (1977) *Financing Strikes* (London: Wiley).

Goldthorpe, J. H. *et al.* (1968) *The Affluent Worker: Industrial Attitudes* (Cambridge: CUP).

Gordon, R. (1977) 'Can the Inflation of the 1970s be explained?', *BPEA*, 1, pp. 253–77.

Gramlich, E. M. (1976) 'Impact of Minimum Wages . . .', *BPEA*, 2, pp. 409–51.

Granick, D. (1975) *Equality of Promotional Opportunities in British Industry* (London: IEA).

Grant, W. and Marsh, D. (1977) *The CBI* (London: Hodder & Stoughton).

Hannah, L. (1976) *The Rise of the Corporate Economy* (London: Methuen).

—— and Kay, J. A. (1977) *Concentration in Modern Industry: theory, measurement and the UK experience* (London: Macmillan).

Harbison, F. and Myers, C. (eds., 1959) *Management in the Industrial World, An International Analysis* (New York: McGraw Hill).

Hartmann, H. (1959) *Authority and Organisation in German Management* (Princeton: Princeton UP).

Hayek, F. von (1978) "The Powerful Reasons for Curbing Union Powers", *The Times*, 10 October, p. 12.

Heckscher, E. F. (1954) *An Economic History of Sweden* (trans. Ohlin), (Cambridge, Mass.: Harvard UP).

Hicks, J. R. (1963) *Theory of Wages*, 2nd edn (London: Macmillan).

—— (1975) 'What is Wrong with Monetarism' *LBR*, October.

Hill, J. (1977) *The Social and Psychological Effects of Prolonged Unemployment; A Pilot Study* (London: Tavistock Institute of Human Relations).

Hinton, J. S. (1973) *The First Shop Stewards Movement* (London: Allen & Unwin).

Hirsch, F. (1976) *Social Limits to Growth* (London: Routledge & Kegan Paul).

—— and Goldthorpe, J. H. (1978) *The Political Economy of Inflation* (London: Martin Robertson).

Hunter, L. C. (1978) (with P. B. Beaumont) *Labour Shortages and Manpower Policy*, Manpower Services Commission, Manpower Studies, 2 (London: HMSO).

Hyman, H. H. and Singer, E. (eds., 1968) *Readings in Reference Group Theory and Research* (Glencoe: Free Press).

Hyman, R. and Brough, I. (1976) *Social Values and Industrial Relations* (Oxford: Blackwell).

Hymer, S. (1972) 'The Multinational Corporation and the Law of Uneven Development', in Bhagwati (ed., 1972), pp. 113–40.

Incomes Data Services (1979) *International Report*, No. 92.

Jackson, D., Turner, H. A. and Wilkinson, F. (1972) *Do Trade Unions Cause Inflation?* (Cambridge: CUP).

Jacquemin, A. P. and de Jong, A. W. (1976) *Markets, Corporate. Behaviour, and the State* (The Hague: Nijhoff).

Jühe, R., *et al.* (1977) *Gewerkschaften in der Bundesrepublik* (Köln: Deutscher-Institut Verlag).

Kendall, W. (1975) *The Labour Movement in Europe* (London: Allen Lane).

Kervyn, A. (1965) 'Politique des revenus: L'expérience Hollandaise', *Revue d'économie politique*, May.

Keynes, J. M. (1936) *A General Theory of Employment, Interest, and Money* (London: Macmillan).

Kolb, E. (1962) *Die Arbeiterräte in der deutschen Innenpolitik* (Düsseldorf: Droste).

Korpi, W. (1978) 'Workplace Bargaining, the Law and Unofficial Strikes: The Case of Sweden', *BJIR* (November), pp. 355–67.

Kuhn, T. S. (1970) *The Structure of Scientific Revolutions*, 2nd ed. (Chicago: University of Chicago Press).

Laidler, D. E. W. and Parkin, J. M. (1975) 'Inflation: A Survey', *EJ*, December.

Maki, D. and Spindler, Z. A. (1975) 'The Effect of Unemployment Compensation on the Rate of Unemployment in G.B.', *OEP*, 27 (November), pp. 440–55.

Mant, A. (1977) *The Rise and Fall of the British Manager* (London: Macmillan).

Marshall, A. [1890] (1916) *Principles of Economics*, 8th edn. (London: Macmillan).

McCarthy, W. E. J. *et al.* (1971) *The Reform of Collective Bargaining at Plant and Company Level*, D. E. Manpower Papers No. 5 (London: HMSO).

Miller, E. with Lonie, A. (1978) *Microeconomic Effects of Monetary Policy: The Fallout of Severe Monetary Restraint* (London: Robertson).

Miller, M. and Williams (1976) 'Money, Output and Inflation: A Synopsis and Critique of Some Recent Developments in Monetarism in the UK', Manchester University, mimeo (Autumn).

Mitchell, D. J. B. (1978) 'Union Wage Determination: Policy Implications and Outlook', *BPEA*, 3, pp. 537–82.

Miller-Jentsch, W. and Sperling, H. J. (1978) 'Economic Development, Labour Conflicts and the Industrial Relations System in W. Germany', ch. 7 in Crouch and Pizzorno (eds.) (1978), vol. I.

National Board for Prices and Incomes (1970) *Third General Report*, No. 77, Cmnd.3715 (London: HMSO).

NEDO/Stout, D. K. (1977) *International Price Competitiveness, Non-price Factors, and Export Performance,* April (London: NEDO).

Neild, K. R. (1963) *Pricing and Employment in the Trade Cycle*, NIESR Occ. Pap. 21 (Cambridge: CUP).

Nickel, W. (1973) *Zum Verhältnis von Arbeiterschaft und Gewerkschaft* (Köln).

OECD (June 1977) *Towards Full Employment and Price Stability* (Paris: OECD).

Paige, D. C. *et al.* (1961) 'Economic Growth: the Last Hundred Years', *NIER*, pp. 24–49.

Parker, S. (1975) *Workplace Industrial Relations, 1973* (London: HMSO).

Parkin, J. M. and Zis, G. (eds., 1976) *Inflation in the World Economy* (Manchester: Manchester UP).

Parkin, M. and Sumner, M. T. (1978) *Inflation in the UK* (Manchester: Manchester UP).

Partridge, B. E. (1979) 'Influence and Responsibilities of First-line

Supervisors', *University of Aston Management Centre W.P. No. 129*, February.

Patchen, M. (1961) *The Choice of Wage Comparisons* (New York: Prentice-Hall).

Penrose, E. (1959) *The Theory of the Growth of the Firm* (Oxford: Blackwell).

Perry, G. L. (1978) 'Slowing the Wage-Price Spiral: The Macroeconomic View', *BPEA*, 2, 259–91.

Phelps, E. S. (1967) 'Phillips Curves, Expectations of Inflation and Optimal Unemployment over Time', *Eca.*, 34 (August), pp. 254–81.

Phillips, A. W. (1958) 'The Relation between Unemployment and the Rate of Change of Money Wage Rates in the UK, 1861–1957', *Eca.*, November, pp. 283–99.

Pigou, A. C. and Robertson, D. H. (1931) *Economic Essays and Addresses* (London: King).

Pollard, S. (1969) *The Development of the British Economy, 1914–67*, 2nd edn. (London: Arnold).

Pribicevic, B. (1959) *The Shop Stewards' Movement, 1910–22* (Oxford: Blackwell).

Pryor, F. L. (1972) 'The Size of Production Establishments in Manufacturing', *EJ*, June.

Regalia, I. *et al.* (1978) 'Labour Conflicts and Industrial Relations in Italy', ch. 4 in Crouch and Pizzorno (eds) (1978), vol. I.

Robinson, J. (1972) *Economic Heresies* (London: Macmillan).

—— (1974) *Reflections on the Theory of International Trade*, (Manchester: Manchester UP).

—— (1977) 'What Are the Questions?', *JEL*, 15, pp. 1318–39.

Rosenblum, G. (1973) *Immigrant Workers: Their Impact on American Labor Radicalism* (New York: Basic Books).

Ross, A. M. (1948) *Trade Union Wage Policy* (Berkeley: University of California Press).

Samuelson, P. A. (1948) 'International Trade and the Equalisation of Factor Price', *EJ*, 58 (June).

Schuster, D. (1976) *Die Deutsche Gewerkschaftsbewegung* (Köln: DGB).

Serrin, W. (1974) *The Company and the Union* (New York: Vintage Books).

Shonfield, A. (1965) *Modern Capitalism: The Changing Balance of Private and Public Power* (London: OUP, for Royal Institute of International Affairs).

Simon, H. A. and March, J. G. (1958) *Organisations* (New York: Wiley).

Stein, G. (ed., 1954) *Unternehmer in der Politik* (Düsseldorf).

Stromberg, A. H. and Harkness, S. (1978) *Women Working* (New York: Mayfield).

Taylor, A. J. P. (1961) *The Course of German History* (London: Hamish Hamilton).

Teschner, E. (1977) *Lohnpolitik im Betrieb* (Frankfurt: Campus).

Tobin, J. (1970) 'Money and Income: *Post Hoc Ergo Propter Hoc?'*, *QJE*, May.

—— (1974) *The New Economics One Decade Older* (Princeton: Princeton UP).

Troy, L. (1965) *Trade Union Membership, 1897–1962*, NBER Occ. Pap. 92 (New York: Columbia UP).

Tylecote, A. B. (1975) 'Determinants of Changes in the UK Manufacturing Wage Hierarchy, 1954–70', *BJIR*, March.

—— (July 1975) 'The Effects of Monetary Policy on Wage Inflation', *OEP*, 27, pp. 240–5.

—— (1976) 'The Fall of the Phillips Curve: the Effect of the Level of Demand on Wage Inflation in British Manufacturing', University of Manchester, Dept. of Economics, DP No. 4.

—— (1977) 'Managers, Owners and Bankers in British and German Industry: Causes of the German Industrial Superiority', University of Sheffield, DP No. 77.10.

US Dept. of Labor (1978) *Handbook of Labor Statistics, 1977* (Washington: Bureau of Labor Statistics).

Vernon, R. (1966) 'International Investment and International Trade in the Product Cycle', *QJE*, 80, pp. 190–207.

Ward, T. and George, K. D. (1975) *The Structure of Industry in the EEC*, DAE Occ. Pap. (London: CUP).

Weber, A. R. and Mitchell, D. J. B. (1978) *The Pay Board's Progress: Wage Controls in Phase II* (Washington: Brookings Institute).

Worswick, G. D. N. (ed., 1977) *The Concept and Measurement of Involuntary Unemployment* (London: Heinemann).

Index

Two methods of reference are used: '71, n.38 (202)' indicates that the subject is mentioned *directly* on p. 71 *and* in note 38, which appears on p. 202; '72 n.42 (206)' indicates a reference to the subject on p. 72 but only by way of note 42.